Stuck at Home

Stuck at Home

Pandemic Immobilities in the Nation of Emigration

Yasmin Y. Ortiga

Stanford University Press

Stanford, California

Stanford University Press
Stanford, California

Library of Congress Cataloging-in-Publication Data

Names: Ortiga, Yasmin Y., author.

Title: Stuck at home : pandemic immobilities in the nation of emigration / Yasmin Y. Ortiga.

Description: Stanford, California : Stanford University Press, 2025. | Includes bibliographical references and index.

Identifiers: LCCN 2024042819 (print) | LCCN 2024042820 (ebook) | ISBN 9781503641846 (cloth) | ISBN 9781503642812 (paperback) | ISBN 9781503642829 (ebook)

Subjects: LCSH: Foreign workers, Filipino—Government policy—Philippines. | Nurses—Philippines. | Cruise lines—Philippines—Employees. | COVID-19 Pandemic, 2020—Social aspects—Philippines. | Philippines—Emigration and immigration—Government policy.

Classification: LCC JV8685 .O88 2025 (print) | LCC JV8685 (ebook) | DDC 325/.25990905—dc23/eng/20241228

LC record available at https://lccn.loc.gov/2024042819
LC ebook record available at https://lccn.loc.gov/2024042820

Cover design: George Kirkpatrick
Cover collage: Michael Lorenzana

For Ama Nene and Ama Ruth

Contents

Acknowledgments

At some time while I was editing the final manuscript for this book, my sister messaged me to say that she had found a copy of my first monograph among my grandmother's things. There was a bookmark—a real one, with a gold tassel hanging from its end—wedged between pages x and 1. "Well, at least she made it to the acknowledgments," my sister typed, with a laughing-while-crying emoji. Maria Belen Ortiga, "Ama Nene" as we called her, was never one to read through an entire book about Philippine emigration, even if it was written by her eldest granddaughter. While curious enough to interrogate family members about what they did, whom they dated, and how much money they made, she was always impatient with my efforts to explain my work. "How am I supposed to brag about you to my friends if I can't understand what you do?" she once asked me, smiling, but not joking.

Paano kita ipagyayabang sa mga kaibigan ko kung di ko naman maintindihan ang ginagawa mo?

I thought a lot about Ama Nene in the development of this book, my second monograph on emigration in the Philippines. Having conducted this research amid a global pandemic, I felt the need to tell a story that was not only scholarly and relevant, but also engaging enough for people to understand and, hopefully, share with others. As I went through each draft, I couldn't help but remind myself of Ama's question. If grandmotherly pride could not translate my research to nonacademics, then who else would possibly make sense of it?

In many ways, this book reflects my attempt to become a stronger storyteller, to write about people's experiences with the goal of having them read and heard. Such skills are often not part of graduate school training. The making of this book relied on people who were willing to provide honest feedback on how I could communicate my research more effectively.

The nurses and cruise workers who took part in this study served as my main source of inspiration. Under "normal" circumstances, few would have volunteered to share their lives with a researcher who contacted them via Facebook. The events of the pandemic made them want to impart their frustrations, struggles, and experiences of immobility. They asked me, "Where will this research go?" *Saan mapupunta ang research na 'to?* They reminded me of the purpose of my work, beyond theory-building and academia.

The project itself would never have happened if not for my collaborators: Karen Anne Liao, Luis Macabasag, and Michael Joseph Diño. I had pitched the project to them as a need to document what Filipino nurses and cruise workers had gone through during the pandemic. To this day, I am amazed that this reason was enough for them to spend eighteen months conducting online interviews, and many more months writing, planning, and disseminating project findings. Mike Quilala, Exequiel Cabanda, and Diuzza Aragon also contributed their time and effort during our early days of data-gathering. Meanwhile, grants from the Singapore Management University and the Social Science Research Council provided us with the financial support to sustain this project for two years.[1]

To craft research participants' stories into a coherent narrative, I leaned heavily on colleagues and writing groups to read through countless drafts of this manuscript. Kellynn Wee, Menusha De Silva, Dean Dulay, Sahana Ghosh, and Andy Chang reviewed early versions of my chapters. They asked, "What do you want us to take away from this, Yas?" When I struggled to answer this question, they quickly offered encouragement and commiseration. Another group of friends gamely read through the final manuscript: Ishani Mukherjee, Cheng Cheng, Seulki Lee, Charlotte Setijadi, Jiaqi Liu, and Sneha Annavarapu. Few of these friends were migration scholars, many were not sociologists. But they understood the book's goals. And when I needed time to process, they provided immeasurable support.

In developing this narrative into an academic argument, I needed the advice of scholars who had a broader view of the field where my work was situated. Chandran Kukathas, my former dean, generously hosted a book workshop at Singapore Management University. The workshop's panelists— Rhacel Parreñas, Rubén Hernandez-Leon, and Natasha Iskander—helped me finalize my book's argument. They asked: Why should the book matter to people who do not know or care about migration from the Philippines? What ideas am I pushing against? These questions were even harder to address but helped define the story I wanted to tell.

While academics are often driven toward getting others to agree with their arguments, it was actually a disagreement with Marla Asis that formed the foundation of this book. Ma'am Marla pushed me to consider: What if a migration policy is also a national policy? Can immobility be justified? I am thankful to her for challenging me, and for referring me to Ricardo Casco, whose thoughtful reflections on the Philippine civil service contributed so much to this study.

As my argument took shape, Rhacel Parreñas encouraged me to see my story's future as a book—as a publication that would need to be marketed, taught, and distributed to a wider audience. I am grateful to her and to my good friend Maria Hwang for believing in this story before it was fully formed.

As the world moved on to its post-pandemic era, there were times when I began to doubt the significance of my stories. Was there still any value in a book about immobile workers? My development editor, Jenny Gavacs, gave me much-needed perspective. Why be in a rush? A well-crafted story will continue to be read. A summer spent at the Stockholm Centre for Global Asia provided the space and distance to write. I appreciate the efforts of Rebecca Ye and Johan Lindquist in giving me that time to move away (literally) from the distractions of my everyday life.

Eventually, the book found a home in Stanford University Press. I am grateful to Marcela Maxfield and the editorial team for ensuring that the book received constructive reviews and found its way into the world.

Throughout this process, my family had a different relationship to this book. My parents, Sergio and Nancy, as well as my siblings, Marco, Kara, and Selena, could easily relate to the nurses and cruise workers who took part in my research. While I wrote the book in my faculty apartment in Singapore, they were stuck at home in Manila, where constraints on people's mobility dragged on for years. They heard about the book's inception, witnessed my struggle to write it, and celebrated its completion. Still, the specific world of migration scholarship was always a strange other place. While my parents liked to ask, "Is this book a big deal?" it was unlikely they would ever read it.

Perhaps, in the end, family members are really meant to shape the making of the author, even if they have only limited impact on the making of the book. Marvin Montefrio, the life partner I was lucky to find, taught me to be a kinder and wiser person. Meanwhile, my children, Pepe and Tala, now constantly ask, "What happened during the pandemic, *Nanay*?"—making them the best part of learning to become a better storyteller.

After my sister found my first book among Ama Nene's things, I took out a copy from my office bookshelf and flipped to page x. I didn't include Ama Nene in my acknowledgments then; whether she was annoyed by this omission, she didn't let on. I never got the chance to ask her, either. Having lived through World War II, two Philippine revolutions, and a global pandemic, Maria Belen Ortiga passed away in August 2023. She was ninety-four years old.

I was able to see Ama Nene during a trip to Manila, the month before she passed. We were sitting in her car, on the way back to her apartment, and she wanted to gossip about my sister, who was visiting home with a new boyfriend from Australia. As always, Ama Nene was curious. Is he good-looking? Does he have a real job? I cautioned her against asking too many sharp questions. "I know that!" she said, smiling, but only half-joking. "We don't want to scare him off." She turned to the topic of my work at the university. At that time, I chose not to mention the book. I didn't feel like being grilled about my project.

Now, having completed this monograph, I wish that I had heard Ama Nene's unasked questions. Would they have helped me write a better story that she could relay to her friends? I am thankful to those who helped me try to do so, nevertheless.

Introduction

Ricardo Casco spoke with the confidence of a bureaucrat who liked explaining things to people outside the bureaucracy. Not that he was expecting difficult questions from his audience of students and academics—most of whom, like me, studied labor migration policies. While officially retired, Mr. Casco had spent two decades working for what was then the Philippine Overseas Employment Administration (POEA),[1] a state agency tasked with managing the outmigration of Filipino workers. I later found out that he was also a man of many hobbies, one of which was keeping fit with ballroom dances like the cha-cha. This bit of trivia seemed apt, given the metaphor he chose to describe his work. "Migration governance is really about dancing," he began, swaying his hands. "It's about moving and making changes depending on the market."

To anyone listening in, Mr. Casco might have sounded like he was running a global business instead of a public office that regulated the movements of Filipino migrants. In many ways, one could argue that both were true. The Philippines is widely known as one of the most successful labor-exporting nations in the world. Close to 10% of the country's population lives and works abroad, dominating professions in seafaring and health care, as well as blue-collar jobs in factory and domestic work. Mr. Casco personally disliked the word "export" ("We are not packing people into boxes like bananas!"), but he conceded that there was a corporate theme in how the Philippine state treated its outgoing migrants. After all, his former office was nicknamed the "marketing department." While he scanned the globe for potential employers in need of Filipino labor, his colleagues vetted migrants' job contracts and facilitated their departures. Meanwhile, overseas Filipinos remitted their earnings home, funneling millions of dollars into the country's national coffers. If governing emigration was indeed like dancing, it seemed that the Philippine state had followed all the right steps in turning its citizens' mobility into a lucrative enterprise.

Yet, around the same time that Mr. Casco made his statement, the Philippine state was performing a completely different set of moves. It was 2021, and the world had just entered the second year of a pandemic caused by a novel coronavirus called COVID-19. Airborne and frighteningly contagious, this virus would eventually kill more than 5 million people across the world and sicken hundreds of millions more. To contain COVID-19 infections, governments closed international borders, shut down schools, and ordered their citizens to isolate themselves at home. Mr. Casco was cohosting an online conference to discuss the pandemic's impact on Philippine migration policies just as a mutated version of the virus brought a new wave of deaths in Metro Manila.

Immediately, the pandemic made thousands of workers redundant, while others, especially within the health care field, became indispensable. And in a matter of months, the Philippine state moved from mainly deploying aspiring migrants toward retaining essential workers and reintegrating those who lost their jobs overseas.

First, rising numbers of infected patients compelled the Philippine government to redirect aspiring nurse migrants toward hospitals at home. After years of sending nurses to health systems across the world, state officials chose to ban Filipino health professionals from leaving the country for overseas work. Hundreds of nurses found themselves stuck, unable to depart for jobs waiting in places such as the United States, United Kingdom, Saudi Arabia, and Singapore. Second, the pandemic triggered return migration at a scale that blindsided Philippine officials. Service workers in tourism and hospitality were the first to lose their jobs. But they were only a portion of the 316,858 Filipinos who returned home in 2020 (Zurbano 2020).[2] If the Philippine state had governed emigration by "dancing" between global demands and local needs, the COVID-19 pandemic required that it execute its most difficult pivot yet.

"Our policy, in the interest of the state, is that when our own industries and our stakeholders demand that we should stop [migration] or have some restrictions, we must respond," Mr. Casco explained gravely. "There is that obligation." Listening to him speak from my family's on-campus apartment in Singapore, I couldn't help but feel skeptical. On the one hand, Mr. Casco seemed to be describing a dilemma that the Philippine state had always known, but that migration scholars have mostly ignored. While deploying migrant workers led to profitable returns, states had the mandate to tighten regulations over cross-border movement in line with national interests, whether related to economic or public health concerns. On the other hand, it was hard to see how migrant-sending states like the Philippines could shift away from labor export while maintaining the support of a highly mobile and globally oriented citizenry. For decades, Filipino workers had been encouraged, trained, and governed to emigrate. What would happen when they were suddenly told that they could not or should not leave the country? While the state could adjust its policies to fit the nation's changing needs, people's own migration plans are not as easily paused, altered, or restarted. In other words, how does the world's model for labor export manage its workers when they are unable to move or must be kept in place?

I found that the answer lay in a tense negotiation process that occurred well before would-be migrants left their homes.

———————

In making sense of how nations govern emigration, social scientists have largely focused on state efforts to control people's mobility, spurring countless studies on who gets to move, how they do so, and where they end up going. This book argues that migration governance involves not only regulating people's movement, but also managing the meaning and implications of how they remain in place. Set in the context of a global pandemic, *Stuck at Home* is a story of how the Philippine state and its aspiring migrant workers negotiated what it meant to be stranded in a country where international migration is a way of life. Far from simply the failure to emigrate, I discuss how immobility can have a specific value and purpose, which defines public perceptions of those who do not move. For Philippine state agencies, the immobility of some workers can bolster the image of a government that prioritizes the needs of local citizens and cares for migrants forced to return home. In contrast, Filipinos can use their immobility to demand aid from state officials while criticizing the problems of an ill-prepared administration. Controlling the narrative of immobility has high stakes for both the migrant-sending state and individual migrants. This book shows how the story that dominates public discourse eventually determines how aspiring migrants are treated by others in their home country and how government agencies are expected to attend to their needs.

This book draws from eighteen months of qualitative research, conducted in the first two years of the COVID-19 pandemic. To tell the story of how the Philippine state attempted to frame the immobility of its would-be migrants, I analyzed media reports, state documents, and online recordings of Philippine Senate meetings and debates. I compared this discourse with workers' views of their own immobility and how this shaped their engagement with government officials and agencies. With a research team divided between Manila and Singapore, I interviewed two groups of workers who were stuck in the Philippines during the pandemic. The first group is composed of fifty-five aspiring migrant nurses whose labor had become critical to the Philippines' COVID-19 response—a situation that pressured the state to prevent them from leaving for jobs overseas. The second group comprises forty-five service workers who returned home after losing their jobs in the global cruise line industry—waiters, entertainers, and kitchen staff whose work had been labeled "nonessential." In response to these migrants' needs, Philippine state agencies encouraged them to pursue self-employment or reskill for jobs within their home communities.

Both groups of workers actively pushed against government narratives of their immobility and advocated for support in restarting their migration journeys. Throughout these discussions, tensions arose around the question of skill. Philippine state officials constructed different meanings of "skill" to retain some workers at home and prevent them from emigrating while reintegrating those who were forced to return due to job loss. Nurses and cruise workers, however, opposed these justifications, emphasizing the time and effort they had already invested in honing their skills for overseas work. They claimed that their skills were misrecognized and devalued within the Philippines, making their immobility oppressive and involuntary. Yet, by the end of the pandemic's first year, only one of these groups received nationwide sympathy and, eventually, government assistance and commiseration. The other was castigated by the general public and left with only a grudging compromise from the state.

I do not write this book to argue that Filipino workers are exceptional or unique. During the pandemic, governments across the world had immobilized their own citizens—imposing self-isolation measures, hardening internal borders, and banning all forms of travel. Migration studies have analyzed these pandemic-era regulations in detail, emphasizing how discourses of public health justified the immobility of certain groups over others (Lin and Yeoh 2021; Xiang et al. 2022). What this book does argue is that such controls are not mere aberrations in the relationship between the state and its aspiring migrants. While the COVID-19 pandemic magnified these practices, they have long been part of state approaches to managing people's movement. And the Philippines, as the world's model for labor export, serves as an ideal case to understand how aspiring migrants negotiate this process.

Growing up in Manila, I witnessed the Philippine government's exuberant celebration of emigration. Local newspapers headlined the remittances that migrant workers sent back every year, and state officials trumpeted the success of those who had "made it" in other countries. But when I myself became a migrant in my twenties, I realized that such acclaim for overseas workers did not necessarily lead to free movement across borders. To leave my own country, I went through a lengthy state-mandated process for departure that included paying for local insurance and an assessment of my employment contract. Every time I visited my parents in Manila, I needed to obtain a certificate that endorsed my exit to Singapore—the country where I was employed as a migrant academic. Filipinos I met abroad constantly complained about these requirements, wondering how the same government that depended on their remittances also made emigration so difficult. Beyond exporting their citizens' labor, Philippine state agencies took charge of regulating migrants' departures while facilitating the long-term resettlement of others. Immobility seemed to be an integral part of this entire process.

In this book, I wish to underscore how the meaning of such immobility can also be negotiated, as state officials navigate changing public sentiment and aspiring migrants advocate for their own right to international mobility. This negotiation has important implications for broader conversations on who eventually deserves to move, yet it remains largely absent from studies of international migration.

Studying the Migration State

Weeks before reports of an unknown respiratory virus first appeared in the Philippine media, the biggest headline in January 2020 was a government decision to ban Filipinos from migrating to the Gulf state of Kuwait. Jeanelyn Villavende, a Filipino domestic worker, had succumbed to internal injuries shortly after her employers abandoned her at a Kuwaiti hospital. When doctors reported signs of physical abuse, then-president Rodrigo Duterte ordered state officials to block the departures of all Filipino workers bound for Kuwait (Gita-Carlos 2020). Caught in this diplomatic fracas were migrant professionals—mostly teachers and engineers—who could not comprehend how one domestic worker's death had somehow compromised all their overseas careers (Jimenez 2020). Still, the ban would remain in effect until the Kuwaiti government signed a joint memorandum ensuring new protections for Filipino workers. To apply pressure on their Kuwaiti counterparts, the Duterte administration believed that imposing a "total ban" on all workers was more effective than only preventing the departures of some (Aben 2020).[3]

The discord over Villavende's death was not the first incident to upend Filipino workers' migration plans.[4] Since the beginning of the country's labor export program, the Philippine government has either suspended workers' deployments or extracted its citizens from destinations deemed unsafe or "noncompliant" in preventing cases of migrant abuse. As COVID-19 grew into a global pandemic in the following weeks, Kuwait was no exception to these shifts. In an ironic sequence of events, President Duterte finally allowed labor deployment to Kuwait in February 2020, only to later repatriate thousands of Filipino workers back to the Philippines after the coronavirus spread to the Gulf states. This case illustrates perfectly the "dance" that Mr. Casco had earlier described in defining migration governance: state institutions must respond to external events by moving flexibly from deployment to protection to repatriation and return. Yet migration studies offer limited tools to explain how and why governments act in these ways. In writing this book, I realized that telling a story about the Philippine state and its immobile workers meant telling a different story about migration governance as well.

People are often surprised to know that for a time, emigration was mainly a problem for governments in the West. Afraid of losing productive workers, European nations enforced strict exit bans on specific groups, depending on occupation and class status. When restrictions were finally removed in the late nineteenth century, the mass departure of aspiring migrants led to an "exit revolution," which eventually shifted mainstream scholarship away from emigration (Zolberg 2007). Today, most academic discussions of migration and the state revolve around issues of immigration, or the entry of foreigners into a nation's territory. Sociologists, in particular, have produced numerous studies on how states manage the influx of immigrants and, subsequently, their incorporation within their host society (D'Appollonia 2012; Stokes-DuPass 2015; Yuval-Davis, Wemyss, and Cassidy 2019). Far fewer scholars examine how migrant-sending nations oversee the departure of their citizens and handle their possible return (Fitzgerald 2009; Green and Weil 2007; Iskander 2011; Rodriguez 2010).

As countries in the Global North became major migrant destinations, the task of governing emigration shifted to source countries in the developing world. But until the 2000s, few social scientists regarded these sending states as subjects worthy of scholarly attention (Massey, Durand, and Malone 2002; Ostergaard-Nielsen 2003). Instead, there was a pervasive belief that poor nations lacked the capacity to control their borders and, as such, simply allowed emigration to happen (Natter and Thiollet 2022; Talani 2021). Globalization in the late twentieth century further diminished the salience of studying emigration governance, as scholars questioned whether states could truly control their citizens' movements in the context of a highly interconnected world (Torpey 2007). As a result, research on migration governance revolved mainly around regulating immigrants. Perhaps most telling is Hollifield's (2004) seminal work on the "migration state," where he refers only to the challenges of maximizing the benefits of immigration amid domestic pressures to restrict the influx of foreigners.

Stuck at Home is situated among a growing number of studies that have pushed for greater recognition of the role that sending states play in shaping international migration. Contrary to the image of governments rendered helpless by globalization, these studies reveal how sending states can shape the conditions of people's departures, their absences from their origin communities, and their future returns home (Fitzgerald 2009; Rodriguez 2010; Tyner 2004; Xiang 2016). However, this book also diverges from the underlying theme that defines much of this research. In studying the sending state, scholars have painted a picture of a government that uses emigration for economic development. For example, scholars have studied how sending state agencies reach out to overseas citizens in the hope of involving members of the diaspora in national projects (Gamlen 2008; Ragazzi 2014; Setijadi 2023).[5] Researchers have also examined how states have deliberately facilitated people's departures to maximize the monetary remittances that these migrants will eventually send home (de Haas 2005; Tyner 2004). In this book, I argue that, aside from monetizing people's labor and mobility, governing emigration is also about balancing the benefits of emigration with the demands of a nonmigrant constituency. To understand how states achieve this balance, scholars need to look beyond the issues of labor export, widening the scope of current research to focus on the broader concerns of a migrant-sending nation.

This is not to say that the Philippine state cares less about the economic gains of emigration. Among other sending states, the Philippines has always stood out for its aggressive efforts at channeling Filipino workers to jobs abroad (Lee 2017). Migration studies reveal the wide range of activities involved in such work, from establishing bilateral agreements with destination countries to skilling and marketing Filipino labor to foreign employers (Cabanda 2017; Guevarra 2014; Lee 2021; Ortiga 2018a). In describing the scale at which the Philippine state coordinates this process, sociologist Robyn Rodriguez (2010: xiv) went as far as calling the country an "export-processing zone" that manufactures "ideal" workers for foreign employers.

However, the developmental story of emigration governance has its limitations as well. While remittances can explain why some governments promote emigration, there are many sending-state regulations that are not motivated by economic development. For example, Iskander's (2011: 33) careful history of Morocco's policies reveals how state officials used emigration to quell local unrest, directing labor recruiters to "areas where popular resistance to the monarchy's policies was strong." Meanwhile, Eritrea restricts return migration as a means of punishing political dissidents who left without authority from the state (Milena and Cole 2022). Even within the Philippines, state campaigns to protect women from illegal trafficking have made their movement more arduous and expensive, inadvertently preventing many workers from leaving the country (Encinas-Franco 2016; Hwang 2017). More recent events, such as President Duterte's "total ban" on emigration to Kuwait, also signal a willingness to put migrant professionals' jobs in jeopardy even if these workers are not directly involved in heinous cases of employer abuse. These examples show how states can justify immobilizing their own citizens, regardless of the economic benefits their emigration may bring.

Such incidents are not deviations from the sending state's labor export agenda. While it is true that remittances bring many benefits to migrants' countries of origin, an overemphasis on developmental needs risks type-casting the migrant-sending state as a monolithic entity, driven solely toward accumulating economic returns. In reality, scholars have shown how government regimes can alternate between tightening and loosen-ing controls over migrants, depending on local or international pressures (Iskander 2011; Xiang 2016). Beyond maximizing remittances, states must also manage other issues related to migration, such as worker abuse, local labor needs, and its own legitimacy among potential voters at home. Mi-gration governance is indeed a dance, and states cannot simply rely on one set of moves to get by.

In this book, I emphasize how governing migration also requires new engagements with those who have yet to leave, those unable to do so, and the majority with no intention of leaving at all. As Fitzgerald (2009) argued, international migration forces sending states to create a new social contract with their people, changing how government agencies address emigration issues within the country. While he was referring mainly to sending states' relations with overseas citizens, I argue that such new forms of governance also cater to both aspiring migrants and nonmigrants alike. To make sense of how this works, scholars must first envisage an emigra-tion story that begins from a point of immobility.

Moving beyond the Mobility Bias

When I first reached out to Rachel in June 2020, the thirty-six-year-old nurse was isolating at home, just outside the Philippine city of Cebu, sell-ing a homemade version of milk tea to her neighbors. "I'm just keeping busy. This is a diversion from my problems," she said, only half-joking. Six months before our interview, she had had a job offer from a nursing home in Ireland—a long-awaited opportunity. It had taken three years of paperwork and exams before she could even interview for open positions in the United Kingdom. When Rachel received the offer, she promptly resigned from her hospital job in Cebu and devoted all her time to pre-paring for her departure. By the time COVID-19 hit the Philippines and the government announced its first lockdown, she was just waiting for her work visa to be approved.

For two weeks, Rachel sent emails to the UK embassy in Manila, beg-ging it to reopen. She never received a response. Then, President Duterte declared a deployment ban on all health care workers, and she was left with no choice but to defer her departure for Ireland. "My mom keeps telling me that this is God's plan, and my brother keeps telling my mom to stop saying that," she said, laughing bitterly. It was becoming hard to fall asleep at night. Irish hospitals and nursing homes were starting to rescind their offers to Filipino nurses who were stuck at home. Rachel worried that her employer would do the same if she was unable to leave the Philippines in the next few months.

Larry, a thirty-one-year-old bartender, was also anxious to leave the country. But unlike Rachel, for Larry the pandemic interrupted not a highly anticipated change but a dependable overseas routine. Larry began 2020 as he had always done for the previous nine years: manning the largest bar of an international cruise ship. The New Year holiday was peak season for the travel industry, and the ship was packed with tourists, enjoying a weeklong excursion along the Caribbean Sea. Suddenly, in March 2020, the cruise line announced an outbreak of a mysterious virus in several of its ships. Company management decided to ground its entire fleet, forcing the captain of Larry's ship to disembark all passengers at the nearest port. Crew members stayed onboard as the cruise line searched for ways to repatriate its employees back home. It would take another twelve weeks before Larry returned to his wife and two children.

Stuck at sea, Larry isolated himself in one of the guest cabins of his ship, leaving his room only for meals and mandatory temperature checks during the day. A fellow cruise worker organized Zumba dance sessions on the ship's deck, just to keep everyone "healthy," but Larry was never really scared of the virus. Instead, he worried about what to do once he arrived home. "I knew I would be stuck in the Philippines for some time," he explained. "If my wife and I don't do something fast, we'll end up grinding salt to feed our kids." The first time we spoke, there had been several failed attempts to restart cruising in 2020. A resurgence of the virus had foiled company plans to begin limited voyages in Europe. Larry was steeling himself for a few more months of unemployment, hoping he could find a part-time job that would cover the family's daily expenses. Neither of us had known then that it would take another two years before the cruise industry would fully resume operations.

Numerous academics had written about people like Rachel and Larry— mobile workers whose care and service labor had become integral to the global economy (Chin 2008; Guevarra 2010; Terry 2014; Yeates 2012).

However, most of these studies frame their experiences as immigrants outside the Philippines. Even at the height of the pandemic, international news was mainly centered on stories of Filipino health care workers dying in American hospitals or reports of cruise employees stranded at sea (Carr 2020; McCormick and Greenfield 2020; Shoichet 2020). Little was said about nurses like Rachel who were unable to emigrate and cruise workers like Larry who were repatriated back to their countries of origin. Instead, there was an implicit belief that because these workers were at "home," their struggles had either ended or were yet to begin.

Kerilyn Schewel (2020) criticizes this logic as a symptom of the "mobility bias" in migration studies, or an overfocus on the experiences of those who can and do move. Immobility is a "default situation" or a condition of normalcy that is only significant when interrupted by emigration (Mata-Codesal 2015; 2017). In many ways, this bias is present in frameworks of migration governance as well. Among studies of source nations, researchers have generally painted a picture of unremitting movement, with people progressing smoothly from recruitment to overseas deployment (Acacio 2008; Rodriguez 2010). Thus, scholarly attention has mostly centered on how states manage mobility, specifically among temporary migrants who cycle between their homes and work sites abroad.

But for every migrant who successfully leaves the country, there are many more who fail to overcome barriers to international opportunities. The Philippines' own labor export history has been marked by constant disruption—whether armed conflict in Libya, a tsunami in Japan, or diplomatic spats with Kuwait.[6] The COVID-19 pandemic simply pushed these stories to mainstream attention, revealing how much of the migration cycle includes periods when people are unable to move or are made to stay in place. Today, there is a growing body of research on the topic of immobility, mostly outside the discipline of sociology. However, these studies have tended to cluster around two major themes, each with its own limitations.

On the one end, scholars examine how structural barriers can impede migrants from pursuing international opportunities or block them from traveling to desired destinations (Carling 2002; Stock 2019).[7] Much of this work investigates the phenomenon of involuntary immobility or situations where individuals are prevented from moving despite their high aspirations to leave (Carling and Schewel 2018; Cresswell 2012).[8] Current scholarship mostly attributes the rise of immobility to border security and immigration control (Bakewell 2008; Glick Schiller and Salazar 2013). Writing from the perspective of receiving states, scholars theorize how forced immobility results from an expansion of state power—often driven by a discourse of "crisis and chaos" at the national border (Mountz and Hiemstra 2014). Political geographers provide insightful work on how governments in places like the United States push their borders "outward," enforcing policies that prevent asylum seekers and refugees from entering national territory. In such cases, aspiring migrants are immobilized in a third place—separate from their countries of origin yet outside their desired destinations (Hiemstra 2012; Hyndman and Giles 2011).

Such displays of state power extend to source countries as well. Sending states can block the movements of their own citizens by refusing to issue travel permits or preventing access to documents required for emigration (Fitzgerald 2009; Weinar 2017). In such situations, surveillance and bureaucratic controls can immobilize even migrants traveling through legal channels, as the requirements for moving become more complicated and expensive. While some of these measures may be intended to protect migrants' interests, they reinforce existing social inequalities. Individuals who possess privileged passports or high economic capital can move more quickly and smoothly across borders. Meanwhile, low-wage laborers, asylum seekers, and migrants from the developing world experience more delays, longer periods of waiting, and mobility constraints (Bélanger and Silvey 2020; Johnson and Lindquist 2020).

While important, these studies have tended to treat immobility as an "opposite concept" (Salazar 2021: 4) or a condition where the goals of migration remain unfulfilled. Such research provides insight on how immobility results from state authority, but we know less about how individuals themselves define their immobility in the first place.

At the other end of the spectrum, researchers have emphasized how individuals perceive and interpret their international immobility. Rather than a condition imposed upon aspiring migrants, immobility can be part of people's imagined identities, shaping how they see themselves and their place in the world (see Bissell 2007; Salazar and Smart 2011). Anthropologists, in particular, have introduced detailed accounts of the many ways people make sense of immobility (Chu 2010; Stock 2019). Some may feel depressed and anxious in navigating "stuckedness" or what Ghassan Hage (2009) describes as a condition of going nowhere. Meanwhile, others can voluntarily choose to be immobile due to an attachment to a place or community (Ortiga and Macabasag 2020; Schewel and Fransen 2022). Taking things further, scholars such as Noel Salazar (2011) argue that mobility and immobility are intertwined—shaping one another as people's thoughts and imaginations remain constantly "in movement" (see also Bissell 2007; Hannam, Sheller, and Urry 2006; Smets 2019).[9]

Anthropological research provides a more nuanced view of how individuals interpret their immobility. But few of these studies adequately explore how ideas about immobility can also be opposed, used, or bolstered by institutions and organizations. In this sense, immobility is mainly a subjective experience that defines individual identities and perspectives.

Stuck at Home occupies the space between these two approaches to immobility. Research under these two themes has effectively shown that immobility is a fundamental part of the migration process, as people spend time navigating the bureaucracies, assessments, and opportunities that allow their movement to progress.[10] However, this book is not just a story of closed borders and lockdowns. Neither is it a tale of how extended periods of waiting affected migrants' identities and imaginations. Rather, this book examines how dominant narratives of immobility are negotiated between both state institutions and individual migrants, justifying who deserves to move and who must remain in place.

Telling Stories of Immobility

How can we make sense of how states govern immobility? *Stuck at Home* focuses on the negotiations that occur in telling stories about those who are unable to move. As social scientists have long argued, public narratives often reveal how powerful institutions, like the state, maintain political legitimacy. Within migration studies, researchers have shown that the image of the migrant—as victim, opportunist, or criminal—animates social discourse meant to either increase or block immigration (see Allen et al. 2018). When it comes to labor export, the Philippines rationalized its own emigration policies through stories that valorize overseas workers as modern heroes whose monetary remittances keep the nation's economy afloat (Aguilar 2009; San Juan 2009).

Conversely, we know very little about the public narratives of immobility. While existing research recognizes the many state policies that prevent or delay migrants' international mobility (Bélanger and Silvey 2020), few scholars investigate how these practices are rationalized or how would-be migrants respond to the way others depict their immobility (Chan 2017). As Polleta and her colleagues (2010: 110) argue, public narratives are "interactively constructed, institutionally regulated, and assessed by their audiences in relation to hierarchies of discursive credibility." In other words, examining immobility narratives entails an in-depth study of how relevant stakeholders interact in creating these stories in the first place.

Stuck at Home focuses on two factors that shaped the narratives of immobility that emerged in the Philippines during the COVID-19 pandemic. First, this book investigates how state institutions and two groups of aspiring migrants negotiated what it means to remain in place, pushing for a public narrative that would fit their own interests. To date, scholars have mostly focused on how international organizations, commercial agencies, and civil society groups can influence public discourses on migration (Goh, Wee, and Yeoh 2017; Rother 2022). This book is centered on how Philippine state institutions interact with migrants themselves in responding to the effects of the COVID-19 pandemic. Specifically, it shows how both aspiring migrants and government officials tried to convey a narrative that best appealed to a broader Filipino society, altering parts of their stories to gain sympathy, commiseration, or support.[11] In doing so, *Stuck at Home* echoes Salazar's (2021: 16) call for scholars to examine the experience of remaining in place "across very dissimilar scales"—one that involves both state interests and individual perspectives of immobility.

Second, this book highlights how the concept of skill served as a key part of each group's narrative, creating tensions between state interests and would-be migrants. There is a vast literature on how skill itself is socially constructed and often defined by dominant norms surrounding race, class, and gender (see Iskander 2021; Liu-Farrer, Yeoh, and Baas 2021). In this book, I discuss how ideas about skill became a sticking point in how Filipino workers and their government negotiated the meaning of their immobility. Filipino workers were stuck at home during a time when governments faced rising demands to mitigate the spread of the virus while responding to the economic repercussions of the pandemic (Patterson 2021). This book reveals how the stories told about immobility varied depending on general perceptions of workers' skills. Whose immobility was necessary and whose was simply unfortunate? The comparison between nurses and cruise workers underlines how public narratives of immobility can have varying strategic objectives. And as the rest of this book will show, not all stories were successful in legitimizing the state's authority or migrants' right to leave their own country.

What Is the Philippines a Case of?

Migration scholarship is replete with typologies of how states govern international movement. Researchers have contrasted "Western" and "non-Western" nations, often comparing policies between "democratic" and "autocratic" regimes (Natter 2018). Within this literature, the Philippines' aggressive approach to labor export has made it an example of a neoliberal government that commodifies its own citizens for the global market. Scholars have used the Philippines as a case of how emigration allows state institutions to avoid improving social conditions at home, leaving individual workers with the responsibility of seeking better employment prospects abroad (Rodriguez 2010; Tyner 2004).

In contrast, this book presents the Philippines as a compelling case of how migration governance goes beyond labor export. Even as states seek to benefit from the outmigration of their citizens, they must also preserve political legitimacy among those who remain in the country. The struggle to maintain this balance was not just an isolated problem borne in by the COVID-19 pandemic, but an ongoing issue that runs through the country's history as a migrant-sending nation. This history shows how the Philippine state is not a static entity that functions only to export its citizens' labor. Rather, it is an institution whose approach to emigration has evolved through time, in line with the changing demands of its citizenry both within and beyond the national borders.

To begin, the Philippines' popular image as a democratic, neoliberal emigration state did not emerge fully formed. In fact, the country's labor export system was established during a time of martial law, under the authoritarian regime of former president Ferdinand Marcos. It was President Marcos who in 1974 first decided to institutionalize the migration process, establishing state agencies to take charge of the "development, promotion, regulation and implementation of the labor export program" (Rodriguez 2010). He justified this move as a provisional measure meant to address domestic unemployment rates and the rise of unscrupulous placement agencies that took advantage of aspiring migrants. As such, government bodies were initially focused on directing aspiring migrants toward official channels (Acacio 2008).[12] It was almost a decade later that administration officials sought to capture migrant remittances through Philippine banks, thus generating an abundant source of revenue for the national government.

The Philippine emigration state we see today is a product of subsequent efforts to amend the Marcos administration's policies in line with officials' own political agendas and priorities. Some had deliberately reinforced the country's labor export system, mainly as an opportunity for economic development.[13] However, other Philippine administrations faced pressures to amend the government's migration policies, even if it meant slowing the outmigration of future migrant workers. For example, the 1990s saw a rise in heinous cases of worker abuse, causing public uproar and protests from local advocacy groups in the Philippines. In response, then-president Fidel Ramos instituted the Migrant Workers and Overseas Filipinos Act of 1995,[14] a law that granted state agencies the power to ban overseas deployment, assess workers' contracts for necessary protections, and receive additional funds for repatriation and reintegration. This law also altered the state's stance toward migrant workers, placing more emphasis on gender and the protection of women (Encinas-Franco 2016). Despite these new regulations, the Ramos administration was also the first to publicly acknowledge that emigration was no longer a short-term solution to unemployment. In an annual report for the Department of Labor and Employment (DOLE), Ramos praised overseas Filipino workers as "internationally shared human resources" whose presence "benefits both their host countries and the Philippines" (DOLE 1995: 3). However, the former president stopped short of saying that the state explicitly encouraged workers' departure, arguing that government agencies would continue to ensure proper protections for outgoing workers (Ortiga 2018a).

This ambiguous stance toward labor export defined future administrations as well. President Rodrigo Duterte, a highly popular politician, initially declared that his administration would focus on creating better jobs within the country, eventually making overseas work "just an option" for Filipino workers (Corrales 2017). Yet his administration also spearheaded the creation of an entirely new state department specifically devoted to addressing the needs of overseas Filipino workers (Avendano 2017). Aside from making the deployment process more "efficient," state representatives underlined that the new department would also ensure better support and international safeguards for Filipinos working abroad.

In many ways, these tensions have been relatively invisible in discussions of Philippine policies on emigration. Globally, international organizations regarded the Philippines as a "model" for migration management (Acacio 2008). However, the country's own approach to emigration was also constantly changing, as different administrations tried to maximize the benefits of labor export while managing the sentiments of Filipinos within the country. In this book, I present the Philippines as a powerful case of how, even within a highly successful labor-exporting nation, state officials must continuously balance the needs of citizens within and beyond national borders. I show how doing so entails not only regulating movement but also controlling a narrative of immobility.

Organization of the Book

Stuck at Home is a story of how Philippine state agencies and aspiring migrant workers negotiated two different narratives of immobility in the context of a country that had thrived on encouraging outmigration. Specifically, this book focuses on the state's interactions with two groups of workers caught in separate junctures of the migration process: deployment and return. Contrary to the image of a sending state driven solely toward exporting labor, I show how Philippine government agencies were quick to pivot toward retaining essential workers and reintegrating those sent home from abroad. However, such strategies relied on constructing a narrative that defined these workers' immobility as an ideal response to the ongoing crisis—one that bolsters the state's image as a responsible and competent authority (Xiang et al. 2022). This book examines how both Philippine government agencies and aspiring migrants worked to construct a story of immobility in line with their own interests and how these narratives led to two very different results.

To understand how the Philippine state governs emigration, it is essential to first recognize how workers are prepared, directed, and channeled toward a global market of migrant labor. Chapter 1 provides an overview of how Philippine society came to associate professions such as nursing and hospitality services with overseas opportunity. Specifically, I discuss how the Philippine state cultivated a postsecondary education system driven toward training graduates for foreign employers. I also show how for-profit private schools enabled this system to flourish, as school owners catered to the aspirations of Filipino families eager to provide their children a pathway to emigration. This chapter serves as an important context for the rest of the book, as Filipino workers' orientation toward global careers would later make it difficult for state agencies to manage their immobility.

The next two chapters delve into the competing narratives of deferred departure. Chapter 2 focuses on the narrative of immobility from the Philippine state, where government officials justified a ban on nurses leaving the country as a means of addressing the effects of the ongoing pandemic. This chapter shows that while immobilizing nurses seems at odds with the logic of labor export, the state's narrative was popular among the Filipino public, cementing the administration's legitimacy in the context of a quickly spiraling crisis.

Chapter 3 directs our attention to the narratives of nurses themselves—specifically, the stories that they wanted to emphasize among state officials and the broader Philippine society. I show that while most nurses had opposed the state's ban on their overseas movements, there were two variations in how they viewed their inability to leave the country. Specifically, I discuss how Filipino nurses saw their immobility as either an opening to new overseas possibilities or as a quickly closing gap that put their emigration plans in jeopardy. This chapter explains how this division among nurses weakened efforts to counter the state's narrative of their immobility as a necessary measure for national safety.

Later chapters focus on the narratives of reintegration, as state agencies sought to frame the immobility of cruise workers who lost their jobs overseas. Chapter 4 examines how Philippine government officials tried to promote a story of forced return as an opportunity for permanent resettlement—a time for migrants to start their lives anew without the hardships of working far from home. Pushing against the image of a sending state only concerned with labor export, I show how there were high stakes in the state being able to show a successful reintegration of former migrants. However, this narrative eventually failed to gain support from both Philippine politicians and returning migrants, despite massive public funds and support. Chapter 5 delves more deeply into why Filipino cruise workers rejected the state's narrative of permanent resettlement, by analyzing how these former migrants viewed their own immobility. I discuss how cruise workers emphasized their struggle to gain recognition for their service skills, reinforcing the belief that their immobility should remain temporary. In many ways, the cruise workers' narrative emphasized the struggles of their involuntary immobility. Yet, unlike the case of their nurse counterparts, state efforts to reframe their immobility were destined to fail, given that most of Philippine society saw little use in their remaining within the country.

The conclusion brings us to the end of the COVID-19 pandemic, as the Philippine state turns back toward governing emigration in a post-pandemic world. I discuss how state agencies and aspiring migrants continue to negotiate the meaning of their immobility despite the reopening of borders and the resumption of international travel. Drawing on follow-up interviews with nurses and cruise workers, I share the outcomes of their immobility and how their negotiations with the Philippine state affected their lives during the pandemic. I end this book with a discussion of how attention to narratives of immobility is essential to migration governance, as would-be migrants and government agencies negotiate the questions of who gets to cross national borders. Such findings have important implications as to how migration scholars have understood the state, those who move, and those who remain in place.

One

Prelude to the Pandemic

Skilling to Seize Global Opportunities

In recalling how she first made plans to leave the country, Rachel began with the story of choosing her undergraduate major. Her mother and brother—both teachers—were already permanent residents in the United Kingdom. Rachel wanted a career that would allow her to follow them there, but she had no interest in working in a school. Becoming a nurse was the practical choice. "I wanted to be a pediatrician, but my dad got leukemia, so we didn't have the money to pay for medical school," she explained. "My aunt was the one who suggested nursing. At that time, it was so in demand. That was way back in 2002."

Rachel had entered university at a time when countries such as the United States and the United Kingdom were aggressively recruiting foreign nurses. This international "demand" for nurse labor fueled a subsequent demand for nursing degrees, spurring a proliferation of private nursing schools within the Philippines (Ortiga 2018a).[1] "I just felt like I was riding a wave," Rachel said, sweeping her hand across her face, as if to demonstrate the surge that pushed her toward her profession. She wasn't exaggerating. By the time Rachel obtained her license in 2006, nursing programs in the Philippines had close to half a million enrollees—ten times the number of students just a decade before (Ortiga 2018a).

Five years after this nursing "boom," another academic program saw a major increase in enrollment. This time, students were pursuing degrees in tourism and hospitality management, mostly inspired by news of mass hiring in tourist hubs such as Singapore and Dubai (*Channel News Asia* [CNA] 2012). For Larry, a former cruise worker, the sudden popularity of these degrees was what led him to a career bartending on ships. "When I was a kid, I always wondered why my friend's house was so much nicer than ours," he shared. "His dad was a seaman, so I decided I wanted to be a seaman too." This friend would show off postcards from the different cities his father's freight ship touched at, and Larry remembers examining the glossy photos very closely, just in case he too would one day visit a place like Helsinki or Rotterdam. This friend also told Larry that there were plenty of ships in need of good workers, and cruise lines, in particular, employed Filipinos by the thousands. "My parents couldn't afford a degree in marine engineering, so I took HRM [hotel and restaurant management] instead. It was really trendy then. I mean, it was either HRM or nursing."

The "trends" that Rachel and Larry described were all too familiar. Around the same time they pursued their globally oriented degrees, I was a PhD student, studying how overseas labor needs impacted Philippine colleges and universities. Part of this work involved charting student enrollments throughout the 2000s, trying to make sense of how one "in-demand" degree made way for another (Ortiga 2018a). The Filipino students I spoke to then were much like Rachel, Larry, and many of the other workers featured in this book. They began the emigration process with a decision to acquire certain skills—often with the hope that such capacities would lead them to opportunities overseas.

The dissertation I submitted in 2015 described how the Philippine state had fostered this system of educating its own graduates for other countries. It was the government that allowed schools to explicitly train students for care and service work, establishing the Philippines' reputation as an ideal source of such labor. It was also the state that encouraged Filipino parents to invest their savings in degrees that would lead their children to global opportunities. I had no idea that this tale of export-oriented education would eventually become a prelude to the events documented in this book. Suddenly, the nursing and service skills that Filipino students pursued to access overseas jobs became the very reason for their international immobility. Meanwhile, the government that had actively supported their departures became the institution responsible for keeping them in place.

To make sense of how nurses and cruise workers negotiated their im-mobility with the Philippine government, it is essential to first understand how both groups prepared themselves for emigration and what challenges they would face if they were unable to leave the country. Scholars have long documented how Philippine state agencies marketed nurses and service workers to foreign employers by highlighting Filipinos' "natural" propensity for care (Choy 2003; Guevarra 2010).[2] In this chapter, I dis-cuss how state agencies also promoted the education of these workers for "export," effectively redefining occupations such as nursing and hospitality as stepping stones to emigration. Meanwhile, health care and hospitality professions were largely neglected within the Philippines, subjecting those who remained to poor work conditions and low social status. Migration scholars often discuss these problems as the factors that push workers to pursue international migration. In reality, these issues also emerge from a system where global labor demands encourage the overproduction of certain professions and diminish attempts to retain their labor within the country. This system will come to cause problems for the Philippine state, when the workers educated for export find themselves stuck at home.

Brain Drain as Business Strategy

Perhaps one of the most striking aspects of the Philippines' labor export system is the wide range of skills the state is able to successfully deploy overseas (Acacio 2008). Unlike those of other source countries, such as Mexico and Indonesia, Filipino workers are highly represented in multi-ple industries, encompassing blue-collar workers to professionals in health care and engineering. Even more astonishing is the fact that Philippine society generally accepts the departure of these workers as a benefit to the nation. Global discourse usually portrays the loss of skills as a form of "brain drain," a problem that undermines national development. How then did the Philippine state come to produce skilled workers mainly for the benefit of other countries?

Until the 1980s, state-led skilling programs geared toward overseas jobs were limited to providing vocational training for out-of-school youth and unemployed adults—workers whose "excess skill" could not be ab-sorbed in the Philippines' domestic economy (Ortiga 2018a). Exporting this excess skill fit the general narrative that Philippine state agencies had used in the early years of the country's labor export system. While the government facilitated Filipino workers' departures, officials claimed that such policy was only meant to address pressing issues of local unemployment (see Acacio 2008; Encinas-Franco 2016). Throughout the 1980s, any mention of emigration was taboo among highly skilled professions that required four-year degrees (Ministry of Education [MEC] 1984). While many Filipino university graduates did emigrate to other countries, their departure was blamed on the pull of better opportunities beyond borders. The idea of intentionally educating university students for overseas jobs would have been considered preposterous, if not harmful to the Philippines' future as a nation.

A turning point came in the early 2000s, as ideas of a new knowledge economy became popular among both local and international policymakers (Powell and Snellman 2004). This ideology exhorted nations to invest in the education and training of their citizens, as the global market competes for innovative ideas and skills. Gloria Macapagal-Arroyo, who took the Philippine presidency in 2001, fully embraced the ideals of the knowledge economy in her plans for labor export.[3] Her strategy was simple: if overseas workers were the key contributors to the Philippines' economic well-being, it was essential that schools provided them with the skills needed to compete for jobs in other countries. Then President Macapagal-Arroyo justified the plan as one that would leverage the country's large population. The domestic labor market was simply too small for the Philippines' young workers. Training young people for overseas jobs would be an effective means of maximizing the nation's human resources.

This approach to migration management encouraged universities to create academic programs geared toward filling foreign labor shortages, with nursing and hospitality services becoming two of the largest degree programs associated with jobs abroad (Ortiga 2017). While local critics raised concerns over the lack of academic programs for domestic industries, there was little public furor over the notion of making Filipino graduates more globally competitive. The nurses and cruise workers I spoke with did not think of their education in terms of its national implications. Their only goal was to allocate family resources to education that could ensure gainful employment. That these degrees led to jobs outside the country was a given, a fact of life. In 2016, a report from the International Labor Office found that Filipino youth constituted half of all unemployed workers within the Philippines. More than one-third of these jobless young people had invested in at least one postsecondary degree

(*Manila Bulletin* 2016). While these numbers have oscillated since then (Yee 2024), Filipino parents continue to look beyond borders in weighing future options for their children.

Such was the case for Jenine, whose father was adamant about her becoming a registered nurse. Jenine admitted that, as a seventeen-year-old entering university in 2007, her plans were far from pragmatic. "What I really wanted was a fancy type of major, the type where all I do is sit in an office and I could wear whatever I wanted—no uniform, fashion show every day," she laughed. "But my father gave me an ultimatum: if I don't pursue nursing, I would have to take a [technical vocational] course instead. I just went along with it. At least, after everything, I would still have my four-year degree." At that time, Jenine's first cousin was already a nurse in London, and it was clear that her family wanted her to chase the same goals. "I guess there's glamor in having one of your children abroad, sustaining the family," she reflected. "So that was the initial goal for my parents: Right after I pass the board exams, I should be able to work overseas."

Not all government agencies had promoted education for export. But most state officials were hesitant to curtail the aspirations of those like Jenine's parents. As the demand for nursing degrees started to grow in 2002, Philippine health officials began to note an increasing number of medical doctors within the country who were entering fast-track nursing programs to access nursing jobs overseas. When members of the public raised concerns over a domestic shortage of doctors, representatives from the Commission on Higher Education (CHED) rejected calls to restrict local colleges and universities from offering these courses. A statement to Philippine media read, "Our concern is to provide quality education to the Filipino youth. The [exodus of health professionals] should be the concern of Congress, the Department of Labor and Employment, and the Department of Foreign Affairs" (*Manila Standard* 2004).

These changes indicated a drastic shift from the government's earlier mandate to educate undergraduates for national labor needs. Embracing the ideology of producing a globally competitive citizenry, Philippine state officials encouraged the training of Filipino graduates who would be desirable to foreign employers. But, as such practices spread throughout the country's postsecondary education system, even the state did not fully anticipate how privately owned schools would turn "education for export" into a profitable enterprise.

Private Interests in Education for Export

Despite the Philippine state's bold emphasis on producing the best workers for the global market, it was the private sector that took on the task of educating would-be migrants. Commercial agencies offered in-house training for domestic and factory workers before deployment overseas. Meanwhile, private colleges and universities dominated an even larger market for degree programs and technical and vocational training.

Although the majority of basic education in the Philippines is publicly funded, postsecondary schooling is mostly run by private institutions (Yee 2024). In 2020, nongovernment entities operated close to 90% of the country's 1,975 colleges and universities.[4] Thus, a significant proportion of Filipino high school graduates were likely to enter schools owned by either private corporations or family businesses. Most of these schools are profit-driven institutions, entirely reliant on income earned from tuition-paying students.

While the Philippine government approved the establishment of private schools and regulated some of their operations, many of these institutions had considerable autonomy in what academic programs to offer and how best to train their students. In the early 2010s, the colleges and universities I visited in Manila were mainly driven toward educating future nurses and hospitality workers. Nursing schools were offering language electives in Arabic and German, in response to anticipated opportunities in the Gulf and Western Europe. Meanwhile, hospitality programs were scrambling to establish ties with hotels and cruise line companies. While Filipino migrants were already highly represented in service positions overseas, school administrators insisted that developing these skills early in their schooling would provide graduates with advantages later on. As the owner of a private school argued, "When inexperienced people go to hotels, they have a lot more to learn. But the hotel people do not have time to teach them. Experienced individuals, on the other hand, can easily adapt in the workplace because they have the knowledge of the working environment" (*Manila Bulletin* 2013a). STI Education Services Group, a for-profit chain of local schools, had even signed an agreement with Royal Caribbean Cruises Limited, promising to follow the company's standards in training its students for hospitality jobs on cruise ships (Loyola 2017). While it was hard to say whether such classes truly gave aspiring migrants an upper hand in obtaining these jobs, Filipino school owners took it upon themselves to anticipate whatever skills were purportedly needed in the global market.

For private school owners, developing export-oriented degrees had an obvious return on investment. Majors that came with the promise of future emigration could be easily sold to potential new students. When I asked school administrators how they determined the demand for a certain degree, their responses were both random and diverse. Some referred to statistics from the country's labor export agencies, such as the Philippine Overseas Employment Administration (POEA). Others put their trust in contacts within foreign embassies or alumni who were based abroad. However, the most important source of information were parents themselves. Private school owners I interviewed in 2013 believed that parents depended heavily on the advice of relatives and friends (many of whom were likely to be working overseas). "The parents will come to our registrar's office and ask if we have a degree program in hotel management or maybe in tourism. If you say you don't have that program, they'll just go somewhere else!" exclaimed one school administrator. "As a business owner, what do you expect me to do? Of course, I will try to see if we can offer that program as well."

As private schools rushed to offer postsecondary degrees that appealed to potential students and their families, the state's loose regulations allowed for the quick establishment of new programs. On paper, CHED has the power to prescribe the baseline requirements for all university curriculums and classroom teaching. Meanwhile, the Technical Education and Skills Development Authority (TESDA) regulates the delivery of short-term courses in vocational skills. All postsecondary schools were legally required to obtain approval from one agency or the other before they could begin accepting students. However, the application process was far from stringent. To propose a new program, private institutions were expected to invest money and resources in proving the school's capability to take in students. By the time school owners had applied to CHED, it was unlikely that their proposal would be rejected. "Basically, anybody can just put up the facilities and submit an application for whatever major," one school administrator admitted. "I guarantee you, I bet there is a 90% chance it will be accepted."

Once private institutions had established a new degree program, it became very difficult for the state to shut down those that failed to maintain standards. For one, state agencies like CHED relied on private school associations to manage their member schools and ensure the quality of classroom teaching. State officials argued that it was simply impossible to monitor the hundreds of education providers in the country. Perhaps even more difficult was that private school owners had their own political clout. In 2013, a Philippine newspaper reported that CHED officials had failed to shut down eighty-three nursing schools that lacked not only qualified faculty but basic facilities, such as a training hospital and library. School owners had successfully filed a temporary restraining order in court, allowing them to continue accepting students (*Manila Bulletin* 2013).[5]

Even as issues of substandard programs featured prominently in the national media, Philippine state officials stopped short of imposing stricter regulations on private colleges and universities. Instead, the Macapagal-Arroyo administration chose to release a list of "low-performing" schools for popular majors like nursing. This list included all schools whose passing rate in the annual board exams fell below the national average, including several institutions where none of their graduates had ever obtained a professional license. The president's spokesperson at that time argued that this system would "give the public an idea on where they should enroll" (Manongdo, Cagahastian, Mabasa, and Roxas 2006). Little else was done in terms of closing these schools.

In the end, government policies had a clear underlying message: Filipino students must take it upon themselves to make better academic decisions, even if it meant navigating a large education market crowded with for-profit schools of varying quality and reputation (E. Tan 2011). While the state encouraged aspiring migrants to pursue particular professions as a step toward international mobility, individual students would be responsible for transforming themselves into employable future migrant workers.

Pushing for Protections

On the surface, it is easy to assume that aspiring migrants simply accepted the imperfect conditions of the Philippines' education system. Many of the nurses and cruise workers I interviewed would not be in their professions if not for the presence of private schools. The few state institutions within the country were highly competitive and often limited in their capacity to increase student numbers.[6] In contrast, Philippine private schools adopted an "open admissions" policy, accepting most applicants into their programs—purportedly with the condition that they maintain a passing grade average.

However, Filipino families also wanted their government to ensure a certain standard among the private businesses that dominated the market. When the state offered only limited protections, dissatisfaction began to simmer among students and their parents. Such discontent came to a boil in 2006, when a group of nursing graduates disclosed that questions from that year's board examinations had been leaked to dozens of test-takers before the exam (Cerojano 2006). Several hospitals in the country, including the prestigious Philippine General Hospital in Manila, paused the hiring of nurses who obtained their licenses in 2006. Meanwhile, nursing graduates agonized over their chances of finding work overseas.

Investigators eventually convicted two members of the Professional Regulation Commission (PRC) of selling the test questions to a company that ran review classes for nursing graduates taking the licensure exam (Napallacan and Umel 2006). But public anger quickly turned to private nursing schools and the state agencies tasked with regulating their operations. In the year of the cheating scandal, the Philippines' 450 nursing schools had accepted tens of thousands of new students, spreading doubts about the quality of teaching within these institutions (*Manila Times* 2007).

As one of the oldest professions in the country,[7] Philippine nursing had built a strong infrastructure around the standards and requirements for practice—including a four-year bachelor's degree and a national board examination.[8] However, nursing leaders argued that the overexpansion of nursing schools had compromised the standards of their profession.

In producing ill-prepared graduates, private schools created a situation where many were tempted to find dishonest ways of obtaining their license. "It is the nursing schools that have primary responsibility to give quality nursing education. The bottom line is the regulation of nursing schools," argued Josefina Tuason, a professor at the University of the Philippines. "They have abrogated their basic responsibility of rendering good nursing education" (Aning 2006a).

Media outlets attributed the problems besetting nursing education to the dubious operations of "fly-by-night" schools that had failed to obtain proper government approval (Bagaoisan and Ching 2009). However, the majority of nursing students were actually enrolled in private institutions that were fully recognized by CHED. In other words, the Philippine state allowed these colleges and universities to greatly increase their student numbers, but later failed to prevent falling standards when these institutions overexpanded their programs. This fact was not lost on the many Filipino families who had invested hard-earned savings in their children's education.

In response to the cheating scandal, the government first proposed that all 42,000 examinees retake the nursing board exam. This announcement was met with widespread anger among the 17,000 nurses who had already passed the test. A group of parents formed the "Alliance of New Nurses" and threatened "civil disobedience" if their children would be forced to go through the exam again (Manongdo et al. 2006). Nursing graduates also held press conferences for the national media, begging President Macapagal-Arroyo to spare them the anxiety of going through the assessment once more. "Let them not take away from me what I and my parents had worked hard for," cried one nursing graduate in an interview with the media (Napallacan and Umel 2006). Such stories generated sympathy among Filipino politicians, media personalities, and educators, intensifying calls for state agencies to regulate private schools.

Eventually, administration officials walked back the notion of requiring a retake for all 2006 examinees (Aning 2006a). However, the stigma of the cheating scandal was difficult to shake off. The US–based Commission on Graduates of Foreign Nursing Schools announced that it would not accept Filipino nurses with 2006 licenses if they did not retake the board exams (Cabreza and Salaverria 2007). Aspiring migrants were left with no choice but to go through the exam again. To appease angry parents, the Philippine Congress allotted state funds to cover their review lessons and exam fees (Aning 2006a).

Not all the nurses I spoke to were part of "batch 2006." Still, most of them remember the crowded lecture halls and overwhelmed instructors that reflected the popularity of their profession. If given a choice, they would have wanted a different educational experience. "It's harder to get the teacher's attention when there are too many students," complained Miguel, a nurse who obtained his license in 2010. "Your teacher might ask, '*Gets niyo ba?* (Are you following the lesson?)' It feels quite embarrassing to speak up and let the whole lecture hall know that, nope, you don't get it." Miguel had chosen to enter a for-profit university with a long history of nursing education. The family that owned the school was the first to establish programs for health professionals in his province. However, administrators expanded the nursing program from 500 to more than 6,000 students, effectively taking over half of the campus. For Miguel, this expansion came at a cost. "Our instructors are much better teachers when the school gives them fewer students."

While individual aspirations had created the demand for particular degrees, the nurses and cruise workers I met were not blindly chasing trendy credentials. On the contrary, those who managed to obtain their degrees eventually developed a passion for their work, and schools played an important role in fostering such professional development. In Miguel's case, he spent most of his first year in university feeling "lost and unmotivated." He admitted that he only entered the nursing program because his parents wanted him to emigrate to the United States. However, the instructor who led his clinical rotations in the local hospital inspired him to see the hands-on aspect of nursing work. "She really showed me what nursing looks like on the hospital floor. It was amazing. You're just as important as the doctor in helping people get better." Such experiences—those that inspired and piqued students' interests—were sacrificed as for-profit schools expanded academic programs to maximize tuition profits.

In the mid-2000s, nurses were by far the most active group calling for educational reforms. But even their efforts to mobilize support during the 2006 cheating scandal did not lead to tighter regulations for private colleges and universities. Meanwhile, issues within hospitality programs never garnered enough attention to reach headline news. The hospitality students I interviewed also complained about substandard teaching and poor training. However, they only raised their concerns to their own school administrators, and many of those concerns remained unresolved. CHED officials continued to leave individual students responsible for their own education, despite the pushback from students and their parents.

Still, I believe that such reactions to the problems of substandard schools reflect how aspiring migrants saw the connection between postsecondary training and their own migration aspirations. As Filipino students took on the task of skilling themselves for future overseas jobs, they also felt entitled to a positive return on their educational investments. The possibility of becoming internationally immobile, whether due to cheating scandals or poor education, was a problem they felt the Philippine government should help address. For export-oriented professions such as nursing and hospitality services, leaving the country was an outcome of schooling that they felt they deserved. The poor work conditions that both types of workers encountered within the Philippines only fueled their migration aspirations further.

Nursing Other Nations

The development of nursing within the Philippines has always occurred alongside the outmigration of Filipino nurses. While the American colonial government established the first emigration pathways for nurses to the United States (Choy 2003), the Philippine state now deploys nurses to a wide range of destinations. Before the pandemic, more than fifty countries across the world depended on Filipino nurses to staff their health care systems (Acacio 2011; Kingma 2006).

Although other Filipino professionals were also highly represented in the migrant labor market, nursing was one of the few professions that provided a clear pathway to citizenship—especially in destinations such as the United States and the United Kingdom. The appeal of permanent emigration was part of the reason so many parents had encouraged their children to pursue the profession. When I first started interviewing nursing students in 2010, I rarely encountered nurses who intended to practice their profession in the Philippines. There was good reason for their ambivalence with regard to local service. Before the pandemic, only nurses who obtained overseas jobs were celebrated as national heroes due to the remittances they sent home. In contrast, those who stayed in the Philippines were often poorly compensated and overworked (Cabanda 2017b; Ronquillo et al. 2011). Part of this problem can be attributed to the development of nursing as a global profession, where the demand for nurses overseas can impact the status of the profession at home (Timmons et al. 2016). In the Philippine case, efforts to improve work conditions and pay within local hospitals were often hampered by the widespread belief that nurses would leave for overseas work anyway. Local politicians have been mostly concerned about nurses' employability overseas rather than their actual career development at home (Cabanda 2017a).

The state's domestic neglect of the profession was obvious in the lack of full-time staff nurse positions within public hospitals in the Philippines—which also constituted the majority of the country's health care system. Staff nurses within these institutions handle up to forty patients in one shift, often with limited supplies and equipment. In rural areas, nurses take on the work of doctors as well, diagnosing patients, prescribing medications, and suturing wounds (Ortiga and Macabasag 2021). While private hospitals offer a more manageable workload, the wages are much lower, and their patients are seen as more demanding (Ortiga and Rivero 2019).

This is not to say that all nurses were driven toward leaving the country. Cherry, a registered nurse since 2018, had obtained her degree from the University of the Philippines, the country's premier public institution. Raised in a middle-class family, Cherry didn't feel pressured to see her degree as a stepping stone to emigration. "I have lived a comfortable life. We're not wealthy, but I don't think money is the only thing that can bring fulfillment," she explained. "Migration is just not in my plans [pause], but I also don't know if it is because I don't have any family that I need to support." As she began working in local hospitals, she realized she couldn't blame others for wanting to leave: "It's sad, but I can understand why people want to work abroad. Now knowing the system, being in the system, it is so discouraging. I try to keep in mind why I wanted to be a nurse and who I want to serve. But of course, you can't impose your morals on other people, right?"

Given the dire conditions for nurses working in the Philippines, the popularity of nursing degrees has ebbed and flowed along with health worker needs in popular destination countries such as the United States and the United Kingdom (Ortiga 2018b; Smith and Gillin 2021). As discussed earlier in this chapter, the most recent peak in enrollment occurred in the early 2000s, spurred on by news of aggressive hiring among American hospitals and nursing homes (Ortiga 2014). But, just as the demand for nurses rose quickly in the first few years of the new millennium, opportunities for foreign nurses began to decline steadily after 2006. First, the United Kingdom stopped accepting nurses from outside the European Union, drastically cutting the number of Filipino nurses hired for local hospitals (Gillin and Smith 2020). In 2007, retrogression at the US embassy limited the visas available for Filipino nurse applicants to the United States, creating a backlog that would stretch on for years (Acacio 2011). The year after, a global financial crisis devastated national economies, slowing foreign nurse recruitment in North America and Europe (Buchan, O'May, and Dussault 2013).[9]

The decline in demand for nurses overseas did not translate to more opportunities for Filipino nurses at home. Instead, the opposite occurred. Public health institutions claimed that they lacked the funding to open staff positions for nursing graduates entering the domestic labor market. Instead, state hospitals offered part-time, contractual positions that demanded the same amount of work as full-time staff, but with less pay and no benefits (Ortiga and Macabasag 2021). Meanwhile, private hospital administrators saw the large number of new nurses as an opportunity to save on labor costs, offering staff positions with measly salaries that barely paid minimum wage.[10]

Given the lack of available jobs, aspiring nurse migrants found themselves unable to gain the extra work experience that most foreign hospitals required (Ortiga and Macabasag 2020). Moving to places that offered permanent status demanded more time and resources, with multiple exams and countless requirements (Cortes and Pan 2015). While most Filipino nursing students may enter the profession with a desire to gain citizenship elsewhere, this goal became harder to achieve in the mid-2000s, making it more likely for nurses to leave on temporary contracts for places where there is very little success in obtaining even permanent residency, such as Kuwait, Saudi Arabia, Singapore, and the United Arab Emirates. To find their way to more desirable destinations, nurses would need to move through more than one country to build the economic resources and work experience that would bolster their applications for work visas and citizenship (Amrith 2021; Collins 2021). All these factors created a "migration trap," where aspiring nurse migrants invested in obtaining credentials for international work but graduated at a time when those jobs were no longer available (Ortiga 2018b). With few regular positions within local hospitals, thousands of nursing graduates gave up looking for clinical work. Instead, nursing graduates found better employment conditions in other industries, such as hospitality, education, and sales (Depasupil 2020; Thompson 2019).[11]

The Filipino nurses I interviewed initially thought that 2020 would finally bring the opportunity they had been waiting for. Health policy experts anticipated that the demand for health workers would continue to rise, as the needs of aging societies would eventually force receiving nations to loosen their immigration policies (WHO 2006). Toward the end of the 2010s, it seemed that their predictions were finally being realized, thanks to a noticeable uptick in the number of jobs in countries like the United Kingdom. Yet, as I outline in later chapters, the emergence of the COVID-19 pandemic became a double-edged sword for aspiring migrant nurses.

Nurses' struggles within the Philippines revealed the paradoxical impact of the profession's global demand. On the one hand, the promise of an international career made nursing an important skill for aspiring migrants and a "service" that the state could proudly "export" to other nations. On the other hand, the overproduction of nurses for foreign employers undermined the profession's status and bargaining power with hospital owners within the country. In many ways, nurses' emigration was not merely a reaction to poor work conditions at home; it was also the reason behind the exploitative treatment of the profession in the Philippines. For the nurses who graduated in the mid-2000s, export-oriented education felt like a broken promise. They had poured their time and money into skilling themselves into future migrant workers, and now a poorly regulated education system and changing labor demands overseas left them unable to fulfill their migration dreams.

Servicing the Seas

When opportunities for foreign nurses declined in the mid-2000s, private institutions began to promote hospitality degrees as the next "in-demand" profession for young Filipinos. Philippine colleges and universities had taught courses on the hospitality services since the 1970s, but new demands for service professionals created a market for specialized degrees in this area. Schools began offering a variety of academic programs related to leisure and travel, from the culinary arts to hospitality management (Ortiga 2018c). Students entered these programs in droves, expanding enrollment numbers from barely 80,000 students in 2005 to more than 200,000 in 2012.[12]

Government officials argued that such expansion was necessary for local development, given the Philippines' growing travel industry (*Philippines News Agency [PNA]* 2012; 2016). Business pundits heralded "food" and "fun" as the country's fastest growing industries, calling for more skilled workers in these areas (Villegas 2017). However, the Philippines' labor export agencies also encouraged hospitality degrees as a means to access global opportunity. Throughout the 2010s, officials from the country's labor department regularly advertised opportunities for hospitality workers in the United Arab Emirates or Singapore, with recruitment directed toward people willing to work in kitchens, housekeeping, and guest relations (*Manila Bulletin* 2014).

But unlike nursing, careers in hospitality services did not offer the same pathways to citizenship or permanent residency. Migrants in the service industry worked under short-term contracts, often tied to the companies that employed their labor. Still, Filipino students continued to pursue hospitality degrees in the hope of accessing jobs abroad (*Manila Bulletin* 2014). Like Larry, the bartender introduced at the beginning of this chapter, several of my interviewees regarded hospitality services as an alternative path toward becoming a seafarer. Others simply wanted to save money while traveling the world. Hospitality services seemed like a reliable path toward a global industry that offered higher wages and better opportunities.

The hospitality majors I interviewed did not see service work as a desirable career within the Philippines. There were few full-time positions in local hotels and restaurants, where most employees were hired as contractual workers through third-party agencies. Even then, full-time hospitality workers received compensation that was barely at the minimum wage level and relied on service charges and tips to augment their income. Relying on tips was fine when it was the peak of travel season. However, erratic visitor numbers during off-season periods made the income of service workers unstable—especially for those working in smaller hotels and resorts.

One reason behind the low status of service professionals is that, while nursing is a recognized profession that requires a licensure exam, hospitality jobs are often represented as "unskilled" work (Harkison, Poulston, and Kim 2011). Formalizing credentials in hospitality and tourism was expected to help Filipino service workers gain more recognition as professionals, both within and beyond the Philippines (Ortiga 2018a). However, service professionals were less successful than their nursing counterparts in this regard. While government agencies claimed that the travel and tourism industry paid one of the "highest entry-level" salaries in the country (Crismundo 2014), a careful reading of their data revealed that well-paid jobs in hospitality were mostly in digital marketing and sales. Hospitality graduates who chose to remain in the Philippines were more likely to end up working as waitstaff, cleaners, front desk officers, or restaurant cooks—positions where wages were much less enticing.[13]

Thus, while colleges and universities produced more students with four-year degrees in hospitality management, they merely worsened the already present problem of credential inflation within the country's labor market. The service workers I spoke with complained that Philippine establishments often required at least a bachelor's degree for entry-level jobs such as waiters or receptionists. Even instructors in hospitality management programs admitted that many of their graduates were likely to be underemployed as housekeeping or restaurant staff. Such jobs not only demanded heavy physical labor but also paid very little. As in the case of nursing, the state did very little to improve such work conditions. Instead, an implicit assumption was that those unsatisfied with the domestic labor market could aspire to leave and find work outside the country.

For the cruise workers I interviewed, the notion of working onboard ships became an ideal goal. Cruise companies had historically recruited service workers from the Philippines, and this practice only became more frequent as the industry expanded (*Manila Bulletin* 2016). Scholars estimate that before the pandemic, the Philippines had a pool of at least 30,000 workers who cycled in and out of cruise ships throughout the year (Terry 2014). While all my interviewees were based in the Philippines, their lives were in constant movement, traveling to and from international ports in Milan, Miami, and Singapore. At these ports, they boarded luxury ships the size of shopping malls and spent four to eight months serving passengers traveling through dozens of destinations across the globe.

The number of scholars investigating the experiences of migrant workers onboard cruise ships is smaller than the number who have examined the experiences of nurses. The studies that do exist have painted a sobering view of an industry that mainly enriches a transnational capitalist class. Currently, two companies (Royal Caribbean and Carnival Corporation) own 70% of the cruise sector, and daily operations involve myriad investors and management firms (Sprague-Silgado 2017). Until the 1970s, cruise lines represented the nation where they based their operations, and crew members were either local workers or migrants from nearby countries. Today, contemporary cruise lines can be owned by a company from one place, but registered in another that allows corporate owners to avoid high taxes and stringent labor laws. Thus, cruise ships can now draw their crew members from a global pool of labor—with most workers coming from developing nations, such as Vietnam, the Philippines, and Indonesia (Chin 2008; Oyogoa 2016).

Work onboard a cruise ship can be punishing. International maritime law only allows workers to be on duty for ten to twelve hours a day. However, living and working in the same vessel make it easy for the job to cut into time allocated for rest. Scholars have also critiqued the cruise industry for the short-term nature of workers' contracts. While many cruise workers stay in the industry for many years, they live on six- to eight-month contracts that their companies renew for every voyage. In between these contracts, workers must find other sources of income until their companies call with new assignments to fulfill.

Most of my interviewees entered the cruise industry precisely because it allowed them to return home on a regular basis. Jaiya, who used to teach at her cruise ship's daycare center, explained that she found land-based jobs abroad too rigid for her family life. "I realized I like cruise work because I can earn a better income than I do at home, and I only need to spend a few months overseas. After my contract is done, I can go home to my family," she shared. "Plus, I get a long vacation—about two months—before I go onboard again. For land-based work, sometimes people only get a week of vacation leave. Then, they have to be away for at least two years!" Waiters and bartenders like Larry had longer contracts—about eight to nine months. However, they preferred this arrangement to the yearlong contracts required for land-based migrants. Due to the flexible nature of their work, cruise workers would fill time at home with other side jobs, working shifts at a local hotel or restaurant.

All this frenetic movement came to an abrupt halt with the emergence of COVID-19. It was then that cruise workers realized that the skills they had used so effectively would suddenly be accorded little value at home.

Educated for Export but Stuck at Home?

In the years leading up to the COVID-19 pandemic, the Philippines intensified its role as a global supplier of both care and service workers. Increasing demand for Filipino health care professionals cemented the country's status as the world's primary source of foreign nurse labor (Yeates and Pillinger 2019). Meanwhile, Filipino service workers came to dominate parts of the global travel industry, constituting more than 30% of crew members onboard cruise ships (Terry 2014).[14] In this chapter, I have discussed how such labor was generated by a for-profit education system geared toward training young Filipinos for jobs beyond national borders. This system emerged from a convergence of different factors: the state's embrace of knowledge economy ideals, Filipino families' overseas aspirations, and private school owners' overzealous efforts to monetize "in-demand" majors.

If we are to see migration governance as a dance between competing interests, then the state's shift to export-oriented education may seem like the right step toward addressing both global and local demands. Among policymakers, debates over brain drain tend to revolve around the experiences of countries where the state subsidizes citizens' postsecondary schooling.[15] In the case of health care workers such as nurses and doctors, a controversial question is whether outgoing migrants should first "serve" the people whose taxes had financed their education (Brock and Blake 2015). Yet, in the Philippines, this dilemma is less of an issue. Among the many nurses and hospitality workers I met, only a minority owed their professional training to public funding. Rachel and Larry, the two workers introduced at the beginning of this chapter, had each paid for the entirety of their higher education. In Rachel's case, her nursing degree was made possible through the remittances of her mother who worked in the United Kingdom—the country she hoped to migrate to in the future. Simply put, the Philippine state did not need to invest public resources in producing the skilled workforce it marketed to overseas employers. In fact, administration officials were often negligent in regulating private education providers that compromised quality teaching for profit. The deliberate production of graduates for export also diminished state efforts to retain their labor within the Philippines, thereby encouraging more graduates to simply leave the country.

Rather than presenting a typical "brain drain" story, this chapter elucidates how the Philippine state intentionally produced a particular type of migrant subject: globally oriented and outward-looking in developing their skills. Filipino nurses and cruise workers were not merely pushed out to other countries due to economic or social factors in the Philippines. Rather, they began their emigration journeys as students and trainees, actively investing in specific types of skill to accomplish their goals of working overseas. In the following chapters, we will see how such dispositions would eventually make it difficult for the state to manage the immobility of their aspiring migrant workers.

Two

An Emergency Measure

Keeping Nurses at Home

On March 27, 2020, Philippine media reported the story of a German hospital group that managed to fly seventy-five Filipino nurses from Manila to the state of Hesse. What made this incident newsworthy was the fact that national borders had been closed for weeks. The COVID-19 virus had spread rapidly within the Philippines, prompting then-president Rodrigo Duterte to declare a countrywide lockdown. Undeterred, the German foreign minister had work visas delivered to each nurse's home, completing their paperwork for departure. The nurses left on a special "recruitment flight" procured by their employers—approved and arranged by the Philippine government (Elemia 2020).

Faced with what was then a life-threatening virus, Filipinos reacted to the report with a mix of panic and outrage. The nurses' departure had occurred shortly after six of the largest hospitals in Manila reached full capacity, unable to provide the space or the manpower to treat the deluge of COVID-19 patients (*CNN Philippines* 2020b). On social media, Filipinos questioned why their government would export nurses to other countries amid a public health crisis at home. Filipino congressman Rufus Rodriguez provided the most scathing critique, accusing the Duterte administration of prioritizing the health of other nations above its own. "We need our health care personnel here . . . to attend to sick Filipinos and not to foreigners," he declared emphatically. "We need those nurses bound for Germany and other jobs overseas to augment our dwindling public health workforce" (Colcol 2020).

Two days after the congressman's dramatic statement, the POEA announced that it would suspend the deployment of all Filipino health care workers to jobs abroad until the "national state of emergency" had passed (Jaymalin 2020a). Loosely referred to as the "deployment ban," this resolution barred the departures of fourteen health-related occupations, including physicians, microbiologists, and medical technologists (POEA 2020). Of these, nurses constituted the largest group, with hundreds unable to leave for jobs waiting in the United Kingdom, Saudi Arabia, and Singapore (Depasupil 2020).[1]

The decision to curtail the mobility of health care workers came as a shock to many—specifically the political and media pundits who were accustomed to the Philippines' image as a model for labor export. Even among migration scholars, the Philippine state is often regarded as an institution determined to reap the benefits of its citizens' international mobility, despite the risks that came with working overseas.[2] Nurses, in particular, have been lauded as one of the country's "prime" export products, given the worldwide demand for their skill (Guevarra 2010; Ortiga 2018a).

While the Philippine government had suspended migrants' departures in the past,[3] the deployment ban on health care workers was unprecedented in its scope. In blocking all the possible pathways that nurses had for leaving the country, the state halted not only the deployments of commercial recruitment agencies but also those arranged through bilateral agreements with other nations (Business Mirror 2020a).[4] In this sense, the hard pivot toward retaining health care workers seemed almost absurd, given the state's long history of facilitating their emigration.

However, the deployment ban on health care workers only seems illogical when viewed from a perspective that primarily sees the Philippines as a labor-exporting state. While the Philippine government does broker its citizens' labor to foreign employers, state officials also face pressure to maintain their legitimacy among constituents within national borders. In this sense, underlying health care workers' immobility are other state interests best served by keeping nurses in place.

In this chapter, I show how the Philippine government used nurses' immobility to appease public concerns about the state's response to the

COVID-19 pandemic. By blocking nurses' emigration, state officials sought to demonstrate that they placed the country's health needs first, even if it came at the cost of its labor export programs (Xiang et al. 2022). Doing so entailed developing a narrative that depicted nurses' immobility as temporary—an emergency measure to prevent the loss of essential skill. I discuss how this emphasis on short-term immobility allowed state officials to gain widespread support for policies such as the deployment ban, even as nurses fought for the right to leave their own country.

Shifting Away from "Surplus" Skills

In justifying the immobility of health care workers, the Philippine state first needed to alter a general narrative that it had propagated for many years. Even before COVID-19, chronic problems, such as poor wages and overcrowded hospitals, had pushed generations of Filipino nurses to leave the country for jobs abroad (see Lorenzo et al. 2007; Thompson and Walton-Roberts 2019). Yet, in the two decades before the pandemic, the Philippine government mainly treated nursing as a skill that was in *surplus*. As discussed in the previous chapter, the Philippines had fostered a higher education system that deliberately produced graduates for overseas markets (de Haas 2005; Ortiga 2018a). When the demand for foreign nurses increased in the early 2000s, private institutions rapidly expanded their nursing programs, accepting thousands of new students each year.[5] This practice reinforced the belief that the country had an ample supply of nursing skills—enough to fill the needs of hospitals within and beyond national borders.

Ironically, this notion of a nursing "surplus" undermined the profession's development within the country, filtering through numerous policy discussions and debates. One example was the Philippine Nursing Act of 2002, a law meant to improve nursing education and practice in the country. Just a year before legislators deliberated the bill, more than 13,000 Filipino nurses—many with years of clinical experience—emigrated overseas. But rather than express concern about such losses, Filipino lawmakers mainly focused on discussing the "domestic surplus" of nurses within local hospitals.[6] Analyzing transcripts of congressional debates, Exequiel Cabanda (2017b) noted how lawmakers were mostly worried about ensuring nurses' overseas employability instead of improving their work conditions at home:

> Although the legislators recognized the shortage of experienced nurses due to emigration, the sponsors of the bill and other legislators considered the economic contribution of remittances as far more significant than shortage. Further, their personal stories about their own family members, who are successful nurses in foreign countries and the positive feedback they received about Filipino nurses during their trips abroad, show enthusiasm for nurse migration and a sense of pride as Filipinos. (Cabanda 2017b: 12)

Efforts to legislate higher wages for nurses continued to stall in the subsequent years, even as the pace of nurse departures increased. In 2006, the average pay for entry-level nurses in urban hospitals was only PHP 9,000 (USD 125), an amount far lower than the salaries of other public servants, such as teachers and police officers.[7] Wages were even lower for nurses in private hospitals and rural areas. Nursing leaders warned politicians about the exodus of qualified nurses from local hospitals—a problem that would compromise patient care if left unaddressed (Cueto 2006; Jaymalin 2009).[8] Still, Philippine state officials insisted that the large number of nursing graduates would sustain the country's health institutions even if foreign recruitment efforts were to increase. In 2008, the Professional Regulation Commission (PRC) declared that the Philippines had a surplus of 400,000 nurses—enough to meet the manpower needs of hospitals in Saudi Arabia, Canada, and most European countries. "The vacancies for our nurses in both private and public hospitals reach 60,000. But we are producing over 100,000 registered professional nurses every year," PRC commissioner Ruth Padilla argued in a media interview. "We do not have additional positions in the government for them. Moreover, private hospitals cannot accommodate the surplus of nurses" (*Manila Bulletin* 2008a).

The commissioner's report cemented the belief that the Philippines had an oversupply of local nurse labor. When a few lawmakers proposed a bill obligating nursing graduates from state schools to work in local hospitals for twenty-four months, the Trade Union Congress of the Philippines immediately declared its opposition. The group's spokesperson, Alex Aguilar, argued that the bill was "totally counterproductive and uncalled for, considering the massive oversupply of nurses in the local labor market." Mr. Aguilar believed that bonding nurses to local institutions would waste their potential as global professionals who could remit money back to the country. "Our sense is, if we must advance the export of services, we might as well consciously encourage the deployment of highly skilled surplus professionals, such as nurses, who are generally immune from employer mistreatment," he explained (Gamolo 2008). As a result, the proposal to oblige nursing graduates to remain in the Philippines failed to gain traction among the country's lawmakers (*Manila Bulletin* 2008b).

When overseas jobs for foreign nurses began to decline in 2010, the discourse on the Philippines' "oversupply" of nurses shifted from economic opportunity to domestic problem.[9] As discussed in chapter 1, hospital administrators claimed that they lacked the capacity to absorb new nurses into their staff, given their limited needs and existing budget constraints.[10] In reality, domestic employers were more than happy to take advantage of the thousands of licensed nurses who had entered the local labor market. All nurses, even those who wished to work abroad, needed to first develop their skills in a local clinical setting. Thus, hospital owners recruited nurses to work as volunteers and interns, claiming that such positions would allow new graduates to gain valuable work experience, despite the low pay and nonexistent benefits. Rachel, the nurse bound for Ireland, laughed as she recounted how the manager at a local public hospital congratulated her on becoming a volunteer nurse shortly after obtaining her license. "At that time, people kept saying that there was an oversupply of nurses," she said, rolling her eyes. "If you wanted to work in a hospital, you have to be willing to work for free and get nothing in return except for experience."

Rhea, a registered nurse since 2012, recalled applying for a job in a small private hospital, where she had to pass two interviews and a written exam. After completing the long and tedious process, she was shocked to find that the hospital could only offer her a contractual position that paid PHP 150 (USD 3.50) per day:[11]

> I was like, "Oh my god. That amount won't even be enough to pay for my commute and my lunch!" . . . I wish they told me that before I took their exam. Then the [human resources officer] said something like, "If you become regularized, you'll get an additional 50 pesos." That was it! [laughter] So it's like 150 pesos plus an additional 50 pesos! Wow, I was shocked. Is that really the most they could offer me? (*Hanggang gano'n lang talaga 'yong kaya niyo i-offer?*)

By harping on the problem of "surplus skills," hospitals profited off nurses who had no choice but to accept low-paid, part-time, or volunteer positions within the local health care system. But as overseas jobs for nurses declined, many nurses gave up and chose to explore options elsewhere. In

Rachel's and Rhea's cases, they eventually left their hospital positions and found work in local call centers instead.

Officials from the Department of Labor and Employment (DOLE) did little to stem the number of nurses leaving the profession. In fact, they encouraged the exodus, arguing that unemployed nurses would be better served by moving to another industry.[12] Former DOLE secretary Rosalinda Baldoz actively promoted available jobs in fields such as medical transcription, insurance, and business process outsourcing (BPO) (Estuye 2013). She even highlighted emerging careers in massage therapy, arguing that wellness companies would benefit from applicants with nursing degrees (Crisostomo 2012).

In understanding the poor treatment of nurses within the Philippines, researchers have pointed to a broader social system that devalues care work as a form of labor.[13] However, I argue that the state's general lack of interest in retaining nursing graduates was also rooted in the belief that such labor was only valuable when used to generate remittances overseas (Ortiga 2021). As such, even as nurses' struggles with unemployment began to feature regularly in local media, state officials appeased critics by emphasizing that overseas opportunities would eventually return and allow aspiring migrants to resume their plans of working abroad.

For the nurses I spoke with, this discourse of "surplus" skills haunted the early years of their careers, causing them to doubt their own worth as professionals. Yet, as pressures on public health institutions began to mount during the pandemic, Philippine state officials were suddenly determined to transform this discourse from an issue of surplus to a problem of scarcity. How did state officials manage to justify immobilizing the country's most successful emigrants? The answer was in a little-known policy of retaining "mission-critical" skills that, strangely, had nothing to do with nurses at all.

Maintaining Mission-Critical Skills

The fact that the Philippine state could immobilize its aspiring migrants had shocked both outgoing nurses and their advocates. But perhaps even more surprising was that the state's deployment ban was also completely legal. In the resolution released by the POEA, the government had the authority to retain "mission-critical skills" in the interest of the nation (see table 2.1). The POEA defined these skills as those that were "internally developed and require extensive training, thus, not easily replaceable" (POEA 2020).

While many assumed that the term "mission-critical skills" was born of the pandemic, it actually originated from an earlier resolution, written in 2006. Ricardo Casco, the retired state bureaucrat introduced at the beginning of this book, had witnessed the development of this policy within the POEA. At that time, the skills in question were not in health care but in aviation. The national carrier, Philippine Airlines, had called on the government to stem the exodus of its pilots and aircraft mechanics who were fed up with the low benefits they received at home.[14] In response, the POEA (2006) enacted a resolution allowing the state to moderate the "injurious effect of outward migration" by slowing the departures of skilled workers in specific industries. "There was a time when we slowed down the deployment of welders because our companies complained that they could not compete with overseas contracts. They could not hire enough welders!" Mr. Casco shared. "In fairness to government, we were not in-

TABLE 2.1. **Policies on the Overseas Deployment of Health Care Workers during the COVID-19 Pandemic**

Date	Policy
April 2, 2020	**POEA Governing Board Resolution No. 9** State suspends deployment of 14 health care occupations classified as "mission-critical skills."
April 13, 2020	**Inter-Agency Task Force Resolution No. 23** Health care workers exempted from deployment ban if they have overseas employment contracts signed before March 8, 2020.
April 20, 2020	**POEA Advisory 47** Reiterates that health care workers with signed contracts before March 8 can leave the country. Indicates that health care workers with ongoing contracts abroad can also leave the country (*balik manggagawa*).
Sept 3, 2020	**POEA Advisory 47B** Amends earlier advisory to allow health care workers to leave the country if they have employment contracts signed before August 31, 2020.
Dec 17, 2020	**POEA Governing Board Resolution No. 17** State replaces deployment ban of health care workers with an annual deployment ceiling of 5,000 new hires per health care profession.

sensitive to needs, especially when there was a crisis among certain industry stakeholders and sectors."

Policies that immobilize outgoing migrants, such as the retention of mission-critical skills, are mostly invisible in studies of the Philippine state. Instead, existing scholarship has largely focused on how the country deliberately uses emigration as a development strategy. After all, why would a labor-exporting state deliberately prevent its citizens from moving overseas, given the clear economic benefits that outmigration can bring? For Mr. Casco, the country's success in labor export did not absolve his former agency from considering other needs within the nation. Most times, Philippine state agencies leaned toward the country's economic priorities, seeking new markets for Filipino workers and matching aspiring migrants with potential employers. However, there were also periods when government institutions needed to placate local constituents and employers. The state's resolution on mission-critical skills is one example of how emigration governance can lean more toward domestic concerns.

This logic of balancing local needs with global demands served as the foundation of the government's rationale for preventing nurses from leaving the country. As Mr. Casco liked to emphasize, this was the "dance" that defined his work as a Philippine state official. In the case of the health care worker deployment ban, Filipino bureaucrats defended the policy as a means of putting the needs of Filipino citizens first. POEA administrator Bernard Olalia claimed that there were too many migrant nurses "in the pipeline" to other countries and it was his agency's responsibility to redirect these workers toward local hospitals.[15] Given the alarming number of health workers falling sick with COVID-19, he warned that the unregulated departure of nurses would "lead the Philippine health care system to collapse" (*Business Mirror* 2020a).

However, there were two factors that made the health worker deployment ban different from previous efforts to retain mission-critical skills. First, unlike the Filipino airline pilots and mechanics in 2006, Philippine nursing schools had explicitly educated students to be employable outside the country (Ortiga 2014). During this period, state officials also encouraged the overproduction of nurses and later used the narrative of surplus skills in allowing their exploitation in local hospitals. What happened to the "oversupply" of nursing skills that local schools generated before the pandemic? In a meeting between Philippine senators and officials from DOLE, Senator Nancy Binay presented the same statistics that administration officials had previously cited in referring to the nursing surplus of the 2010s. "There's data that shows we have close to 500,000 nurses who are still in the country, and according to the nursing groups, private and public hospitals have vacancies for only 90,000," she said. "Therefore, our nurses are asking, why ban them from leaving?"

In response, then DOLE secretary Silvestre Bello III questioned the data, arguing that different agencies had provided conflicting numbers on the actual supply of nurses in the country. "There is no consensus as to how many nurses do we have," he said, waving his hands helplessly. "And we don't know how many of those nurses are actually experienced, how many are skilled, how many are fresh graduates (*baguhan*)." The secretary's point on the loss of experienced workers was the very same argument that nursing advocacy groups had used in warning state leaders of the detrimental impact of nurse migration (Jazul 2020). While these groups had called for better work conditions and higher wages, Secretary Bello's solution was to simply prevent these nurses from leaving. "That's why we cannot afford to have unlimited deployment of our nurses," he insisted. "We just have to observe the development of this pandemic."

Second, the POEA's 2006 resolution only required a six-month notice before specific workers could leave for jobs abroad (Aning 2006a).[16] At that time, labor officials believed that while some workers' skills were critical for the nation, they could not be prevented from pursuing better opportunities overseas. In fact, when industry representatives lobbied for a stricter ban on the emigration of aviation workers, former DOLE secretary Patricia Santo Tomas rejected the idea as "constitutionally problematic." She argued, "Barring a worker from leaving his or her firm might be construed as involuntary servitude, and the courts would surely just issue a restraining order against it if someone complained." (Aning 2006b).

In comparison, the 2020 deployment ban on health care workers had no indication as to when it would end. POEA administrator Olalia emphasized that the suspension would be temporary but avoided making any statements on when the ban would be lifted (Santos 2020a). When nurses pressured state representatives to provide an end date for the policy, officials simply asked them to persevere until the pandemic was over. In an online meeting with stranded nurses, Secretary Bello argued that emerging variants of the coronavirus made it hard for the state to determine when to let health workers go. "We cannot afford to deploy our nurses abroad at the expense of losing the services of our nurses," he explained as several nurses in the meeting started to weep. "We have to follow [the deployment ban] first. Let us try to be patient. This is only temporary. (*Pansamantala lang naman ito.*)"[17] In this sense, the health worker deployment ban seemed to come quite close to the "involuntary servitude" that previous administration officials had hoped to avoid.

The deployment ban's uncertain duration contradicted the reasoning behind the POEA's 2006 resolution on mission-critical skills. The 2006 resolution was not meant to block emigration but only to delay the exit of skilled workers. In doing so, policymakers hoped to persuade Philippine industries to provide more incentives for these workers to stay. As Mr. Casco recalled, all pilots and mechanics involved in the 2006 dispute were eventually allowed to leave the country. "They had good remuneration, their [foreign] employers were of reputable standing, and their papers were all in order," he said. "The POEA had no obligation and basis to force them back to their companies."[18]

In the case of nurses, state agencies could only offer temporary rewards and benefits.[19] Administration officials channeled billions in emergency funds to hire new nurses for the country's COVID-19 treatment centers, offering salaries that were much higher than the regular monthly wage of junior staff nurses in public hospitals (Mercado 2020).[20] Still, these contracts came with no promise of permanent employment and needed to be renewed every three months. There was also no assurance that such high wages could be sustained after the pandemic. Given that local hospitals were unable to promise long-term employment for stranded nurses, Philippine state officials needed to show that nurses' immobility was merely an emergency measure that would not compromise their emigration plans. Fulfilling this promise turned out to be much harder than the state had anticipated.

Challenging State Narratives of Immobility

A week after the Philippine state announced the deployment ban for health care workers, a group of twenty nurses were offloaded from their UK–bound flight at Manila's international airport. Most of these nurses had been working in British hospitals for years and were only visiting family in the Philippines when the lockdown occurred. In official terms, they were *balik-manggagawa* or returning Filipino migrant workers. But when the offloaded nurses called the POEA for help, they were simply told to join the state's urgent hiring scheme for local hospitals (Ramirez 2020).

Until that moment, nurses like Marlo had assumed that workers with existing overseas jobs were exempted from the ban. While still a Filipino citizen, Marlo had been living abroad since 2017 and was only back in the Philippines for a brief vacation. After the offloading of nurses hit the local news, he set up a Facebook group for UK–based nurses who were stranded in the Philippines. Membership grew to more than 200 nurses in one day, and suddenly, Marlo found himself giving statements to the media. At the time of our interview, he seemed slightly bemused with his sudden role as spokesperson for his group:

> All we wanted was for the POEA to clarify the coverage of this ban. It's not clear who is covered and how they are classifying health workers! They told one of the members of our group to volunteer [in local hospitals] but as *balik-manggagawa*, we have existing contracts, and we are employed. Even if we're here in the Philippines, we also have to pay bills in the UK because that's actually where we live!

The situation of nurses like Marlo complicated the state's image of the outgoing Filipino nurse. To rationalize the immobility of health workers, Philippine government officials had conjured a particular image of a first-time migrant—an individual just about to embark on a migration journey toward new opportunities abroad.[21] Halting all deployments was a means of compelling health workers to be voluntarily immobile, to put their plans on hold, and to keep local hospitals running for the duration of the pandemic. However, the government agencies quickly realized that not all nurses fit this image. As Marlo noted, he was not a first-time emigrant who could simply postpone his departure to serve his home nation. Essentially, the deployment ban had prevented him from returning to the place where he actually lived and worked.

Faced with the travails of immigrant nurses, the state rationale of retaining mission-critical skills suddenly seemed draconian and cruel. Filipino politicians began to criticize the Duterte administration for compromising the livelihoods of overseas Filipinos, and social media pundits attacked labor officials for their purported insensitivity. Amid such backlash, the Philippine government quickly moved to amend the resolution. On April 13, 2020, the Inter-Agency Task Force (IATF), an ad hoc group of executive officials set up during the COVID-19 crisis, announced that the deployment ban would not apply to health workers who had "perfected contracts" and overseas employment certificates (OECs) dated on or before March 8 (see table 2.1) (Yap and Santos 2020). A "perfected con-tract" was a signed agreement between an employer and an employee, approved by the Philippine embassy in the migrant's destination country. The OEC was an exit pass to prove that an outgoing Filipino worker was registered with the POEA and had gone through all the necessary pa-perwork for departure. To obtain an OEC, Filipino workers exiting the country needed to provide their flight details and a valid work visa.[22]

Philippine state officials hoped that in setting such criteria, the modified deployment ban would cover only "new hires," or health workers who were not tied to employers in other countries. Karlo Nograles, spokesperson for the IATF, declared this amendment a "win-win" situation for both nurses and the government. Nurses with finalized contracts would be allowed to continue to their jobs overseas, while those without required documents would be encouraged to lend their labor to the country's COVID-19 hos-pitals (PNA 2020a). In other words, the state could maintain its narrative of nurses' immobility being only an emergency measure. The deployment ban would not deprive nurses of their migration dreams, but simply oblige aspiring migrants to remain in the Philippines awhile longer.

However, the category of "aspiring nurse migrants" turned out to be much more differentiated than the state had assumed. For some nurses, like Joshua, it was easy to fit into the state's notion of a "new hire." Joshua was leaving the country for his first job, in Singapore, and had worked only in the Philippines since obtaining his nursing license in 2015. He had finalized his contract and exit pass well before the March 8 deadline and was therefore exempted from the ban. When we spoke, his only concern was that he was waiting for Singaporean officials to authorize his entry into the country. Once that day finally came, Philippine immigration would not bar him from boarding his flight.

Viena, a nurse waiting to leave for the United Kingdom, had a more complicated status. Unlike Joshua, she had been working in a Japanese nursing home for three years and was about to start a new job with the National Health Service in the United Kingdom. She was only in Manila to process her final paperwork for departure. However, the fact that she was starting a new contract in a different country meant that she was tech-nically a "new hire" and would therefore be affected by the deployment ban. Viena could have completed all her paperwork in Japan, but before the pandemic, a side visit to Manila seemed like a harmless trip that could save her some money:

I just needed to do the medical exam, and a few other papers, like the TB (tuberculosis) test. I mean, I could have done it in Japan, but they were asking me for 50,000 yen . . . My friend told me, "Eh, 50,000 yen! That's so expensive! That same test will only cost 5,000 pesos in the Philippines." So, I just decided to go home.

Looking back, Viena admitted that she was depressed working at the nursing home and wanted to "recharge" with her family in the Philippines. The job in the United Kingdom brought the promise of a more fulfilling and better compensated career, but she wanted some respite before emigrating to a new place. At the time of our interview, she felt a heavy sense of regret in choosing to come home. While Viena had a valid contract with her employer, she was unable to get her UK visa before the lockdown in Manila and was therefore ineligible for an exit pass.

The label of being a "new hire" glossed over Viena's situation as a migrant nurse stuck *between* contracts, officially resigned from her previous job but unable to begin work with her current employer. This conundrum was also common for nurses coming from the Gulf states, given that they worked on short two-year contracts that required a return to the Philippines once their tenure was completed. If a nurse was to change jobs or move to a different hospital, they would need to go through a new round of paperwork, thus making them newly deployed workers in the eyes of the state.

Again, the plight of nurses like Viena featured heavily in various news outlets as the deployment ban for health workers stretched on for months. Making things worse, the ban continued to suffer from inconsistent implementation. In September 2020, airport officials offloaded another group of seven nurses who were bound for the United Kingdom, arguing that while their contracts were valid, their visas were issued after the March 8 deadline. Stranded nurses intensified their demands to the POEA, and supportive politicians bolstered their appeals to the national government. Skeptical of the deployment ban from its inception, Senator Nancy Binay chastised the government's labor department for causing nurses unnecessary stress and anxiety. "The latest offloading incident involving UK–bound nurses only shows that the policy is disjointed and conflicting and its implementation is prone to lapses," she complained (Aquino et al. 2020). In highlighting the arbitrariness of the state's deadlines, the immobility of nurses like Viena seemed illogical and costly, given the thousands of pesos nurses had already invested in paperwork, visas, and travel documents.

As the pandemic reached its half-year mark, private recruitment agencies joined the opposition to the deployment ban, reproaching the government for compromising nurses' careers without providing reasonable alternatives. At this time, nurses employed in the country's COVID-19 hospitals were still working on limited contracts that were renewed every three months. "If the government cannot provide better working conditions for nurses, at least allow them to seek their opportunities for a greener future for their families," argued one recruitment executive (R. Santos 2020b). Eventually, government bureaucrats admitted that the state's health institutions could not provide the benefits and salaries that overseas jobs would bring. "Our health workers are also looking for jobs that are more stable," conceded one official from the Philippine Department of Health (DOH). "Even if we tell them that [their contracts] can be renewed once the 2021 budget is approved, that is not enough to reassure them," he said (Geducos 2020a). Nursing groups capitalized on these weaknesses in arguing that health care workers had no choice but to take their skills elsewhere (*Philippine Daily Inquirer [PDI]* 2020b; Aquino et al. 2020). As argued by a representative from Filipino Nurses United, "the government has no right to force health care workers, including nurses, to stay if there is an opportunity to work abroad and uplift the lives of their families" (Ramirez 2020).

Such rising discontent made it crucial for state officials to frame nurses' immobility as only an emergency measure. While the deployment ban was technically legal, state officials realized that a blunt implementation of the policy generated strong opposition from both nursing groups and their allies. For example, when COVID-19 cases rose sharply in August 2020, government agencies considered removing all earlier exemptions for nurses with existing contracts dated before March 8. However, this idea was quickly quashed as outraged nurses were able to mobilize support from the media and sympathetic politicians. Local news outlets began to release stories of nurses who were buried in debt because they could not leave for jobs waiting overseas. Even administration officials such as Department of Foreign Affairs secretary Teodoro Locsin Jr. began to openly criticize the deployment ban. The secretary was a member of the IATF, but he made it clear that he disagreed with the decision to immobilize nurses. "I said [to the task force] . . . pay big money if you want keep [our nurses] in reserve," he said. "[We] cannot hold a section of our population hostage for that eventuality" (*CNN Philippines* 2020d). As a result, the narrative of nurses' immobility needed to maintain the possibility that aspiring migrants would be able to leave the country once the pandemic was over. The Filipino public needed assurance that the deployment ban was merely a temporary condition in the context of a national crisis.

Faced with such pressures, the Philippine government agreed to amend the deployment ban once again (Terrazola 2020b). In an advisory, the POEA extended the cutoff date for perfected contracts to the end of August 2020—close to six months after the initial March 8 deadline (see table 2.1). Then presidential spokesperson Harry Roque announced the change as proof of the administration's empathy for the nurses' plight. "The president listened to the appeal of the nurses," he pronounced in a televised speech. "So, for those who have their contracts and complete documents as of August 31, 2020, you may now leave the country." This adjustment allowed another 1,500 nurses to finally depart for their jobs overseas.

Despite these small victories, stranded nurses and their advocates remained unsuccessful in attaining what they saw as the ultimate goal: the complete removal of the health care worker deployment ban. Even after announcing the extension, spokesperson Roque clarified that restrictions on nurses would remain. "There's no decision yet for the total lifting [of the deployment ban]. We just compromised for nurses who had already spent money for their applications abroad (*Pinagbigyan lang po 'yong mga nakagastos na*)," he said (Geducos 2020b). It seemed that while state officials were willing to tweak some policies in response to public critique, they refused to allow all health workers to leave the country. In the end, the administration stood behind its assertion that it needed to prioritize the welfare of Filipinos in the Philippines. As labor secretary Bello argued:

> I for one will not recommend [lifting the ban] because we have to think of our country and our countrymen who will be affected by COVID-19 . . . God forbid, but if the level of transmission and contamination of COVID increased, what will happen then if our good nurses are already abroad? (Aquino 2020b)

The state's insistence on maintaining the ban seemed to indicate that keeping nurses in the country still had a key political purpose. By this time, a few politicians were starting to doubt that immobilizing health workers would translate to greater success in combating the virus. Rather than prevent outgoing nurses from leaving the country, nurse leaders argued that creating more full-time positions with hazard pay would be more effective in recruiting health workers for COVID-19 wards (Cabico 2022; *PDI* 2020b). However, as the number of COVID-19 deaths continued to rise, nurses' immobility served as a powerful symbol of how the administration was willing to forgo dollar remittances to care for Filipinos at home (Xiang et al. 2022). While this move was detrimental to the state's labor export interests, it fulfilled the need to maintain an image of authority and responsibility during the pandemic. Eventually, nurses who opposed the deployment ban were not only stigmatized as unpatriotic, but also criticized as the reason for the country's pandemic woes.

Calling for Voluntary Immobility

President Rodrigo Duterte had always been fond of delivering long speeches, often peppered with curse words in Tagalog and English. The president had built his popularity on being tough enough to get things done, and the pandemic had been a serious test of his leadership. It was perhaps no surprise that, when asked to comment on his administration's controversial deployment ban, he blamed wealthy nations for luring away the country's health workers. Dressed in a blue polo shirt with a small Philippine flag stitched over his left chest, the president spoke directly to these nations, saying: "You should rely on your own people. Now, you just depend on taking them away from the Philippines. Then when there is a shortage, we'll be the ones who will be sorry." Pausing for effect, President Duterte moved on to what he felt was the solution to this problem: appealing to Filipino nurses' sense of nationalism. His next set of comments targeted the nurse migrants themselves:

> So now, our [COVID-19] task force is just saying, "You can't all leave at once. We need you." I understand that [nurses want to leave]. That is self-preservation. You have to work. They have job offers in the US, so you go there . . . I'm not blaming the nurses. I'm not mad. I have no emotions about this. But if you want to serve another nation, another people, I think we should just remember, there will come a time when [the Philippines will suffer] (*PNA* 2020a).

In reminding nurses of how the Philippines will "suffer" from their loss, President Duterte placed the onus on individuals to forgo personal gain for the good of the nation. This narrative drew from a gendered ideal that portrays Filipina women (who constituted the majority of nurses) as naturally caring and self-sacrificing (Encinas-Franco 2023). However, the president's speech also had a clear emphasis on retaining nursing skills—resources that other nations had supposedly taken away from the Philippines. In fact, state officials had no qualms about allowing the departure of migrant domestic workers during the pandemic—a group entirely composed of women. It was clear that the president's appeal for "care" was only directed at outgoing nurses.

As the Philippines' health institutions buckled under the pressure of rising numbers of COVID-19 cases, state officials pointed to the outmigration of Filipino nurses as one reason for the administration's beleaguered pandemic response. As President Duterte suggested, the deployment ban was merely a desperate plea for their help, given that few nurses were willing to remain in the Philippines. Other administration officials reinforced the president's narrative as well. In a public webinar held in August 2020,[23] secretary of health Francisco Duque III shared his experience of meeting a group of 1,000 stranded nurses in the hope of encouraging them to work in the country's COVID-19 hospitals. He expressed disappointment with their response:

> So, someone tried to facilitate a discussion with me, to convince these health care workers to come serve in our hospitals. And you know what? Only 25 signed up! The others refused! (*'Yong iba, ayaw!*) This is where I am asking for help. I appeal to the sense of nationalism, the sense of patriotism of every health care worker. We are at war. Let us be united and help each other . . . Let's change our mindsets and be selfless. It's not going to be easy anytime soon.

When Secretary Duque revealed the number of stranded nurses who eventually agreed to serve in local hospitals, his eyes widened in disbelief, signaling that 25 out of 1,000 nurses was a ridiculously low figure. National news outlets reported this statistic accordingly, with the *Philippine Star* promoting the misleading headline (Crisostomo 2020).

In reality, 7,849 nurses had already filled the 10,468 available positions in the state's urgent hiring scheme (Yee 2020). And despite government promises of higher pay and additional benefits, social media was flooded with complaints of delayed salaries and the lack of personal protective equipment (PPE) such as hazmat suits and masks. Advocacy groups argued that such spotty protection had led to a high number of Filipino health workers who died from the coronavirus (Ranada 2020). One could argue that having twenty-five nurses who were still willing to work in the Philippines' COVID-19 hospitals was a surprising number in itself.

Still, the image of nurses selfishly refusing to share their skills percolated among members of the general public. As Filipinos struggled with local unemployment, state officials explicitly referred to the millions of pesos devoted to paying high wages for nurses working in COVID-19 hospitals. Presidential spokesperson Roque argued, "We gave them an additional allowance, free lodging, life insurance, and free COVID-19 testing . . . I do think we have a good package for our medical frontliners" (*Manila Bulletin* 2020). As a result, nurses who refused to be voluntarily immobile were seen as eager to "jump ship" and escape worsening conditions in the Philippines. It did not help that, while nursing groups were immediately vocal in demanding the freedom to pursue overseas jobs, the Philippine Medical Association supported the deployment ban. Association representatives even released a public statement arguing that Filipino doctors must "serve the country first, before anything else" (Ramirez 2020).

By the end of the pandemic's first year, the Philippine state had effectively constructed voluntary immobility as a form of heroism among health care workers. Suddenly, nurses' aspirations for international mobility were criticized as opportunism and a lack of empathy for fellow Filipinos. In a strange twist, the "heroism" that state agencies used to associate with migrant nurses was redefined to apply to those who decided to work in Philippine hospitals. Presidential spokesperson Roque exemplified this shift in a press briefing, where he praised health care workers in local hospitals for their "dedicated and compassionate service" as frontliners in the fight against COVID-19. He added, "We consider them our modern-day heroes as they have responded to the call of duty during these challenging times" (*PNA* 2020a).

As state officials valorized those who served in Philippine hospitals, nurses who actively critiqued the deployment ban found themselves on the receiving end of online attacks from strangers. Rhea, who was bound for the United Kingdom, remembered being frustrated with the negative comments she read on Twitter and Facebook:

> My friends and I had a lot of bashers. They would say, "Why can't you understand that we're in the middle of a pandemic? It's a national emergency!" Or sometimes, people will comment, "Why are you in such a

hurry to leave anyway? *(Bakit atat na atat ka umalis?)*" Those are the kind of comments nurses were getting online. The problem is they don't understand. None of them understand what nurses went through.

Rhea's complaint emphasized the poor treatment that Filipino nurses had experienced before the pandemic, when their skills were seen as a "surplus" that local hospitals could exploit. Still, the vitriol Rhea faced on social media reveals how other Filipinos had readily accepted the narrative of nurses' immobility as an important emergency measure. Nurses who pushed for their right to leave the country were criticized as self-interested individuals, unsympathetic to the country's dire situation.

Another nurse, Chenie, was disturbed by the sudden shift toward celebrating the heroism of nurses who worked within the Philippines. When she emigrated to the United Kingdom in 2017, the public hospital in her home province had little interest in convincing her to stay. Chenie's supervisors deliberately chose not to endorse her promotion, arguing that she would likely leave the country anyway. Chenie only returned to the Philippines to visit her mother, who had been living alone since she left. She protested:

> So my decision to go overseas and be far from my family, that was me being selfish? How about all those remittances I sent from the UK and the competence I showed as a Filipino nurse in the NHS? We don't count that as national loyalty anymore? Why am I suddenly a bad person for choosing to care for myself, my family, and to take care of the responsibilities I have in the UK?

Like Rhea, Chenie felt frustration as a result of relentless commentary on social media, where the narrative of voluntary immobility had put nurses like her on the defensive. Even as nursing groups gained ground in pressuring state officials to amend the deployment ban, it was still common to see Filipinos calling for nurses to fulfill their oath as "health care heroes." Elmer, an emergency room nurse, sounded almost nostalgic as he recalled his time as a migrant nurse in Saudi Arabia. "I used to really tell people in Saudi, Filipino nurses do not only provide world-class care; we also have the brains to back it up *(may utak din 'yan)*," he said proudly. "Sometimes, the foreign doctors in the ER would ask me what to do. I'm not belittling them, ha. I'm just saying, this is what it meant to be a Filipino nurse!"

However, when we spoke, Elmer was stranded in the Philippines, with his new work visa pending at the UK embassy. While still proud of his profession, he admitted that the pandemic had made it hard for nurses like him to celebrate their personal achievements, such as getting a job overseas. He explained:

> These days, if you don't serve local hospitals, you get shamed right away. They'll say "You're useless. We should revoke your license! You don't deserve to be called a Filipino!" You can't do anything about it. I feel like people just jumped on the bandwagon.

Elmer's experiences revealed the outcomes of the Philippine state's narrative of keeping nurses in the country. In redefining nursing skill as a dwindling essential resource, government officials promoted a widespread belief that nurses needed to volunteer their immobility for the good of the country. Those like Elmer, who actively opposed the ban, not only found it difficult to garner public sympathy but also faced condemnation from fellow Filipinos at home.

Essential Immobility

This chapter has explained how the Philippine state managed to pivot its emigration policies from facilitating nurses' departures to retaining their labor for local hospitals. Among migration studies, researchers have tended to portray sending states as either helpless in stemming emigration or relentless in profiting off their citizens' labor (Rodriguez 2010; Tyner 2004). The Philippines is a popular example of the latter case, with the country's labor export system largely seen as a model of how to use emigration as a development strategy. Yet, as noted in my introduction, not all migration policy is driven toward economic remittances (Iskander 2011). In this chapter, I have discussed how government officials used nurses' immobility to appease an anxious citizenry grappling with the effects of an ongoing pandemic. At stake was the legitimacy of an administration concerned with maintaining an image of a government that could manage the country through an ongoing crisis.

To justify keeping nurses in place, the Philippine government promoted a narrative with two main themes. First, the state framed nurses' immobility as an emergency measure, using a 2006 resolution that gives the government the right to retain mission-critical skills. This move effectively reconstructed nurses' capabilities as resources that were in short supply and, as a result, simply too valuable to let go. In tying the deployment ban to a national crisis, administration officials also portrayed nurses' inability to leave the country as a temporary condition—one that would eventually pass and allow nurses to fulfill their long-term plans of emigration. Second, the state celebrated as national heroes nurses who chose to remain in the country, framing their voluntary immobility as a key part of battling the coronavirus. In contrast, nurses who continued to oppose the deployment ban were seen as individuals eager to abandon the country and unwilling to serve fellow Filipinos, even for just a "temporary" period.

In the end, the deployment ban on health care workers was meant to do more than augment the nation's supply of nursing skills. Migration governance can also serve as a means of maintaining political authority within borders, and this chapter has revealed how such motivations can lead to increasing controls over people's international movements. In the case of Filipino nurses, their immobility allowed administration officials to bolster the image of a responsible government that was putting the health of its citizens first. The public's support for the deployment ban strengthened the state's resolve to keep health workers in the country, despite strong opposition from foreign governments, professional associations, and nurses themselves.

Still, the actual task of redirecting nurses' labor to local hospitals led to mixed outcomes, despite the state's success in keeping nurses in place. In the next chapter, we turn to how nurses defined their own narrative of immobility, complicating government efforts to subsume their labor in the country's pandemic response.

Three

Windows of Opportunity

Divided Nurses Respond to Their Immobility

When I first began interviewing nurses in 2020, the Philippine government had just announced its decision to ban the overseas deployment of health care workers.[1] The nurses who agreed to speak to me then had all been immobilized—legally prohibited from leaving the country for work. Despite their common predicament, my interviewees were divided into two very different groups.

Rachel, the nurse unable to leave for her job at the Irish nursing home, immediately took to social media, where she easily found others who shared her frustration and disbelief. Hoping to get the deployment ban repealed, she joined an online community of stranded nurses who called themselves the *PrisoNurses*—a play on the word "prisoners." True to their provocative name, the PrisoNurses accused the Philippine state of forcing health care workers into local hospitals against their will. In protest, the group's leaders called for a boycott of all attempts to recruit nurses for the state's pandemic response.

Rachel had already resigned from her hospital job when the deployment ban was first announced. But she received a call from her former manager, begging her to come back to work. Staff nurses were falling sick, and the wards were severely understaffed. Would she be willing to take on a few shifts? Rachel declined, using the excuse that she needed to be home with her son. "It's not as if I intended to leave my colleagues to deal with the virus. I know that's what it looks like," she said defensively. "But nurses should not be forced to work. Especially during a pandemic."

While Rachel and the PrisoNurses framed their advocacy as a campaign against forced labor, there were actually a number of nurses who willingly entered and continued to work in Philippine hospitals. Jenine, a registered nurse since 2011, was in one of the first cohorts to join the government's "urgent hiring scheme," a program that recruited health care workers specifically for the country's COVID-19 treatment centers. She was waiting to leave for a job in Saudi Arabia when state officials declared the deployment ban and closed national borders. "I mean, I had my visa, I submitted my biometrics, I was ready to go," she recalled. Before the pandemic, Jenine had moved through multiple jobs in Manila, trying out a two-year stint as a school nurse before finding another position as a company nurse. Neither of those jobs paid well, so she left for the Gulf states and spent three years working in an aesthetic clinic in Riyadh. Looking back, she sometimes finds it hard to believe that she was suddenly handling patients in one of the largest COVID-19 treatment centers in Manila. At the time we spoke, Jenine was living in a temporary shelter built for health care workers who wanted to avoid infecting their families at home. The work was dangerous, but she had no regrets. "Better to be doing something and earning an income rather than just wasting time at home," she remarked candidly.

Rachel and Jenine's stories reflect the schisms among Filipino nurses immobilized during the COVID-19 pandemic. In chapter 2, I discussed how the Philippine state used nurses' immobility to promote the image of an administration that prioritized its citizens' health, even if it came at the cost of the country's labor export interests. State officials also pressured nurses to accept their immobility as a temporary sacrifice and join local efforts to mitigate the effects of the virus. This chapter shifts our attention to how nurses themselves constructed a narrative of their immobility and how these perspectives resulted in two contrasting responses to their government's call to service.

In many ways, nurses' stories highlight the value in understanding what it means to remain in place. While broader social structures can control people's movements, individuals can perceive their immobility negatively or positively—as either a barrier to opportunity or a voluntary way of life (Salazar 2021). However, studies of how people define immobility are quite nascent in sociological research. Compared with the many frameworks that explain why people migrate, fewer scholars investigate how individuals come to either accept their incapacity to move or choose to forgo such opportunities altogether (see, for example, Ali 2007; Ortiga and Macabasag 2020; Schewel and Fransen 2022; Wyngaarden et al. 2022).[2]

In the case of nurses like Jenine, public discourse highlights many of the themes that scholars have used in explaining voluntary immobility: the need to remain close to family, social obligations, and an attachment to place manifested in a desire to serve one's community (Somaiah et al. 2020; Thalang and Auikool 2018). These factors may hold true for some nurses, but there is a danger in assuming that those who opposed their immobility do not have the same reasons to stay. As noted in chapter 2, state officials had used a narrative of national service in portraying nurses like Rachel as selfish and opportunistic. How else can we understand why some nurses accepted their immobility while others fought for their departures? How did these two groups negotiate the various meanings placed upon their inability to leave the country?

This chapter shows how nurses stuck in the Philippines perceived their immobility as one of two windows of opportunity: a space that opened to new prospects for emigration or a gap that was quickly closing out a future that they had worked so hard to attain. I argue that nurses' inclination to see one or the other depended on how remaining in the Philippines affected the value of their clinical skill for overseas work. This value involved not only individual perceptions of their own capabilities but also a global regime of skills assessment that determined nurses' ability to practice their profession abroad. I reveal how the nurses' divergent narratives countered state efforts to channel their labor into local hospitals. But as I will discuss later, this division also weakened nurses' attempts to dispute the government's rationale for curtailing their international mobility.

The Invisible Work of Building Nursing Skill

Stories of nurse migration are often centered on the challenges nurses face at the point of departure as they embark on the process of integrating themselves in their new homes abroad (Amrith 2017; Guevarra 2010; Showers 2023). Yet, to understand how nurses make sense of their immobility, it is important to focus on an earlier phase of their migration journeys, when they first begin the process of building the required skills for overseas work. Nursing is one of the most regulated professions in the world, and nursing associations often require foreign applicants to demonstrate a specific level of "clinical exposure." Aspiring migrants must prove that they can meet these standards, by listing the type of hospitals where they have worked and their duration of tenure in each place (Collins 2021; Walton-Roberts 2021). Before the pandemic, popular destinations such as the United States required applicants to have spent at least three years working in a tertiary hospital with functioning operating rooms and an intensive care unit. In countries like Singapore, foreigners applying for staff nurse positions needed to have worked in hospitals with at least a hundred beds—a rarity for many source countries such as the Philippines (Marcus, Quimson, and Short 2014).

For the nurses I interviewed, accumulating such hospital experience was perhaps the most difficult and demeaning phase of their professional lives.[3] Most of my interviewees had graduated in the mid-2000s, during a time of intense competition for certain types of clinical exposure (see table 3.1).[4] Philippine health institutions, both public and private, saw the large number of nursing graduates as a chance to save on labor costs and started hiring nurses on temporary contracts with low wages and poor benefits. Such practices left nurses with few employment opportunities within their own country's health care sector. Thus, many were faced with the dilemma of whether to remain as a professional nurse or move to a nonclinical career that at least paid a living wage.

Those who chose to persevere in accumulating clinical skills relied heavily on the social and economic capital of their families. In Rachel's case, it was her UK–based mother who supplemented the meager wages she earned at the private hospital. After obtaining her license in 2006, Rachel spent close to a decade working in a local call center agency. She had given up on finding a hospital job that could cover her son's school fees and their everyday expenses. It was only after receiving her mother's support that Rachel could return to clinical work and finally begin clocking in the experience needed to qualify for jobs abroad.

Alma, a registered nurse since 2011, used her brother's networks to find a part-time position in a rural hospital within her province. She worked three days a week, receiving only a small allowance as compensation. "Technically, I was supposed to be considered a 'volunteer nurse,' but I needed a COE [certificate of employment] to go abroad. Luckily, my

TABLE 3.1. **Profile of Nurse Interviewees**

	Nurses
Year passed the nursing licensure examination	
2019	2
2018	1
2016	1
2015	4
2014	1
2013	6
2012	7
2011	10
2010	7
2009 and earlier	16
Response to deployment ban	
Oppose	51
Support	4
Able to leave for overseas?	
Yes	24
No and working in Philippine hospitals	25
No but still waiting	4
No and unable to leave*	2

*Based on interviews conducted at the end of 2020. This number includes nurses whose documents had expired or who had had job offers rescinded.

brother was good friends with a doctor there, so they still gave it to me," she recounted. Her three-year stint at the small hospital was not enough to apply for jobs in the United States, but an agency recruiting nurses for Saudi Arabia offered her a position. Looking back, Alma was thankful that she had obtained a valid certificate for her skills. She knows of many friends who also worked part-time for local hospitals but were denied COEs. "We all did the same work, even if we were not full-time staff," Alma said, clucking her tongue. "In the end, my friends couldn't go anywhere. They just wasted their time."

A number of the nurses I interviewed (11 out of 55) were able to emigrate to overseas jobs despite never having worked in an actual hospital. However, their employment options were limited to dental clinics, pharmacies, and rehabilitation centers—places that provided care for patients but where employment failed to count as a valid form of clinical exposure. Jenine, the nurse bound for Saudi Arabia, understood that her position at the aesthetic clinic would be useless in seeking hospital jobs in the United States—her dream destination. She was frank in explaining the reason for accepting the job anyway. "I just needed to earn more money! That's how I became a dermatology nurse in Saudi Arabia," she laughed. "It was okay, but it wasn't a hospital setup. Our patients were only there for aesthetic procedures, so they weren't really sick. At that time, it was better than nothing."

Jenine never gave up on her dreams of working in an established hospital. But as a "derma nurse," she couldn't qualify for jobs in other health care institutions within Saudi Arabia, much less potential employers in the West. If given a choice, she would have liked to begin her career in a "real hospital" and develop her bedside skills right away. However, unlike Rachel, Jenine didn't have parents who could offer monetary support; she was responsible for handling her family's household expenses and sending her younger siblings to school.

In many ways, nurses' work experiences within the Philippines were a crucial part of determining their prospects for future emigration. While destination countries have been known to relax requirements for clinical exposure during times of urgent labor need (Gillin and Smith 2020), waiting for such changes could take many years. As such, nurses faced with poor domestic opportunities needed to find their own way of moving forward in their careers.[5] Their varied experiences would later determine how individual nurses responded to the state's decision to immobilize them within the country.

Filling in a Skills Gap

Jenine remembered feeling restless when she returned to the Philippines in September 2019. She had just concluded her second contract with her employer in Saudi Arabia, and while the job paid well, she was tired of the temporariness that came with working in the Gulf states. "I just wanted to rest. I wanted to be left alone," she said. "So I decided to just stay home first, catch up with my family, and think about what I really want to do."

After a long period of limited opportunities, destinations such as the United Kingdom were starting to hire foreign nurses once again, and there was a demand for applicants with hospital experience. Friends encouraged Jenine to look for work in a Philippine hospital so she could start gaining clinical exposure. However, local hospital wages were still too low for her family's needs. At that point, Jenine resigned herself to returning to Saudi Arabia. "I just thought maybe I should just let go. I still had my Saudi license, the derma job paid well. Maybe I'm never going to work in a hospital, and I should just be a derma nurse," she explained. "That was my mindset then. I was like, I'm never going to work in a local hospital."

Jenine was just waiting for her recruitment agency to issue her plane ticket to Riyadh, when the pandemic hit the Philippines. Shortly after, the government declared its deployment ban for health care workers. "I had no idea what was going on!" she exclaimed. "I couldn't contact my agency. I wasn't sure if they went out of business. I didn't even know if I could leave the country! I was only talking to my Saudi employers, and they were even more lost than me."

At first, Jenine thought of waiting out the deployment ban. Her work visa for Saudi Arabia was still valid, and the aesthetic clinic offered to delay the start date of her contract. Then, she heard about the Philippine government's urgent hiring scheme for nurses. Health officials had used emergency funds to offer renewable three-month contracts with salaries double the usual amount paid to entry-level nurses. For Jenine, this was the opening to finally move beyond the limits of her work in the Gulf states. She explained:

> Personally, for me, the deployment ban gave me a chance to get hospital experience so I can put something on my resume that will lead to a better offer from other countries. I will not only have hospital experience; I will also be working in a government tertiary hospital. That is the only consolation I have for myself (*'Yon lang naman 'yong pakunsuelo ko*).

Jenine's story reflects a common sentiment among nurses who chose to respond to the state's call for health care workers' voluntary immobility. While government officials praised nurses like Jenine as self-sacrificing heroes, they mainly saw their immobility as a chance to accumulate the hospital experience needed for future emigration. Having been shut out from clinical careers in the mid-2000s, these nurses saw the COVID-19 crisis as a time not only to work in the country's best hospitals but to do so while being paid a proper wage. In this sense, remaining in the country allowed these nurses to fill a gap in their skills—one that had put their migration plans on hold for too long.

One nurse, Sarah, sheepishly admitted that she had not treated an actual patient since passing the nursing board examinations in 2016. She was working as administrative staff in a government office when she heard that the Department of Health (DOH) was recruiting new hires for a prestigious university hospital in Manila. She immediately sent in an application, even if it meant caring for patients infected with COVID-19. "I've always wanted to return to clinical work, but the problem was that I could never find a job that would pay me as much as my office job did," she shared. "Now, the pay is better, and I get to help people. But my main purpose is to start gaining experience because I want to migrate with my daughter in the future."

Jenine's and Sarah's stories reveal how the Philippine state's deployment ban had become an unlikely opportunity. The fast-spreading virus had made health care workers essential, so the government was finally willing to pay a dignified wage for nurses' labor. The state had also established COVID-19 wards in Manila's largest and most prestigious tertiary hospitals: the Philippine Lung Center, the National Kidney Center, and the Philippine General Hospital. For nurses who needed to fill a gap in their skills, entering these hospitals promised a type of clinical exposure that would open more opportunities to more desirable destinations like the United States.

However, this opportunity to gain clinical skill came with much risk. The pandemic created an impetus for hospitals to quickly hire new nurses, relaxing the usual requirements needed for staff positions. While the deployment ban was meant to retain mission-critical skills, the nurses who responded to the state's call for service actually had little to no clinical experience at all. In Jenine's case, she started rotations in her government hospital with a nursing license from Saudi Arabia. She had not renewed her Philippine license since 2018. "At first, I was afraid they would reject me because all my local papers were expired! Because I wasn't planning to practice nursing in the Philippines anymore, right?" she explained. "But a nurse friend from Saudi advised me to just say my license is 'to follow' (*Pwede 'yan to follow*). I could just renew my license later on."

Jenine was fortunate in that she had actually worked in an allied health clinic. Ilyn, a nurse who obtained her license in 2008, had spent nine years running her family's beach resort in the province. She even explored an alternative career as an online English teacher. The notion of entering the COVID-19 wards was even more daunting to consider, but Ilyn was far from alone in terms of her lack of experience.

> When I went for the interview, I remember the person sitting next to me had been working at a bank. Another one came from a call center. On my first day on duty, I worked with a nurse with some experience, but she was only a company nurse. There was only one senior nurse who would check in with us. She said we shouldn't bother her unless we're really desperate and someone's about to die.

Given their lack of clinical exposure, nurses who entered the state's urgent hiring scheme grappled with relearning clinical procedures while also managing their own fears of getting infected with the virus. In 2020, there was no known vaccine for COVID-19. The rate of deaths among health care workers was high, and despite state efforts to recruit nurses, hospital staff struggled to attend to the many sick patients desperate for care. Almira, a nurse who obtained her license in 2004, admitted that she continued to feel paranoid about catching the virus, even when the hospital had her wear a full hazmat suit and three layers of gloves. "Some patients will panic . . . they're scared. They will start shouting, 'I can't breathe! Please help me, I'm suffering! (*Hindi ako makahinga! Hirap na hirap ako!*)'" she recalled. "So, I will rush to check. Is something leaking? Is there enough oxygen? They start drooling and coughing. There are droplets everywhere. I'm so afraid, but you have to provide care. There's no one else."

If working in a COVID-19 ward was not stressful enough, nurses also had to carry the emotional burden of caring for patients who were battling the virus on their own. Before the pandemic, Filipino nurses relied heavily on patients' family members to help with care work, ensuring that meals were consumed and medications were taken on time (Ortiga and Rivero 2019). Fears of infection removed such support while also imposing a strict limit on the time nurses could spend with their patients. Almira complained that her hospital administrators allocated only five minutes for nurses to see each of their patients. This time frame would have been laughable in the context of regular patient care; it was simply ludicrous for nurses in the COVID-19 wards.

One time, Almira found one of her patients slumped on her bed, hospital lunch and medication untouched. Knowing that the patient was diabetic, Almira tried to coax a few spoonfuls of rice into her mouth then hurriedly crushed the prescribed pills into powder so they could be easier to swallow. The whole process took twenty minutes. "Imagine, that patient was just a regular COVID patient! She didn't even have an NGT [nasogastric tube]," Almira said sadly. "Just a regular sixty-year-old who couldn't even sit up and didn't have the energy to eat by herself. She just had nothing left. Nothing."

Making things worse, the government's implementation of its urgent hiring scheme was also far from perfect. In some government hospitals, there were still problems of delayed salaries and missing benefits. One nurse, Raymond, complained that while state officials applauded nurses as national heroes, he still felt undervalued because his salary was always at least a few weeks late. "It would be fine if all their applause and praise could put food on the table," he mused. "Can I go tell people, 'I'm a hero, so please exempt me from all my bills'?"

Still, the nurses I interviewed felt that entering Philippine hospitals would pay off in their future careers. Despite the potential costs of their decision, they knew that working in the country's COVID-19 hospitals would give them access to a wide range of medical procedures and specialized areas, providing plenty of opportunities to accumulate valuable skills. True enough, the pandemic hastened nurses' exposure to hospital procedures in unprecedented ways. Nurses with no prior hospital experience found themselves thrown into the deep end in their first week of clinical duty, as the lack of staff meant having to quickly perform tasks that usually required several days of training. When I first spoke to Sarah, she was only a few weeks into her contract with the DOH. However, she had already completed several intense shifts in the COVID-19 ward. She described the experience as tough but fulfilling:

> I remember on my first day, they wanted us to handle ten patients each. I told the charge nurse, "It's my first time to handle patients, Ma'am." Because it really was my first time! She told me that, well, the other nurse on duty was an operating room nurse, so she did not have bedside experience either! No choice. So, we split the load . . . I learned so much: how to prepare medication, how to do a blood transfusion. I didn't come in with zero knowledge, but you know . . . I never had any bedside experience until I got to the COVID ward.

While Sarah dealt with the needs of ten patients in one shift, Marjorie, a registered nurse since 2013, found herself going through what she called a "crash course on hemodialysis." Originally treated as a respiratory illness, COVID-19 was eventually found to also cause serious damage to people's kidneys. Marjorie's hospital quickly became overwhelmed with a large number of patients who needed to undergo dialysis, a type of treatment where patients' blood is filtered through a machine. In pre-pandemic times, such tasks were only performed by a "Certified Renal Nurse" or CRN. Faced with a surge of COVID-19 patients with failing kidneys, the hospital had little time to search for more CRNs. Marjorie was quickly reassigned to the dialysis unit, where a senior staff nurse taught her the basic procedures of caring for patients undergoing dialysis. While the experience was frightening, Marjorie felt lucky to have gained such a useful skill. Under normal circumstances, she would have had to pay for a six-month training course to work in a dialysis unit. These opportunities to learn new skills motivated nurses in COVID-19 hospitals to keep working even as the pressures of the job increased.

As such, the nurses I interviewed seemed determined to stay in their jobs—at least for a year. Jenine admitted that she often cried during her shifts because she felt so overwhelmed. But six months after our first interview, she was thankful for the clinical expertise she had acquired on the job:

> I remember we had to intubate a patient in the first week. It was my first time to intubate a patient and I was so clueless. It was just me and the doctor because the senior nurse wasn't available. I was so nervous! I didn't know all the terms the doctor was saying . . . But now, I'm confident because I know what to do. I know what to prepare, what to expect. I know it sounds shallow, but I'm proud that I know how to apply tape on an intubated patient. I had no idea how to do that before! Now, I don't need a senior nurse to guide me. I can go at the doctor's pace (*Kumbaga, nakikipagsabayan na rin sa doktor*). Before, the doctor had to slow things down for me. It's so embarrassing when they do that.

Jenine's statement reflects how nurses took pride in the new capacities and techniques they learned as health workers in the Philippines' COVID-19 wards. For many of my interviewees, these learning opportunities were an important rationale for their decision to work in such dangerous conditions. While the state deployment ban had immobilized nurses within the country, it also opened a window of time to accumulate the skill needed in pursuing their future migration plans. Specifically, nurses like Jenine hoped that the time they devoted to the country's COVID-19 response would fill in a skills gap that had hindered their personal dreams for so many years. It was this opportunity for skilling that led them to accept their temporary immobility.

Skilling for the "Safe Window of Practice"

Not all the nurses who responded to the state's call for service were novice professionals with limited skills. Out of the twenty-seven nurses working in Philippine hospitals during our study, nine already had more than two years of clinical experience. For these nurses, the motivation to enter the COVID-19 wards was not to learn new skills, but rather to ensure that foreign employers could recognize the skills they already had.

One nurse, Raymond, had spent close to five years as a staff nurse for the intensive care unit at a private hospital in Manila. In 2019, he resigned to care for his grandfather who had fallen ill. When the DOH launched its urgent hiring scheme in 2020, Raymond had only been a "nonpracticing" nurse for a year. Still, he felt compelled to resume his hospital experience as soon as he could.

Raymond's anxiety was due to the way nursing skills were certified and recognized overseas. Nursing associations in destination countries such as the United States were widely known for scrutinizing even brief interruptions in migrants' clinical careers (Walton-Roberts 2021). Foreign hospitals only recruited nurses who fulfilled a "safe window of practice" or at least two consecutive years of clinical exposure at the time of their application (Ronquillo et al. 2011). While nurses like Raymond may have had valid reasons for taking time off from hospital work, these breaks in their careers disqualified them from jobs abroad. Working in the Philippines' COVID-19 wards provided strong evidence that his nursing skills were viable and up to international standards.

For Dianne, a registered nurse since 2007, the gap in her resume resulted from a common case of work burnout. After six years of working as an emergency room nurse in Saudi Arabia, she returned to the Philippines in 2017, hoping to try something new. "During that time, I just needed a different environment," she explained. "I had been in the hospital setting for so long, I thought that it would be nice to move to an office-based job." Dianne tried working at different call center agencies and even spent a few months as a company nurse. Yet she missed being in the hospital and decided to return to clinical practice in 2020. While she already had extensive hospital experience, the few years she had spent exploring office-based work forced her to rebuild her clinical exposure from scratch. The pandemic became an unlikely opportunity to do so more quickly. She explained:

> This is actually a good time to go back to the hospitals. I can't go any-where abroad because I have a three-year gap in my CV, when I was not working in the hospital. This is the best time to return to the hospital be-cause you can get really good experience and all the best tertiary hospitals are open to you.

Dianne's statement shows how the government's urgent hiring scheme also served as a means of accelerating her chances of leaving the country. Yet, unlike nurses who were entering the clinical setting for the first time, she had no desire to learn new skills. Instead, Dianne needed to adhere to the safe window of practice before resuming her career as a migrant nurse. The pandemic and the Philippine state's deployment ban provided an ideal setting for her to polish her skills.

While international skills standards compelled nurses like Dianne to reenter Philippine hospitals, pressures to maintain the validity of one's skills kept other nurses from leaving jobs they already had. This was the case for Julie Ann, a nurse who had been wanting to leave the private dialysis center where she worked. At the time of our interview, Julie Ann already had a job offer and was only waiting for her work visa to the United States. Unfortunately, the pandemic created a backlog at the US embassy in Manila, delaying her interview for months. The American immigration lawyer working on Julie Ann's case told her not to leave her job until she received her visa. Sudden unemployment before the visa interview might prompt a denial, which would compromise her entire application. While Julie Ann understood the lawyer's concerns, she worried about the worsening conditions at her workplace:

> There was a time when I wanted to resign because we were so under-staffed. Three of my friends resigned one after another. They had been wanting to leave, even before COVID-19, so I understand. But now I'm so exhausted. From a regular eight-hour shift, I now work 15 hours every other day. I don't think the company cares about us, to be honest.

If Julie Ann's job was already stressful before the pandemic, the threat of COVID-19 made everyday work simply unbearable. Even as the number of patients increased, the company offered no hazard pay or extra benefits. Julie Ann complained that she even had to buy her own PPE: a dozen face shields and a pair of hazmat suits. She would bring one suit home after every shift and handwash it herself. "Everyone in my family keeps telling me that this is not worth it, it's not worth getting sick," Julie Ann shared in frustration. "I said, 'This is nursing! This is my job! I can't just leave because I feel like quitting.' And of course, I'm pretty sure my agency will not approve. They don't want a gap in my timeline."

While Julie Ann expressed the need to serve her patients, it was also clear that she remained on the job to avoid creating a gap in her work as a registered nurse. Even if she wanted to stay at home, her pending visa application prevented her from quitting her job. Julie Ann felt compelled to keep working because of the skills standards set by foreign employers. Avoiding a skills gap in one's career meant ensuring that the window for overseas opportunity remained open despite the pandemic. Unlike nurses who were excited at the chance to finally practice their profession, nurses like Julie Ann felt trapped in jobs they no longer wanted to have.

These stories reveal how the multilayered recognition of migrant nurses' skills defined how Filipino nurses assessed the value of working in Philippine hospitals during the pandemic. Contrary to the Philippine state's narrative, these nurses did not view their work in local hospitals as a selfless contribution to the nation's pandemic response. While they felt fulfilled in caring for COVID-19 patients, they also wanted to take advantage of an opportunity for skilling that they had been deprived of for years. The decision to treat COVID-19 patients did not mean that nurses were blind to the possible risks of contracting the virus. Rather, they chose to endure these conditions in the short term, believing that the experience would eventually be worth their time. Not all nurses shared the same view.

Racing against Expiring Skills

John Paul was one of the first nurses who responded to my call for interviewees. He introduced himself as founder of the PrisoNurses, the group at the forefront of opposition to the state's deployment ban. "So what media agency are you from?" he asked bluntly, shortly after he answered my call. I explained that I was an academic, not a reporter—was he receiving interview requests from the press as well? "Oh yes. We talk to anyone who would listen," he said quickly. "We talked to all the nursing organizations, we talked to the media, we even got an audience with the president."

Prior to the pandemic, John Paul claimed, he was "just another Filipino nurse," working in the operating room of a government hospital in Saudi Arabia. His main goal was to emigrate to the United Kingdom, so he spent close to two years working on his papers for a job with the National Health Service. He finally secured an offer in 2019 and returned to the Philippines for a one-month break before starting his new life. He was waiting for his work visa when the pandemic hit the country and the Philippine government suspended all overseas deployments for nurses.

John Paul was sympathetic to the nurses serving in the country's COVID-19 wards, where they were likely to be underequipped and understaffed. He had worked for free at a private hospital in Manila after obtaining his license in 2009. He remembered how the hospital had charged him PHP 9,000 (USD 190) just to enter the program and had proceeded to subject all volunteers to a punishing workload with few opportunities for rest ("Pay to enter and work yourself to death! That's what it was."). His experience as a nurse in the Philippines was so traumatic, John Paul claimed, that leaving for Saudi Arabia actually brought immense relief. "That was the only time I felt I could enjoy some comfort in my life (*Dito lang guminhawa buhay ko*)," he sighed.

When the Philippine government called on Filipino nurses to join their urgent hiring scheme, John Paul responded by starting an online petition against the deployment ban instead. "I think this whole petition was just brought on by my emotions," he laughed. "I'm not an activist or anything like that. I was just a nurse who tried to endure working in this country . . . But at this point, I'm just fed up."

Close to a thousand nurses signed John Paul's petition. Several nurses volunteered to lead the group, and they began protesting the state's deployment ban as the PrisoNurses. They sent appeals directly to Philippine state officials on social media, granted interviews to reporters, and even wrote letters to the embassies of destinations such as the United Kingdom, Germany, and the United States. Among my interviewees, twenty-eight nurses were either active members or supporters of the PrisoNurses' advocacy. While not all had signed the petition, these nurses shared a belief that their immobility was forced and repressive. As such, they refused to work for Philippine hospitals.

Unlike those who saw the pandemic as an opportunity to accumulate skill, nurses who actively opposed the deployment ban had already gained the hospital experience needed to leave the country. Rather than filling in a skills gap, they argued that their prolonged immobility would compromise the limited validity of documents that certified their skills for overseas work. The reason for their anxiety was that, while employers sponsored work visas and immigration papers, individual nurses were responsible for obtaining professional recognition from their destination countries. This work entailed completing numerous competency tests, all of which were only valid for short periods of time. Even before the pandemic, aspiring migrant nurses needed to plan their applications carefully, ensuring that their test results did not expire until their departure. Faced with border closures and the Philippine state's deployment ban, nurses worried that the sudden delay had put all their documents at risk of expiry. While the state tried to frame nurses' immobility as only a temporary condition, nurses like John Paul argued that remaining in the Philippines was closing a small window of time they had in pursuing their overseas careers.[6]

Nurses bound for the UK were especially concerned about their International English Language Testing System (IELTS) results, an assessment of English-language capacity that had a validity period of only two years. For John Paul, the risk of having his IELTS certificate expire would be a painful blow, given it had already cost him close to PHP 70,000 (roughly USD 2,000) to pass this exam. He had to take the exam while he was working in Saudi Arabia, and the only testing center in the country was a one-hour flight from the city where he worked. He recounted:

> So imagine, first, I needed to save up for my transportation. That's about 5,000 pesos for a round trip from my city to Riyadh. Of course, I also needed maybe two or three nights at a hotel—20,000 pesos. Plus, the actual exam fee is 12,000 pesos. Then, I had to take the exam twice to get the minimum score! I also had to take it a third time so I could apply for the UK visa. I spent thousands of pesos—and that's just for the English exam!

Aside from costs, the expiration of nurses' language test results compromised the validity of other certificates needed for nurses to leave the country. One important document was the certificate of sponsorship (CoS) from the UK government. Valid for just two months, the CoS served as proof that a migrant nurse had a legal employer in the United Kingdom.

Several outgoing nurses had their CoS expire when the Philippine government placed Metro Manila on lockdown in March 2020. While their employers could apply for a new CoS, nurses needed to wait for a definite date when they could leave the country. Receiving a new CoS would be useless if the health worker deployment ban was still in effect. Nurses like Elmer were nervous because requesting a CoS meant resubmitting one's language test results. "My IELTS results are only expiring next year, so that's good. But who knows how long this pandemic will last?" he explained. "My concern now is to accomplish the documentation process as fast as possible so I can just leave for the UK."

For many nurses, the cost of redoing their paperwork was too heavy to bear. In Rachel's case, her mother had already invested close to PHP 200,000 (USD 4,000) on her application for Ireland. If any of her documents expired before her departure, it would mean having to redo the tedious step-by-step process of obtaining a decision letter from the Nursing and Midwifery Board of Ireland. Meanwhile, the decision letter itself was bound to expire after a year, increasing Rachel's concerns about her chances of leaving the country. Beginning from the first step of the decision letter process would mean retaking several exams and paying the required fees. "Everything will be like a domino effect," Rachel said, her voice sounding tired over the phone. "In order for you to acquire one document, you have to apply for another. Everything has an expiration date and for me, that date is coming soon."

The pressure of impending expiration dates heightened nurses' appeals to state agencies that enforced the deployment ban on health workers. As noted in previous chapters, Philippine state officials had gradually allowed some nurses to leave the country by making some exemptions to the ban. Still, they remained unwilling to lift the entire policy. While there were ways to get around border closures and the lack of international flights, nurses knew that the Philippine government could easily prevent their departures if the ban was still in place. As Elmer and I discussed his options in case his IELTS results did expire, his voice rose with frustration:

> It's not as if I can just say, "OK, I'm banned from leaving the country. Let me just take my time and work here in the Philippines while waiting." I can't do that because I already invested in all these exams even before there was a pandemic!

It is ironic to note that Elmer's first sentence described exactly what the Philippine government expected nurses to do. In framing nurses' immobility as an emergency measure, state officials constructed a story where nurses would temporarily dedicate their labor to local COVID-19 hospitals. State officials claimed that once the pandemic was over, nurses could simply pick up where they left off and continue their migration journeys. Elmer's second statement exposes what the Philippine government failed to mention. As nurses had consistently argued, applying for nursing jobs in the global market was a costly and tedious process of accumulating and certifying one's skill for foreign employers. While intended to temporarily keep nurses within the Philippines, the deployment ban ran the risk of permanently altering their career trajectories for the extended future. Time was a luxury that nurses such as Rachel, John Paul, and Elmer did not have.

Choosing Not to Serve

Unlike many of those who entered the state's urgent hiring scheme, nurses who actively opposed the ban had already spent years working in Philippine hospitals. This experience had taken an enormous toll on their physical and mental health. At the time they labored in local hospitals, there was no COVID-19 pandemic that prompted exuberant celebration of health care professionals. There was no urgent hiring scheme that offered decent salaries and benefits. While nursing groups had long protested stressful work conditions, there was no social media uproar calling for proper protections. The state's deployment ban was merely another example of how the Philippine government mistreated their profession, and in response, some nurses deliberately chose not to serve in any local hospitals during the pandemic.

To justify their protest, nurses who opposed the deployment ban built a narrative based on the losses they had already incurred as health care professionals within the Philippines—from financing their own training and education to working thankless jobs in local hospitals. In emphasizing their previous experiences of mistreatment, these nurses argued that they deserved the right to seek better opportunities elsewhere. As Rouella, a registered nurse since 2009, argued:

> Why should I serve this country? When my mother refused to help me pay for college, did the government give me money? No! I was the one who worked through the night so I could attend nursing school during the day. When I couldn't find work after graduation, did I ask the government for anything? I never asked them for money. They exploited us for years and now, we're the ones being called selfish.

Rouella's frustrations reflected decades of the Philippine state's poor treatment of its own health care professionals, a well-founded argument that struck a chord among the nurses' allies. However, there were other factors that made it possible for some nurses to boycott the government's urgent hiring scheme. Unlike nurses who needed to work toward filling the skills gap in their resumes, those like Rouella enjoyed temporary freedom from the requirements set by nursing associations in destination countries. When the pandemic led to staff shortages across the world, foreign employers exempted migrant nurses from having to maintain a safe window of practice as long as they already had job offers on hand. Recruiters advised nurses to remain at home, avoid falling sick, and wait until they were given a chance to leave the country.

Without the need to maintain clinical experience, the wages offered by the Philippine state's urgent hiring scheme failed to outweigh the hazards of treating COVID-19 patients. Nurses could not easily forget the overloaded shifts and abusive management practices within the country's health care system. Accordingly, they chose to either remain at home or work outside the hospital setting. Dyan, a registered nurse since 2012, found a job as a company nurse at a call center agency after her departure for Singapore was canceled. She wanted to work rather than "do nothing at home," but sought a job that made her feel "safe." The call center's company clinic required her to work the graveyard shift, but at least there were very few patients who needed her care. Returning to the hospital would have meant more risk and more work. "I heard that they were understaffed . . . But no, I don't want to go back there," Dyan said firmly. She feels no qualms about leaving her old hospital job.

Rhea, who was waiting for her papers from the United Kingdom, found a job with a multinational company that manufactured snacks and chocolate products. To adhere to COVID-19 protocols, the company needed nurses to collect health declaration forms from employees who came in for work. While Rhea worried about getting infected, the company gave her a complete set of PPE, down to a full hazmat suit and goggles.

> I felt safer at [the company] than the hospital. I'm at the clinic most of the time, and I only leave to collect the health forms from employees at the entrance gate. I was a little worried when the company wanted us to actually go and check people's temperature, like go into the office and the factory. But they gave me full PPE and everything.

Rhea's statement shows how nurses pursued jobs outside the hospital setting, considering these as a safer place to earn some money while waiting for the chance to leave the country. Ironically, Rhea's company provided a better supply of PPE compared to local hospitals that treated COVID-19 patients.

Stories from nurses like Rhea and Dyan underline how the state's urgent hiring scheme was only attractive to nurses who felt that they could benefit from clinical exposure within Philippine hospitals. For nurses who already had hospital experience, there was no reason to endure the challenges of practicing their profession within the country, especially during a global pandemic.

However, this discussion does not imply that nurses who refused to serve in COVID-19 hospitals did not care about their patients. Even those who were angry with the Philippine government admitted that they felt a sense of guilt in deciding not to join the state's urgent hiring scheme. Rouella, a nurse who began her interview by arguing that the Philippines did not deserve her labor, confessed that she had briefly considered working at a local hospital. "To be honest, yes, I sometimes feel like I want to volunteer," she said. "I am an anesthesia nurse, so when it comes to intubations, I know I can help out with people."

Other nurses felt even more conflicted about helping fellow health workers, many of whom were also falling sick. Gemma, a nurse bound for Saudi Arabia, was ashamed that she remained at home while so many other nurses were battling the virus. When I called her for an interview, she had been unemployed for six months. The fact that she was "doing nothing" made her feel worse about choosing not to serve. She shared:

> I feel guilty because this is my profession. It's true that I took an oath to serve. But—I don't know, I'm scared. It would have been better if there was a vaccine for COVID-19. But we don't have one! And the hospitals won't even give you proper protections. What if I'm the reason my parents get infected? Or my grandmother? [pause] But truthfully, I feel guilty. I see these videos online of frontliners dancing in the wards to keep their spirits up. I feel inspired. But I also feel scared.

Despite nurses' guilt and worry, it was clear that no matter how passionately they cared for their patients, there was a limit to how much they could endure the poor work conditions in Philippine hospitals. Without the pressure of keeping to a so-called safe window of practice, Filipino nurses found that there were few reasons to enter the COVID-19 wards beyond the promises of a government that had long undermined their profession. Rouella argued that this was the reason she held on to her decision not to serve, despite her guilt. "I feel like this is not right . . . They tell us to risk our lives, but they never cared about our lives! Where is justice in that?"

Divergent Stories, Divided Outcomes

While the Philippine state had blocked the emigration of all Filipino health care workers, interviews with stranded nurses revealed two very different narratives about their immobility. Those who opposed the ban tried to push a story of an exploitative government whose unjust policy placed their emigration plans at risk. Meanwhile, others saw their sudden immobility as a chance to accumulate desired skills for overseas dreams that had been put on hold. Despite the dangers of the virus, these nurses chose to enter the government's urgent hiring scheme, hoping that time spent in the COVID-19 wards would open a window of opportunity for future emigration. These outcomes reinforce what scholars had long argued: immobility is not merely a failure to move. Remaining in place had different value and purpose, depending on the different circumstances surrounding aspiring migrants.

This chapter has traced how individual perspectives of immobility affect how would-be migrants negotiate with the broader state structures that govern their emigration. In pushing against the state's deployment ban on health care workers, groups like the PrisoNurses were successful in highlighting the costs of being stuck at home. As discussed in chapter 2, Filipino state officials eventually agreed to adjustments in the conditions of the deployment ban, allowing more nurses to leave the country. The PrisoNurses' narrative of involuntary immobility played an integral role in forcing the state to allow these concessions. Nurses' refusal to render service to their government was a powerful means of bringing to light the profession's poor treatment through the years.

However, the presence of other nurses who readily entered Philippine hospitals dampened the overall campaign to depict the deployment ban as forced labor. Nurses like Jenine, Sarah, and Almira had voluntarily worked in the country's COVID-19 wards, thereby weakening the PrisoNurses' claim that the deployment ban was a coercive policy. Some nurses' willingness to work also allowed state officials to reinforce the government narrative that those who refused to serve did not care about their fellow Filipinos.

Nevertheless, this chapter has also shown that despite such divergent narratives, there remained a common belief that Filipino nurses had been undervalued and mistreated within their own country. Despite state efforts to reframe their skills as critical to the pandemic response, nurses could not forget how these very same skills were poorly paid and barely protected from employer abuse. The nurses I interviewed had pursued their careers in the hope of moving abroad, where they were likely to obtain higher wages and receive better recognition as health care workers. While the pandemic created a sudden shift in how government agencies sought to retain nursing skills, all my interviewees had doubts about whether such change could be sustained in the long term. Thus, the window of opportunity their immobility created—whether opening or closing—was one that faced outward, toward leaving the country.

Four

A Chance to Start Anew

Reskilling Unwanted Service Workers

At first, the news of 500 Filipino workers stranded on a cruise ship was not exceptionally alarming. The problem began when an eighty-year-old passenger tested positive for COVID-19 after disembarking from the *Diamond Princess* in the middle of an Asian tour. While the captain was able to return to their previous port in Yokohama, Japanese health officials prevented both passengers and crew members from leaving the ship (Sim 2020a). In February 2020, the *Diamond Princess* was the largest COVID-19 cluster outside China, with more than 800 infections onboard.[1] But for the Philippines, it was only one of a few coronavirus outbreaks impacting Filipinos overseas (see Liao 2020).[2] On social media, foreign affairs secretary Teodoro Locsin Jr. was confident in addressing the matter. "It's our duty to take care of our overseas Filipinos wherever they are," he proclaimed assertively. "I want them home now" (Tadalan 2020).

Three more weeks would pass before the Philippine government came to realize that the *Diamond Princess* was just the beginning. In a series of events now documented in countless headlines and media reports, the COVID-19 pandemic crippled the global cruise industry, grounding ship operations for more than a year. While cases of infection first emerged among ships sailing within Asia,[3] the virus quickly spread through major cities across North America and Europe, prompting the closure of international ports (Casey 2020; Harris 2020). The final blow to the industry came in March 2020, when the US Centers for Disease Control and Prevention (CDC) issued a "no sail" order and advised Americans to defer all cruise travel indefinitely (CDC 2020).[4]

Suddenly, the Philippines faced the unprecedented task of coordinating the return of all Filipino cruise workers still onboard their ships. As Secretary Locsin eventually admitted, repatriation efforts during the pandemic were the "biggest" in the country's history as a migrant-sending nation. Still, he remained confident with regard to what lay ahead. "Usually foreign governments would say [to their nationals who are staying overseas], 'Well, they're abroad, that's their problem,'" he said in an interview streamed live on social media. "Not us. We brought [our citizens] home" (*PDI* 2020a).[5]

Yet, as the pandemic continued to keep international borders shut and leisure travel on hold, repatriation became the least of the government's worries. Beyond merely transporting migrants back home, Philippine state agencies also needed to determine what these workers would do upon arrival. While the repatriation process was difficult on its own, returning migrants faced the more daunting task of finding a place for themselves within a country still reeling from the pandemic. Unlike nurses, whose labor was in high demand, cruise workers found their service skills rendered useless with the shutdown of the hospitality industry. While the Philippine state pronounced its duty to care for Filipino migrant workers "wherever they are," the government's actual challenge was to fulfill this promise within its own borders.

Compared with research on how states deploy workers overseas, fewer studies investigate how governments incorporate those who return home after a period of living abroad. Existing research has mainly critiqued the lack of support for returnees, as states tend to either ignore the challenges that former migrants face or stigmatize forced returnees as criminals (Cuttitta 2018; Hagan and Wassink 2020). For years, international organizations called on governments to support former migrants in reestablishing social, economic, and psychosocial ties within their home countries (Graviano et al. 2017). However, initiatives within developing nations are often found to be inadequate or simply absent in all three aspects (Arowolo 2000; Vathi, King, and Kalir 2022). In the case of labor-exporting nations such as the Philippines, scholars have criticized the state for prioritizing deployment over reintegration, given the massive economic benefits of monetary remittances (Banta 2023; Ruhs 2013).

Still, it would be a mistake to assume that all sending states are un-interested in returnees' welfare. In the Philippine case, failing to protect former migrants can be problematic for incumbent officials (see Liao 2020). The COVID-19 crisis heightened public expectations even further, as the plight of returnees dominated news headlines. Administration of-ficials needed to convince anxious constituents that the government had a plan in place and that the return of migrant workers would not worsen social problems that the country was already struggling to solve. Inad-vertently, the task of reintegrating former migrants became a test of the Duterte government's pandemic response.[6]

In this chapter, I discuss how a key part of the Philippines' reinte-gration efforts was framing former migrants' immobility as a chance to rebuild their lives at home. This narrative reconstructed migrants' forced return as a positive opportunity—one that the Duterte administration would help former migrant workers maximize in their favor. I will discuss how state agencies used the promise of skills training to reinforce this ap-proach, emphasizing how new entrepreneurial or pandemic-oriented skills would allow former migrants to thrive within their communities. But, as this chapter shows, such positive portrayal of cruise workers' immobility eventually collapsed, as government officials failed to maintain its narra-tive of successful return.

Pivot to Reintegration

In a budget hearing at the Philippine Senate, administrator Hans Cacdac had the unenviable task of explaining how the Overseas Workers Welfare Administration (OWWA) was reintegrating the 80,000 Filipino cruise workers repatriated home. It was October 2020, seven months since the cruise industry had suspended all operations. A small agency attached to the DOLE,[7] OWWA had existed since the beginning of the country's labor export policies in 1977.[8] Yet never in the administration's history had it received so much scrutiny and attention.

At the onset of the pandemic, the Philippine Congress approved an unprecedented amount of PHP 5 billion (USD 98 million) to aid former migrants, with a significant portion of this fund dedicated toward rein-tegration programs. The senators wanted to know how cruise workers, one of the largest groups of returnees, benefited from taxpayers' money (Canlas 2020).[9] Watching a recording of the session online,[10] it was hard to read administrator Cacdac's expression through his face mask and black-rimmed glasses, and the acrylic divider that separated him from the other state officials attending the budget hearing in person. While the OWWA administrator had traveled from his home to the Philippine Senate Building in Manila, most of the senators were joining the session through the online conferencing platform Zoom. This hybrid session conveyed a sense of normalcy—that somehow, government affairs were still going on—but it was also a stark reminder that the Philippines' COVID-19 infections were still in the thousands. Cacdac's answer was straightforward:

> The general strategy for cruise workers has been first, financial assistance through our cash-out programs. *Pantawid* (To tide them over). The second is through livelihood projects . . . [OWWA] has a sense that the seafarers, including the cruise ship workers, can get into a group livelihood endeavor. They can easily organize themselves into a business endeavor of about five.[11]

The "cash-out" program that Cacdac referred to had emerged during the pandemic (see table 4.1). Under the acronym AKAP (*Abot Kamay ang Pagtulong*), this program disbursed a one-time package of PHP 10,000 to "displaced migrant workers." But Cacdac's emphasis on livelihood projects was not new. OWWA had promoted self-employment initiatives in the past, targeting former migrant workers who no longer wanted to work abroad (Banta and Pratt 2021). In the mid-2000s, then-president Gloria Macapagal-Arroyo had launched several aggressive campaigns encouraging former migrants to invest in the country (Guevarra 2010). However, the economic impact of COVID-19 had made these programs take on a sudden urgency.

In many ways, the ongoing pandemic had dampened any hope that overseas opportunities would return soon. International border closures had curtailed the Philippines' deployment numbers, creating a 75% drop in the number of Filipino workers leaving the country for jobs abroad (IOM 2021). Similarly, the national economy remained in dire straits, with a record-high unemployment rate of 10.3% in 2020.[12] Before the pandemic, Philippine labor export agencies had used emigration as a "safety valve," facilitating an outflow of workers to ease the pressures of a poor

TABLE 4.1. **Programs for Repatriated Migrant Workers during the COVID-19 Pandemic**

Date	Policy
July 2020	**OWWA *Abot Kamay ang Pagtulong* (AKAP)** Repatriated migrant workers receive PHP 10,000 as cash aid.
Sept 2020	**OWWA *Tulong Puso* Livelihood Assistance Program** Returning migrant workers can avail themselves of support to fund business ventures. Grants range from PHP 150,000 to 1 million.
Sept 2020	**President Duterte allocates PHP 13 billion to fund support programs for repatriated migrant workers** Additional funds allocated to cash-out programs (AKAP) and other livelihood programs.
Sept 2020	**Free training programs for repatriated migrant workers** Skills training directed toward jobs in call center agencies, contact tracing, and education.
Dec 2020	**DOLE "Cash for Work" program** PHP 4.9 billion allocated to provide temporary jobs for workers affected by the pandemic.

domestic job market (Ruiz 2014). Suddenly, the government needed to find other ways of absorbing its jobless citizens at home.

While public funds were essential in running the state's programs for reintegration, officials like administrator Cacdac also needed to promote a vision of what lay ahead for migrant workers who were forced to return home. The result was a narrative of opportunity, where migrants' sudden return was depicted as a chance for permanent resettlement. Rather than waiting for the pandemic to pass, government representatives argued that unemployed migrants could take advantage of their time at home to establish their own livelihood projects—endeavors that would eventually provide an alternative to working overseas. To bolster such initiatives, state agencies offered a wide range of grants specifically for "displaced" migrant workers who wanted to set up their own companies (see table 4.1).[13] Cacdac described these livelihood programs as an important break "for those affected by the COVID-19 and those who no longer think that they will be able to return to their host countries." He added that in establishing a successful business, former overseas workers would be able to "start anew" and reestablish their lives in the country (Terrazola 2020a; 2020c).

This plan was not entirely misguided, nor was it unique to the Philippines. Studies of return migration have shown that many migrants regard self-employment as an ideal end goal (see Hagan and Wassink 2018 for review). While there are stories of migrants who return to reestablish their careers in their home countries, such cases tend to involve highly educated professionals (Harvey 2008; Ortiga et al. 2019; Saxenian 2005). For the majority of migrant workers who take on blue-collar jobs abroad, self-employment is often considered the best option upon return (see Hagan, Hernandez-Leon, and Demonsant 2015). Some scholars have even argued that accumulating the capital to start a new business is the main reason migrants choose to move abroad in the first place (Lindstrom and Lauster 2001; Massey and Parrado 1998).

Similarly, a survey from the DOLE claimed that 60% of overseas Filipinos dream of building their own businesses upon returning to the country.[14] If emigration was meant to finance such endeavors, state agencies argued that their reintegration programs would simply accelerate this process, providing the initial funds for Filipino workers to start their own livelihood projects.

However, the push toward entrepreneurship had many weaknesses as well. Despite migrants' efforts to build economic and human capital for their return, studies find that few successfully establish viable livelihood projects within their home communities (Banta 2021; Riaño 2022). Economists have also pointed out that high rates of self-employment are actually correlated to high rates of poverty (La Porta and Shleifer 2014). In the context of the Philippines, being self-employed is similar to working in the informal market, where jobs are often precarious and pay is low. While running one's own business may offer more control to returning migrants, it does not always provide the stability and safety net of a full-time job (Dulay et al. 2021). Thus, scholars have argued that state programs that promote entrepreneurship simply push the burden of reintegration to individual migrants (Banta and Pratt 2021).

In this vein, Filipino politicians were immediately worried about the administration's promotion of entrepreneurship, given that a large portion of public funds had been funneled toward small business grants. In a Senate session held in August 2020, Senator Imee Marcos questioned whether livelihood projects should be the only option for returning migrants.[15] She argued:

> Not every single OFW [Overseas Filipino Worker] is really ready to be an entrepreneur, to be self-employed. In addition to the OFWs' own busi-

nesses, is there a way for us to help them shift to local employment alternatives or perhaps co-investments and partnerships? . . . We have seen too many tragic stories of OFWs squirreling away funds for years and years, then suddenly blowing it all away on a bad business decision.

Given such concern, OWWA needed to reassure the public that funding migrant businesses would not lead to fleeting ventures that would waste limited resources. Instead, the move toward self-employment needed to be seen as a permanent shift central to former migrants' long-term settlement in the country. To reinforce their narrative of reintegration, state agencies turned to encouraging former migrants to acquire particular forms of skill.

Skilling for Self-Employment

If self-employment was the Philippine state's attempt at defining cruise workers' immobility as a time to start anew, entrepreneurial skills training was the answer to all doubts regarding the success of such endeavors. To respond to hesitant politicians in the Philippine government, labor officials qualified that not all migrant workers had the capacity to be successful entrepreneurs. However, they also used this fact to reinforce the need for skills training focused on business management. DOLE undersecretary Joji Aragon emphasized this in response to criticism from members of the Philippine Senate. "You've said that not all [migrant workers] are cut out for entrepreneurship or small business startups. That's true. I think that's an observation shared by all units under the Department of Labor," she admitted, before quickly adding, "That's the reason why we are [teaching] financial literacy."

In this statement, undersecretary Aragon implied that, despite the difficulties of entrepreneurship, training migrant workers in the "right" skills would help ensure their later success. Thus, migrant returnees who wished to access state funds were first required to learn entrepreneurial concepts in a series of seminars and workshops. Skilling was a key feature of all eligibility requirements, whether the available monies were large or small. For example, one grant program required applicants to present a "certificate of entrepreneurial development training" in order to obtain a "micro fund" of PHP 20,000 (USD 390) (*Manila Bulletin* 2020a). Meanwhile, the group livelihood program that administrator Cacdac promoted to cruise workers obliged beneficiaries to take a seminar on business regulations and financial literacy (see table 4.1). Successful applicants could receive up to PHP 1 million in grants (USD 20,000) (Aquino 2020c).

Such optimism about teaching entrepreneurial skills filtered into state partnerships with the private sector as well. In another highly publicized program, state labor agencies partnered with Coca-Cola Beverages Philippines in recruiting former migrants to train as soft drink distributors, wholesalers, or "community resellers." Under this partnership, government workers took charge of identifying potential beneficiaries among migrants who had been repatriated home. Meanwhile, Coca-Cola managers trained these migrants in how to develop a business model, manage cash flow, and handle inventory. Those who took part in these workshops became OWWA's models of resilience and hard work. In an online channel for overseas Filipinos, administrator Cacdac told the story of a woman who signed up for the Coca-Cola program after being repatriated home and completed the online training curriculum during her mandatory quarantine period in Manila.[16] He proudly shared that this former migrant was now running a full-fledged business reselling Coca-Cola products from her home. "If she continues to do well, OWWA is willing to give her more resources to grow her business," he said, drawing exclamations from the show's hosts. "We will reinforce her work so she can develop her business further."[17] In telling this story, Cacdac emphasized how former migrants could turn their unexpected return into a long-term opportunity.

Coca-Cola Philippines' president and CEO, Gareth McGeown, repeated the state's hope for migrant returnees, saying, "Our goal is to help repatriated OFWs who have lost their livelihood abroad to start anew via owning and operating their own business and being successful here, at home, with their families" (Cahiles-Magkilat 2020). Such statements implied that those who reskilled themselves for entrepreneurship would be most likely to survive the disruptions caused by the virus. In glossy photos featured in the media, government officials and Coca-Cola representatives posed with former migrants in their homes, often in a semicircle surrounding a bright red cooler with a solitary bottle of Coke at the center. Former migrants were asked to hold up a framed plaque, certifying their status as soft drink entrepreneurs.

Entrepreneurial skills training strengthened the state's narrative that migrant initiatives toward self-employment would have longevity. Drawing the comparison with cash handouts or other forms of aid, government agencies highlighted the potential of small businesses in helping migrants establish new sources of income. Eventually, even migrant advocacy groups promoted entrepreneurship as an ideal means of coping with the pandemic. In one newspaper feature, a well-known nonprofit organization upheld small businesses as a chance for former migrants to "earn a living without the need to leave their homes." The article also featured a program providing former migrants with a seed grant of PHP 4,000 (USD 78) to purchase and resell chicken products from a local corporation. Unsurprisingly, such benefits came with a training curriculum on how to sustain and expand one's initial capital investment (*Business Mirror* 2020b).

By skilling former migrants for self-employment, the Philippines' labor agencies promoted the idea that entrepreneurial knowledge and financial literacy would suffice in pivoting returnees toward permanent resettlement. Providing support for home businesses was an effective means of not only helping migrant returnees recover from the loss of their overseas jobs, but also molding future contributors to the country's development. Cacdac argued that the Philippines' recovery from COVID-19 would come to rely on the entrepreneurial skills of returning migrants. "[All these programs] will work alongside the state in jumpstarting our economy," he declared. "[Returning migrant workers] will be part of jumpstarting our economy" (Cahiles-Magkilat 2020).

Self-Employment without the State

At first, it seemed that the state's push toward entrepreneurship had been fully embraced by returning cruise workers. In the first round of interviews my team conducted in 2020, thirty-two of the forty-five cruise workers we spoke with were running their own home business. Every person seemed to be selling something new—face shields, hand sanitizer, "gently used" clothes, chiffon cakes, spicy local sausages, and milk tea.[18] Larry, a former bartender, had hedged his bets on selling *hopia,* a bean-filled pastry popular in the Philippines. "There's this brand that was popular in my hometown. So what I do is buy the hopia there then bring it back here to sell to our neighbors," he explained. "We're happy because we sell all 50 boxes in less than four hours." Like other cruise workers, Larry had set up shop in his home, advertising his products on Facebook or through private messaging groups in Viber or WhatsApp. In some cases, former migrants ran "free deliveries" themselves, ferrying purchases to their customers on scooters and bicycles.

One interviewee, Glaiza, was very much a model entrepreneur. She had worked as a massage therapist for a luxury cruise line, but Glaiza's official employer was a smaller private company that ran the ship's spa. She did not qualify for any of the benefits that cruise lines provided for their full-time employees. Still, she made the most of the money she received from the government's cash-out program:

> I always wanted to start my own business, so I decided that this was the time to do it . . . Even before we left the ship, my employer gave us a link to the government site where we could apply for the PHP 10,000 aid package for returning migrants. I applied as soon as I got home, and they sent me the money in three weeks. Whatever I had, I put it into my business . . . I have a shop in Lazada and Shopee,[19] I sell PPE and face masks in bulk. Thank God, the shop is actually doing well.

In many ways, Glaiza fit the image that Philippine state officials promoted in their narrative of "successful" return. Even after losing her source of income, Glaiza found other ways of sustaining her family, turning government aid into a productive business. But unlike Larry, Glaiza wasn't a novice entrepreneur; she had set up her business years before the pandemic, selling random items online between cruise voyages. The sudden suspension of cruise travel gave her the time to fully concentrate on her business. It also helped that she already had the right contacts to quickly update her shop. Her previous suppliers helped her find good products to sell on such short notice. "It's not what you know, but who you know," Glaiza told me pointedly. *"Para-paraan naman nating mga Pilipino eh.* (You just have to find your own way to make a living. That's how we are as Filipinos.)"

Larry's and Glaiza's experiences served as powerful stories for state agencies hoping to construct workers' immobility as an opportunity for more permanent ventures at home. Similar narratives gained quick appeal on social media, where viral videos featured other workers who supposedly were flourishing in their new careers. State agencies publicized features of former migrants who had taken advantage of government aid. One popular video presented the success of seven migrant women who set up their own poultry business selling chicken.[20] With upbeat music in the background, one woman recounted how she retired from her job in Saudi Arabia and formed a cooperative with other former migrants. As she speaks, the video shows the women tending to a row of bamboo cages where their chickens were housed. "Our group's strength is that we're all united in finding ways to grow our business," the women say proudly. The video ends with photos of the migrant women receiving a check from OWWA representatives.

Indeed, it was amazing to see not only the variety of products people managed to sell, but also the speed at which these businesses emerged during the pandemic. Philip, a former bar waiter, started a Facebook group chat for cruise workers to exchange advice on obtaining support from the government and their cruise companies. Immediately, the group started to see growing numbers of workers advertising their new businesses. There were so many new products being sold, Philip had to create a new chat group just for cruise workers to publicize their products. "It was motivating for me to see how creative my coworkers were," he said. "People were making the most of our situation."

However, none of the cruise workers I interviewed had actually availed themselves of government grants meant for establishing home businesses. Some, like Glaiza, had merely relied on the one-time cash handout distributed to all returning migrants. When I asked why, the cruise workers complained that state agencies required them to devote too much time to learning about business models, budgets, and marketing plans. While state agencies released multiple online tutorials to guide migrant workers through the process of submitting their applications, cruise workers remained averse to applying for such programs, despite assurances of available monies and support. They argued that government programs simply entailed more effort than they had to give.

Philip himself had started a business that would have been a perfect fit for OWWA's reintegration programs. He set up a water-refilling station, a shop where people could purchase one-gallon bottles of filtered water for their homes. To get the business started, Philip invested a considerable part of his own savings, while his best friend contributed the other half of the required capital. When I asked if he had thought of seeking extra funding from the government, Philip explained that he did not have the time to undertake the required training to qualify for the grant. His wife was a nurse in Saudi Arabia, and he was caring for their two-year-old daughter at home. He also wasn't sure if the application process was worth his time and energy. OWWA officials had emphasized that they offered grants that would not count as loans. However, Philip remained suspicious of government initiatives that demanded specific outcomes from beneficiaries. He said:

> I don't know anyone who tried to get money from the government. It's like, you got some money, but then you added more problems to your life because you have to pay them back somehow . . . I would rather do what my friend did. He used to be a bartender on the ship. With his last 2,000 pesos, he started selling barbecued meat on the street. He doesn't pay any rent, he doesn't have any debt. He just went outside his house and set up a barbecue stall.

Unwilling to add more problems to their situation, cruise workers complained that government grants were filled with conditions that made the process of starting a business more stressful. One aspiring entrepreneur, Clariza, said that while the state offered attractive opportunities, it was difficult for her to put together an application. "I want to put up my own business, but the government has so many requirements!" she complained. "You need a feasibility study and all these certificates. It takes a lot of effort and patience." Clariza had graduated with a bachelor's degree in business administration. But after years working as a waitress, it was hard for her to recall the tedious process of putting together a business plan. Rather than go through a weekly seminar on entrepreneurship, she started her own online business instead. At the time we spoke, Clariza was selling rice cakes from her parents' home.

For all their complaints about state bureaucracy and paperwork, cruise workers were undeterred in seeking other types of government aid. Upon their repatriation home, my interviewees quickly researched available support, filled out applications for aid, met with local officials, and sent appeals to politicians via social media. Those with children dutifully completed applications for tuition subsidies, while others advocated for unemployment benefits from government insurance. At the height of local restrictions on people's movement, many continued to travel to government offices to avail themselves of cash aid. One interviewee, Adnan, recalled leaving his home at 3:00 a.m. just so he could join the queue at the provincial office of the DOLE. He claimed that there were already more than a hundred people in line when he arrived at 5:00 a.m. It was obvious from my interviews that cruise workers were willing to expend tremendous effort in obtaining more support from the Philippine state. However, they were less likely to put in the same energy toward applying for small business grants despite government campaigns that invited them to do so.

This situation created an unlikely problem for Philippine state officials. In studies of reintegration, scholars have mostly critiqued migrant-sending states for their lack of effective programs for migrant returnees (Arowolo 2000; Kandilige and Adiku 2020). In contrast, Philippine state officials had the opposite problem: They had poured massive funds into reintegration efforts that few returnees were truly interested in.

Even if cruise workers engaged in entrepreneurship, it was obvious that these businesses would not be the enterprises that could help in national development. While state agencies such as OWWA framed these livelihood projects as a means of rebuilding the economy, most of the small businesses that cruise workers established could barely sustain their daily expenses. For example, Jessamine and Kenneth, a cruise photographer and a line cook, respectively, were able to set up an online food store in their first six months back in the Philippines. They had a steady stream of customers, but neither was hopeful that the business would last a year. "Basically, what's happening is you sell things online and your friends buy from you. But because your friends are also selling something, you have to buy something from them too. The money is just going in circles (*parang paikot-ikot lang*)," Jessamine explained. "I think we're both just hoping we can return to cruising soon." In many ways, Jessamine's worries reinforce the work of scholars who have warned against viewing self-employment as a "homogeneous category expected to promote social mobility" (Wassink and Hagan 2018: 1075). Although some migrant endeavors can generate a stable profit every month, others provide only intermittent sources of income.

The disconnect between state programs and former migrants became even more apparent in the requirements for small business grants. To ensure that government funds for migrant returnees would be used for their reintegration, state agencies obligated applicants for certain grants to provide proof that they no longer intended to leave the country. Nilo, another cruise photographer, said that this requirement discouraged him from applying for OWWA's small business grants:

> I needed to provide a certificate saying I am no longer affiliated with my company. I'm just afraid that if I do that, my agency will not give me a new contract when cruising resumes. You need to get some paper that says you've resigned, and you're not connected to the company at all . . . You need all of that before they give you the PHP 20,000 grant.

In trying to frame migrants' return as an opportunity to start anew, Philippine state agencies structured their programs with the goal of permanent resettlement. This narrative assumed that cruise workers would welcome opportunities to remain with their families back home. Nilo's concerns reveal that not all cruise workers saw their immobility in the same way. On the contrary, cruise workers seemed to be caught in what Karen Liao (2024: 3) terms the "grey window of return," a liminal period when migrants deal with the circumstances of their involuntary immobility while seeking opportunities for remigration. Compromising the chance to return to the cruise ship was simply a risk that few former migrants were willing to take.

Unraveling the Resettlement Story

As the COVID-19 pandemic entered its second year, the weaknesses in the administration's narrative of permanent resettlement began to receive increasing scrutiny. Former migrants continued to call for more government aid and support. Meanwhile, Filipino politicians began pressing the administration's labor officials for evidence of their skills training outcomes. During a 2021 meeting of the Senate Committee on Labor, Employment, and Human Resource Development, Senator Nancy Binay raised the question of how migrant workers who obtained government funds were faring with their livelihood projects. "For those workers who received 10,000 pesos or 20,000 pesos, does OWWA have any data on their success rate in setting up their businesses?" she asked.

Attending the meeting in person, administrator Cacdac paused before responding, "We don't have any firm data on the success rate." He explained that, while OWWA officials stayed in contact with aid recipients for three months, this was mainly to ensure that the money had been committed toward building a business. The agency had no means of determining whether these businesses actually prospered. "We do have success stories," Cacdac added quickly. "We identify success stories and give them recognition, but we don't have data on their success rate."

Despite the grainy quality of the meeting's recording online, it was hard to miss the incredulous expression on Senator Binay's face. "I'm feeling a little disturbed that we have no data on the success rate of our livelihood programs," she said, laughing a little in disbelief. "I think we should allot some funds or some time to make sure that these programs are actually working. Because if not, I feel like we're just throwing this money away."

This exchange highlighted the flaws in the state's story of how former migrants could use their immobility as a time to start anew. In advancing their approach to reintegration, government officials needed to show how entrepreneurship would allow former migrants to shift from overseas work to local livelihood projects. Yet there was little proof that such enterprises provided return migrants with the stability to rebuild their lives in the country.

Even among the cruise workers I interviewed, less than half of those who established their own businesses (fifteen out of thirty-two) were still operating the same business six months after our first interview. Pandemic disruptions had worsened people's economic situations, and the arrival of more repatriated workers from overseas led to a glut of online businesses with too few customers. Philip, the bar waiter who had invested in a water-refilling station, was an unfortunate casualty of the tough market. He and his business partner initially thought they had chosen a good location for their shop, but they failed to attract regular customers. When I reached out for our second interview, he told me that he had folded his business within four months. "The money we earned wasn't enough to cover our daily expenses," he explained sadly. "It just wasn't worth it." I was taken aback at how different Philip's voice sounded over the phone. It seemed that whatever energy he had had six months ago had simply faded away. While he still felt the need to publicize the plight of seafarers like him, he no longer mentioned mobilizing his friends through their Facebook group. Instead, he had devoted himself fully to his new home business: building study desks for children who were attending classes from home. His income was just enough to pay for his toddler's milk and diapers. He relied on his wife's wages in Saudi Arabia for everything else.

Other interviewees who maintained their home businesses faced similar challenges. Earnings from their small businesses could help pay for food or groceries. However, this income could not cover larger expenses, such as school tuition or rent. Thus, cruise workers often had to take on other forms of work. Glaiza, who initially did well selling face masks online, shifted to selling beauty products and kitchen appliances when other sellers started offering face masks at cheaper prices. To support herself and her two daughters, she decided to return to her original occupation as a massage therapist. Local spas were still closed due to COVID-19 restrictions, so Glaiza resorted to offering "home service" massages for people living in her neighborhood. I recalled how, at the beginning of the pandemic, Glaiza had been afraid of catching the virus from her American clients at the ship's spa. Did she feel the same fear in entering other people's homes? In her response, Glaiza sounded more resigned than afraid:

> It's not bad . . . I charge 450 pesos for an hour and a half. Sometimes, I have two clients in one day. Sometimes, I'll only have one client a week. People aren't scared of the virus anymore, but I still do all my massages wearing a mask. I wash my hands with alcohol before and after. I also wash my hands when I get to my customer's home. What can we do, right?

Cruise workers' experiences exposed the trickiness of relying on migrant businesses as an avenue to reintegration. As Riaño (2022: 6) notes, successful migrant businesses need to meet people's "fundamental, existential, and security needs." Unfortunately, none of my interviewees could make enough profit to cover even their basic expenses. In the first few months of their return, the cruise workers I interviewed were mainly concerned about applying for government aid and earning enough to avoid exhausting their hard-earned savings. When I followed up with them in early 2021, they were defaulting on household bills, borrowing money, and folding up failed enterprises.

I noted that, despite state emphasis on permanent resettlement, cruise workers felt extremely unsettled upon their return home. Aside from the loss of a stable overseas career, the interviewees also grappled with the possibility of losing all that they had built during their time abroad. Manuel, one of the oldest cruise workers I spoke with, had spent more than two decades in the industry. He left his home province of Siquijor at twenty years old, hoping to find better opportunities in Manila, but ended up washing dishes for a Japanese restaurant. When he got hired as a galley steward for a US–based cruise line, it seemed like a dream come true. "I finally felt like I achieved something in life," he admitted ruefully. As a wine steward in his ship's dining hall, Manuel was able to support his parents while investing in a condominium unit in Metro Manila. When the cruise industry failed to resume after a year, Manuel's savings dried up and he failed to keep up with bill payments. The week before we spoke, the management office of the condominium cut their access to water because they failed to pay their utility bill for two months. Manuel's brother was forced to buy gallons of water from a water station a few blocks away from the condominium, just so the family could go about their daily routine. "It's so embarrassing, especially to our neighbors," Manuel says softly, his voice breaking. His biggest fear was that the bank might eventually take away his condominium unit if he was unable to keep up with his mortgage payments as well.

As stories such as that of Manuel became more prevalent in public discourse, it grew harder for state agencies to push the idea that former migrants' immobility was an opportune time for permanent resettlement. Local politicians began to heighten their call for strategies beyond training former migrants for entrepreneurship. Senator Imee Marcos, already unconvinced of the administration's small-business grants, expressed her frustration as labor officials sought the Senate's approval for their agency's 2021 budget:

> We've given DOLE [the Department of Labor and Employment] so much money, but until now, we have not seen any long-term job strategy. Cash grants and temporary work schemes are good—we all like that. But as we well know, these are all emergency strategies. All these supports, these strategies, they're fine as temporary initiatives . . . but we all know that the economic crisis will outlast the health crisis.

The senator's concern was well founded. A survey by the International Organization for Migration found that 83% of Filipino migrant workers were still unemployed three months after their repatriation in 2020. Close to a year after the emergence of COVID-19, less than half of this sample (45%) expressed an intent to start their own businesses. In many ways, cruise workers' struggles reflected a general trend that challenged the state's image of the pandemic as a time to start anew. Administration officials needed to amend their narrative—from a push toward self-employment toward a campaign of reskilling for domestic industries.

New Skills for the "New Normal"

Pressured to provide alternatives to entrepreneurship, administration officials began to promote alternative careers for former migrants. To maintain the notion that workers' immobility could be an opportunity for permanent resettlement, state officials argued that returnees should retrain themselves for available jobs within the country. In particular, state agencies encouraged alternative careers in the business process outsourcing (BPO) industry, where companies performed business functions for international corporations mostly located in places like the United States. The pandemic had heightened demand for remote services overseas, and as a result, call center agencies were one of the few industries that continued to accept new hires. Filipino workers were particularly in demand for "voice calls" or direct service for customers calling in with inquiries or complaints.[21]

In an interview with local media, labor secretary Silvestre Bello III claimed that call center representatives had "expressed a demand" for migrant returnees due to their overseas experience (*Manila Bulletin* 2020). Cruise workers, in particular, seemed to be the ideal employees for this industry. They were accustomed to serving foreign clients and, as such, were believed to possess the types of skills that could be easily transferred to call center work. Government officials also assumed that call center work was widely accessible and easy to perform. While call center agents received higher entry-level wages than many other professions in the Philippines, BPO jobs were largely seen as work that did not need specialized education or training.[22] Many of these companies did not require a college degree, and there was a common belief that agencies simply hired anyone who could "carry on a basic conversation in English" (Sallaz 2019: 6). To help former migrants enter these agencies, the Technical Education and Skills Development Authority (TESDA) offered basic courses on computer skills.

Yet, as I spoke to cruise workers about their search for call center opportunities, it became painfully clear that the BPO industry was not truly open to all return migrants. While call center agencies allowed their employees to receive calls from home,[23] they required individuals to purchase their own equipment for their work. One interviewee, Joyce, was comfortable with technology, having worked as an administrative assistant for the cruise ship's hotel department. Still, she struggled to find call center jobs because she did not have the type of gadgets that these companies required. "You have to have your own desktop or laptop; the specs of your computer have to be good . . . they want you to have very fast internet at home," she complained. "You know, all these are not really things that seafarers spend on . . . because we're gone most of the year anyway." Frustrated, Joyce borrowed money from her parents to buy herself a new laptop and headset. Other cruise workers were not as privileged, having depleted most of their savings in the first few months of their return.

Beyond call centers, state agencies also tried to reskill former migrants for alternative livelihoods in the country. Hoping to take advantage of the "pandemic economy," TESDA ramped up the release of programs meant to retrain former migrants for jobs in the public health sector. In an online forum titled "Creating New Opportunities for OFWs [Overseas Filipino Workers]," TESDA deputy secretary general Lina Sarmiento boasted that her agency had developed seventy-one online courses for migrant workers who had been forced to return home (Depasupil and Pesco 2020).[24] Many of these new courses involved skills related to the ongoing pandemic, including classes on "practicing COVID-19 preventive measures in the workplace" or "facilitating e-learning sessions."

Sarmiento was most effusive about a free contact tracing program, meant to produce qualified agents to help local government units control the spread of COVID-19 infections. During the open discussion, the webinar's host asked Sarmiento if she saw such work as an alternative career for returning migrant workers. "The pandemic will be with us for, not just till the end of the year, but maybe two years more," the host explained. "Do you see this as a new career for OFWs? Do you encourage them [to take the course]?" Sarmiento responded confidently:

> We have a very high need for contact tracers. Local government units will be recruiting at least 100,000 people to do this work. So, this can be a new career for our [Filipino migrant workers]. Let's say, when this pandemic is over, they can also use the certificate for other health-related qualifications . . . they can qualify for other health-related activities. They can be *barangay* (community) health workers.

In this statement, Sarmiento took pains to portray TESDA courses as a chance for former migrants to develop "new" forms of livelihood in the Philippines. In this push toward reskilling, state officials seemed to believe that unemployed cruise workers could be channeled toward the public health sector, where the high need for labor would provide them with post-pandemic opportunities.

However, none of the cruise workers I spoke with had taken the time to retrain for such positions. In fact, they failed to see how such work required specific skills and formal training. While Sarmiento had advertised contact tracing jobs as widely available, my interviewees claimed that such positions were mainly short-term contracts. Only three out of the forty-five cruise workers I interviewed had taken jobs as contact tracers. They had doubts as to whether TESDA training would have made any difference.

Eduardo, a former cruise ship waiter, obtained his contact tracing job through an uncle who worked in his city's local government. He did not recall being interviewed for the job, nor was he asked to present any evidence of previous training or experience. On his first day of work, another contact tracer merely briefed him on what he needed to do. "What usually happens is that a health worker will tell us if there is a positive case in this household or community. I give the person's household a call to see who has symptoms and then I liaise with the hospital to pick them up," he explained. "That's really about it."

While he was paid a decent stipend, Eduardo did not see the work as especially difficult or meaningful. Nor did it cross his mind that this experience could help him transition to other jobs in the public health sector. At the time we spoke, he was trying to borrow money to apply for a driver's license; he was thinking of becoming a taxi driver once COVID-19 restrictions were finally lifted in his city.

Manuel, the former wine steward, worked as a contact tracer with a team of nurses who were interviewing people possibly infected with COVID-19. Part of his job also involved disseminating information about the virus to rural communities. When I asked if he had TESDA training, Manuel snickered and said he would have been better served by motorcycle driving lessons. Many of the households they needed to visit were located deep in his province's mountains. Only a motorbike could get through the narrow, unpaved roads. Manuel was told that if he did not learn how to drive, the position would need to be reassigned to someone else. Given that he had already been unemployed for several months, Manuel decided that he could not afford to lose the job. "I just learned as quickly as I could! And I didn't even have a license!" he laughed. "What happened was that I would drive the bike around the villages in the mountains. But someone had to take over when we got to the city. There are more policemen in the city."

Manuel believed that this work was important. However, he also realized that it was not a long-term career. Even if he did obtain TESDA training and transitioned to working as a public health officer, he would only qualify for low-rank positions. Such limited benefits were outweighed by the obvious risks of constant exposure to possible COVID-19 cases. Eventually, Manuel chose not to renew his contract with the government. His mother was so opposed to his work as a contact tracer that she prohibited him from staying in their home lest he infect other family members. "She told me there are other ways of earning money," Manuel recalled. "My life is irreplaceable (*Ang buhay mo hindi mapapalitan*)."

Eduardo and Manuel's stories indicate that while TESDA officials may have highlighted the potential of COVID-related training as alternative careers, former migrants did not see enough reason to reskill themselves for the short-term, high-risk jobs that were available.

For many cruise workers, reskilling for new careers took time and re-sources that could otherwise be allocated toward other ways of earning money. Those more open to retraining were likely to be younger, single, and free from having to support other members of their families. Donita, a former cruise photographer, was the only one among my interviewees who decided to invest in graduate study. She was offered a scholarship for an online MBA and decided to take the chance. "I always consult my sib-lings and my parents, but the ultimate decision lies with me because I'm not responsible for anyone," she said. "I have no kids and I'm not married. I think I have more freedom when it comes to deciding what I want to do with my career." The majority of the cruise workers I interviewed did not have the money or time to enjoy such privileges.

In the end, state efforts to reskill former migrants failed to serve as an avenue for cruise workers to resettle into their communities. Although funds for training programs did provide opportunities to explore new ca-reers, the government glossed over the many other ways that former mi-grants were excluded from local employment.

Beyond Reskilling for Return

While return has long been part of people's migration journeys, reinte-grating former migrants can become politically urgent in times of acute disruption (Kuschminder 2017). The struggles of migrant returnees can signal how well incumbent state officials are managing a global crisis. A bad experience of return conveys the image of a government that is unable to protect its own citizens from the risks of working abroad, but contin-ually relies on their monetary remittances for national development. This chapter has illustrated how the Philippine state sought to avoid this issue by framing migrant workers' forced return as an opportunity for perma-nent resettlement. A key part of this narrative was an emphasis on skills training and entrepreneurship, placing it upon former migrants to adopt capacities that would allow them to start their lives anew and contribute to the nation's economy.

Undeniably, the Philippine state faced extreme challenges in responding to the needs of its migrant returnees. Migration scholars have shown how the conditions that shape migrants' return can have a great impact on how they eventually reintegrate within their home communities. In the case of cruise workers, the COVID-19 pandemic had cut short their overseas careers, making them unprepared for the long period of immobility that followed soon after. Even worse, the pandemic had devastated the Philippines' hospitality industry, leaving cruise workers with few opportunities in the local job market. For this reason, perhaps, the Philippine state had little choice but to promote a narrative of skilling for self-employment. The prospect of starting anew provided former migrants with some hope that they could still achieve the social mobility that emigration was supposed to bring.

However, the state's story of cruise workers' immobility hinged upon replacing migrants' old skills with new expertise. In pushing for reintegration through reskilling, Philippine government officials also assumed that all migrants had the time and privilege to start new careers. In the end, the state's narrative of immobility failed to gain enough ground among cruise workers. In the next chapter, we see how much of this reticence was rooted in how workers themselves perceived their immobility and defined the value of their own skills.

Five

A Long Time to Stay Afloat

Cruise Workers Reclaim Their Work

Larry had just turned twenty-one when he first tried his luck in the cruise industry. The recruiter who looked over his resume rejected him immediately. "They said I was too young for the job," he laughed, "because during that time, they were only hiring people to work in the bar. I guess they wanted someone older." Undaunted, Larry simply applied again a few months later. For the eldest son in a family of six children, there was always constant pressure to earn more money. After completing the two years required for an associate's degree in hospitality services, he quickly found a job as a server in Manila's Hard Rock Café. He moved up the ranks of restaurant employees, eventually managing his own group of assistant waiters. However, Larry's main goal was always to get onboard a cruise ship.

"The second time I applied, I challenged the interviewer," he recalled. "I told her, 'Why don't you just try me first? Let me participate in the training. If I can pass the training, then maybe you can consider my application.' She was like, challenge accepted." Larry's audacity paid off. He passed the cruise line's training requirements with an impressive score of 90 out of 100 and received a contract for his first voyage in 2011. Still, his relatively young age limited him to working as a pool attendant—what cruise employees considered the lowest position in the bar department.

For the next four years, Larry began work at 5:00 a.m. every day, setting up the pool area for guests. He folded towels, arranged silverware, and ensured that the pool bar was stocked for the 8:00 a.m. opening. Work was difficult and tiring, but Larry was buoyed by the opportunities offered for promotion. The cruise line provided free training for employees who wanted to move up to higher positions or switch to other departments onboard the ship. Eventually, he worked his way toward becoming a bar waiter and later an assistant bartender. Before the pandemic, Larry was already head bartender and leading his own team. He considers this position one of his biggest life achievements.

The COVID-19 pandemic brought his entire career to a sudden end. When the cruise industry shut down, Larry found himself stuck in the Philippines, unsure of what to do with the skills and experience he had built over the past decade. "If I wanted to be head bartender in Manila, it would take me forever because I will need to get a four-year degree," he explained. "On the ship, you can get promoted if they see you working hard and you're efficient. They don't really care about your educational background. It's more about how you deal with your job."

Larry's frustration reveals how cruise workers struggled to find a place within a local economy that suddenly had little use for their skills. This chapter draws from these stories to understand how cruise workers made sense of their immobility throughout the different phases of their return—from the initial months of the pandemic to the resumption of limited cruise travel in 2021. While state agencies sought to frame migrants' return as a chance to start anew, cruise workers like Larry developed a different narrative of their experiences at home. Rather than as an opportunity for permanent resettlement, they saw their immobility as an extended period of treading water, during which they were simply working to stay afloat.

Like the nurses introduced in previous chapters, cruise workers found their experiences of immobility defined by general perceptions of the value and purpose of their skills. Scholars have argued that to ensure successful return, local governments must engage returnees with policies that can leverage their skills for national development (Hagan and Wassink 2020; Saguin 2020). However, recent studies have mostly revolved around the experiences of highly skilled migrants (Cerna 2016; Liao and Asis 2020; Saxenian 2005). While there is extensive literature on how immigrants' skills are often undervalued and underpaid (Eckstein and Peri 2018;

Ozkan 2018; Raghuram 2021), these stories are largely situated within destination countries, where foreigners are excluded from certain occupations and pathways to social mobility. This chapter underlines how return migrants can also face similar problems within their home countries and how these challenges undermine the possibility of reintegration.

Most of the cruise workers I spoke with had pursued postsecondary credentials and training to prepare themselves for the global hospitality market. However, Filipino employers generally treated them as "low-skilled" labor, with little use beyond the hotels and restaurants where they used to work. Philippine state agencies devalued their capabilities even further, encouraging them to retrain and acquire more "useful" skills. This chapter recounts how such experiences left cruise workers with no choice but to see their immobility as a status that must remain temporary. Eventually, this narrative of staying afloat gained much sympathy from Philippine society, forcing state agencies to heighten efforts to redeploy cruise workers to their ships.

Unexpected Returns

In determining what leads to migrants' successful return, an often-cited concept is Jean-Pierre Cassarino's (2004: 271) emphasis on "preparedness" or the readiness to return to one's country of origin. To be considered fully prepared, Cassarino argues, migrants must have "sufficient resources and information about post-return conditions at home." Such knowledge allows migrants to mobilize the networks and capital needed to aid their reintegration upon their arrival.[1]

If preparedness is indeed a key factor of reintegration, one could argue that cruise workers were well positioned to cope with sudden return. Unlike other Filipino migrants,[2] most cruise workers only stay onboard their ships for a maximum of eight months.[3] They return to the Philippines after each contract and spend at least two months at home before leaving for new assignments abroad.[4] As Cassarino (2014) noted, migrants who spend longer periods overseas find it harder to generate the resources needed to prepare for their return. In this sense, the short contracts common in the seafaring industry allowed cruise workers to remain connected to networks and family in the Philippines.

Several of my interviewees had experienced leaving the cruise industry for a few years and then returning when they needed the money. For example, Lianne, an activity host in her ship's entertainment department, retired from cruise work in 2016 to accept a job hosting events in Manila. She later returned to the cruise industry in 2018, when her daughter's school fees became too expensive for her Philippine salary. Looking back, Lianne claimed that reestablishing herself at home was fairly easy:

> Getting a job at home wasn't really a problem at all. Even while I was still a cruise worker, I could do all these side jobs during my vacation period. I couldn't stand staying at home all the time, so I would host events, co-ordinate parties, orient staff for concerts. There were so many freelance opportunities! I had a pretty good network of people in the industry.

In many ways, the cyclical nature of cruise ship jobs allowed Lianne to keep herself well integrated in Manila's events industry. She also owned an apartment in the city and maintained a close-knit group of family and friends.

On the surface, it was easy to assume that cruise workers like Lianne would have the resources to cope with unexpected immobility. However, the pandemic's shutdown of the cruise industry was brutal and swift, making it difficult for any of my interviewees to adequately prepare themselves for their sudden loss of employment. On March 15, 2020, cruise line companies suspended all voyages with little warning, and ships were forced to suddenly stop operations regardless of their planned itineraries. Abegail, an assistant bartender, recounted:

> I remember on March 14, we still accepted passengers. One big group of Australians. And then the next day, March 15, we had to tell them to leave! We had to go back to the Mauritius port . . . The captain had to make an announcement. Our hotel director also made an announcement . . . The passengers were so angry, but they had no choice. They had to disembark.

Similar situations played out in the Mediterranean, where Gerard, an assistant waiter, was working onboard a ship traveling through different Italian ports:

> We had a group of forty people who just joined the cruise. I think they were French. Some of them were eating at the restaurant when the captain announced that everyone needed to disembark in Rome. Then, one of them fainted! In the restaurant! I don't know, maybe they were shocked at what happened. I guess I would be too if I were them. Maybe they were celebrating something important like a birthday, something special.

Once all passengers had disembarked from their cruise ships, crew members lost the potential earnings they received from customer gratuities and tips. Several companies also reduced cruise workers' salaries to just their basic pay, removing the bonuses that workers usually received at the end of every voyage. For waitstaff such as bar waiters, tips and commissions could amount to at least USD 2,000 per month, in addition to their basic pay. Basic salaries varied depending on cruise workers' rank and position (bar waiters shared that they could earn as little as USD 150 a month), so the sudden loss of extra sources of income was especially hard for cruise workers who had just embarked on their ships. Abegail explained:

> There were some crew members who had been onboard for close to eight months. Then, the pandemic came, and they got stuck because there were no flights. So of course, they wanted to go home because they were so tired. They wanted to rest, to see their family, things like that. But maybe half of the crew just started their contracts. Like me! I just embarked on my new contract, so I'm thinking about the money I was supposed to earn, the money I was supposed to send home . . . I just spent two months at home, on vacation. I need to earn money!

The sudden stoppage also blindsided workers like Nilo, who had been taking a break between contracts when all cruise travel came to a halt. When Nilo had disembarked from his last voyage in January 2020, cruise operations were normal. There were reports of a new coronavirus in China, but his company treated the possibility of an outbreak as a distant threat. In February, Nilo's friend encouraged him to apply for an opening at a call center agency. Failing to see the need for another side job, Nilo declined. "I wasn't worried at all because I just assumed I would return to the ship," he recalled. "My friend said, 'Why don't you just apply while you're waiting for your next contract?' But I didn't listen."

The month after, Nilo received an email stating that his next contract had been canceled. Suddenly, he found himself with no job and no income. As he tried to describe how he was feeling at this time, Nilo's voice was heavy with remorse. "If I listened to my friend, at least I would feel safer now. I would at least have a salary to help me survive the next few months," he said sadly. "But now, I have nothing. It's just been so hard . . . Well, what else can we do? I was stupid (*Wala eh, tanga ako*)."

Like Nilo, other interviewees wondered what more they could have done to prepare for the disruptions caused by the pandemic. However,

COVID-19 created challenging conditions that few would have been able to anticipate. The fast-rising number of COVID-19 cases led to prolonged lockdowns in the Philippines' major cities. All of this had taken a toll on the local economy, with the food and leisure industry facing the worst fall in revenue (*CNN Philippines* 2020c; Lim Uy 2020). The country's largest hotels were forced to shrink their manpower pools, leaving thousands of local service workers unemployed. Meanwhile, restrictions on social gatherings shut down Manila's entire events industry.

In many ways, the COVID-19 pandemic disrupted the usual networks and resources that cruise workers had maintained in their frequent visits home. Even those like Lianne, who had easily found local jobs in the past, were suddenly unsure of what they could possibly offer Philippine employers. "I don't think organizing events is an option right now. I mean, even weddings are going online," Lianne said candidly. "I need to think of something else to do. Maybe I can teach English to Koreans online or something." She paused to think of other types of work she could explore. Then, unable to name other alternative careers for herself, she apologized instead. "Sorry, I really don't know."

Waiting Out the Pandemic

Initially, the cruise workers I spoke to assumed that the COVID-19 pandemic would simply blow over, much like the epidemics that had affected international travel in previous years. Thus, they saw their immobility as a temporary disruption—one that they could simply wait out. Joyce, an administrative assistant working with the cruise ship's hotel, explained, "At first, I was not scared because these things have happened before. We had SARS, we had H1N1.[5] It is on the news, but we know people are on it. They know how to handle the situation."

Upon their return home, cruise workers' priorities revolved around finding quick ways to find other sources of income. In the previous chapter, I discussed how cruise workers established their own businesses at home, marketing their products through social media and community chat groups. State agencies had promoted such entrepreneurship as a means of working toward permanent resettlement. However, I found that cruise workers' motivations could not be more different. Government leaders had hoped that self-employment would help returnees establish alternative livelihoods to aid in their reintegration. In contrast, my interviewees only started selling things because they didn't know what else they could do. The "side jobs" that used to be so widely available in the Philippines' leisure industry were suddenly nonexistent. While larger cruise lines provided ad hoc aid for their employees,[6] cruise workers did not have the option of seeking unemployment benefits. Making matters worse, most Philippine cities were still under lockdown, keeping most residents from leaving their homes. Selling products from home was not only the best but also the only option for many returnees.

Abegail was repatriated to Manila in May 2020, two months after her company canceled all voyages worldwide. She conceptualized her business while going through the mandatory fourteen-day quarantine and decided to try her luck selling pastries and "sushi bake," a trendy dish made up of Japanese rice, crab sticks, and dried seaweed. When I asked how she thought of starting a business, Abegail's response was blunt. "I'm not just doing it because it's trendy. If I don't do this, I don't get to eat (*Kung di mo ginawa ito, nganga*)! I'm worried about all my bills; every month, the amount I pay just goes up."

As Abegail's statement revealed, most cruise workers seemed to have started their home businesses out of desperation. Such business ventures were "survivalist" in nature—unstable, generating low earnings, and mainly seen as a temporary project (Wassink and Hagan 2018). It was perhaps no surprise that few of the migrants' small businesses remained in operation as the pandemic continued into its second year. At this point, cruise workers began to realize that their immobility could be more long-term than they had anticipated.

Cruise companies attempted to resume operations multiple times during the pandemic. Cruise lines outside the United States began sailing with limited passenger capacity—mostly within specific geographic areas. In Singapore, the government allowed two companies to offer a "cruise to nowhere," which was mainly a three-day journey around the island. Still, these attempts were hindered by cancellations as new outbreaks emerged within cruise ships and in destination ports (Hines 2020; Yang, Chia, and Low 2021). In such cases, crew members had to be repatriated back to the Philippines, where they underwent another two weeks of quarantine. These cancellations were often unpredictable and last-minute, making them especially disruptive for cruise workers relying on these contracts for much-needed income. Joyce recounted her experience:

My agent called to say I was good to go . . . I had to do my medical exam, renew my training certificates, and pay for a new seaman's book. Then, a week before I was scheduled to leave, they canceled everyone's contract! The good thing is that at least our company refunds all our expenses on paperwork and flights. Not all companies do that.

As more dismal news of the cruise industry began to emerge, cruise workers began to communicate a different narrative of their immobility. From a temporary disturbance meant to "blow over," cruise workers realized, their return to the Philippines could very well become an extended phase of their careers, in need of long-term planning and resources. When I spoke with Abegail again at the end of 2020, she had already stopped selling pastries online and was actively looking for a full-time job. Cruise line representatives had warned their employees of a long recovery period, dashing Abegail's hopes of returning to work:

> A group of us cruise workers heard that the cruise line industry will only resume in 2022. So basically, two more years, right? When all of us heard this, it was like, "Oh my God. What are we going to do?" What about the people who need to take care of their families? And if all Filipino cruise workers are stuck at home, who gets to get back on the ship first? We might end up waiting even longer.

After witnessing their companies' struggles, cruise workers began to have second thoughts about returning to their ships. Some worried about the risk of contracting the virus from passengers, while others could not bear the thought of another long repatriation journey home. For Jaiya, a youth counselor in her ship's entertainment department, the pandemic made her realize the value of being with family. In a follow-up interview at the end of 2020, she wondered out loud if cruise work was worth the risk of falling sick. "The thing is, my daughter is getting older, and I want to be there for her," she shared. "I only entered the cruise industry because I wanted to earn money to buy a house. Now, I'm thinking that it might be better to start settling down . . . I can do some teaching or work for a local tutoring center."

Meanwhile, other cruise workers fretted over whether cruise ship protocols would allow them to do their jobs properly and earn the kind of money that they used to enjoy. Efforts to prevent the spread of the virus had drastically reduced the number of passengers that cruise ships could accept, decreasing the amount that cruise workers could earn from customer gratuities and tips. As someone who benefited from selling drinks, Abegail was particularly unhappy about her company's decision to remove their "commission," an extra incentive that bar staff used to receive for selling drink packages to guests:

> So let's say we have a seven-day cruise. If we sell enough packages to go beyond the quota, we get a big commission as a reward. That amount is divided equally among all the bar staff . . . Now, we don't get commission anymore. They said they will give us a "bonus" instead, which is lower than the commission . . . The company lost so much money because of the pandemic. Like, maybe a billion dollars. I guess they needed to recoup their losses.

Without extra sources of income, interviewees wondered if working in the cruise industry was worth the punishing shifts and backbreaking labor that they often had to endure (Chin 2008; Terry 2011). Adding to cruise workers' hesitation was the implementation of new safety requirements that would make their jobs harder, but perhaps not much safer. As Rheynalyn, a member of her ship's entertainment department, explained:

> I have so many things that I want to do in my life and, you know, all it takes is one infected passenger to set things off. In my work, you really need to interact with guests. As in, we hug them, we hang out with them. Sometimes, there are guests who will kiss you on the cheek! How can I do my work without getting sick? That's why I'm really thinking of just staying [in the Philippines], even if I'm unemployed. Actually, I am really unemployed right now, so that's that [laughs].

Still, even as the ongoing pandemic tempered cruise workers' desire to return to their ships, their views of remaining in the Philippines depended on finding employment that could replace their cruise ship jobs. Cruise workers were mainly concerned about obtaining jobs that paid a meaningful wage. They would eventually come to realize that part of this struggle was finding a place for their skills within their own country.

Skills Out of Place

Unlike the case of the Filipino nurses featured in previous chapters, there was no public clamor for cruise workers to provide their skills to the nation. On the contrary, government officials promoted a narrative where the key to cruise workers' reintegration was to acquire new skills that could be of better use in the country's local economy. The low value that government institutions and Filipino employers ascribed to service work became a major obstacle for cruise workers hoping to reestablish their careers at home. While time spent overseas can help migrants acquire skills that may be in demand within local industries (Hagan et al. 2015), employers must recognize and reward the skills that migrants learn abroad. If not, returnees are likely to experience "downward occupational mobility" or end up becoming self-employed as a last resort (Hagan and Wassink 2020: 547).

Most of the cruise workers I interviewed encountered this problem, even as they managed to find some work in the Philippines' local labor market. Manuel, the former wine steward, recalled a bitter experience working with his provincial government's COVID-19 risk management team. On paper, Manuel was hired to receive people arriving from Manila and escort them to local hotels for the mandatory quarantine. He also sanitized rooms between occupants, stripping bedsheets and wiping down surfaces to prevent the spread of the virus. His pay was only PHP 300 per day, below minimum wage, but Manuel tried to give the job a hospitality spin. "People are tired and stressed. I was in charge of making their quarantine stay as comfortable as possible." But barely a week into the new job, Manuel's supervisor ordered him to help unload 300 sacks of rice that had been delivered for the quarantined guests' meals. Such hard labor was unexpected, and with each sack weighing 50 kilograms, he worried about straining his back. Manuel tried to reason with local government officials, arguing that his skills could be put to better use. Controlling the spread of contagious diseases was not unfamiliar to him. He proudly recounted a time when an outbreak of gastroenteritis occurred during a voyage around Europe. He had led the team in charge of disinfecting the ship's largest kitchen. Sadly, his supervisor was unimpressed. "They said, no excuses. I should just leave if I wanted." Dejected, Manuel resigned from the job the next day.

Even cruise workers who tried to "sell" themselves to other service-oriented companies had difficulty translating their skills to the needs of Filipino employers. Such problems were especially prevalent in the business process outsourcing (BPO) industry. As noted in chapter 4, BPO was one of the few industries in which companies continued to hire new employees during the pandemic.[7] But among the forty-five cruise workers I interviewed, only six were able to successfully gain entry to local call center agencies in 2021. Cruise workers lamented what they saw as a bias toward a specific type of applicant: fluent in English, middle-class, and "professional." Initially, I was surprised to hear that cruise workers felt disadvantaged in seeking call center jobs. Given their exposure to foreign cruise travelers, wouldn't their service skills be an asset for BPO companies? More than half of my interviewees also had university degrees (twenty-eight out of forty-five), mostly in relevant fields such as hospitality management and tourism (see table 5.1).[8] In this sense, they seemed well positioned to take on these jobs.

Still, my interviewees explained that call center agencies demanded certain standards that seemed more stringent than even the five-star service expected of cruise line staff.[9] Although companies did not require specific credentials for entry-level agents, they expected applicants to go through a rigorous training process on handling difficult customers and using the company software. Accessing these jobs required a type of cultural capital

TABLE 5.1. **Profile of Cruise Worker Interviewees**

	Cruise workers
Department	
Dining	10
Bar/beverages	6
Kitchen	7
Entertainment/youth	9
Photography	6
Galley	2
Others*	5
Average no. of years in cruise industry	7
Able to return to ship**	
Yes	29
Waiting for assignment	12
No plans to return	4

*The category of "others" includes workers employed in hotel services, housekeeping, and the spa.

**Based on final interviews for the project at the end of 2021.

associated with Manila's professional class—a level of comfort with technology and a specific way of carrying themselves and communicating with clients.[10] While call center agencies often used general words such as "confidence" or "professionalism" in describing ideal applicants, it seemed that they mainly wanted individuals who could speak English with a "neutral" accent and manage interactions with irate customers. Cruise workers complained that call center recruiters were quick to question their ability to use computers, perform office work, or speak proper English. Richard, a former assistant cook, recounted one interview with a local company:

> So [the interviewer] saw my resume and she said, "Oh, you're a seafarer. Are you sure you know [how] to deal with computers?" Something like that. I really wanted to respond by saying, "Ma'am, if you want, I'll make you a computer right now!" (laughs) . . . I guess she saw in my resume that I only worked in kitchens, but should things be like that? If you're good at one thing, does that mean that's the only thing you can do? (*Kung 'yon ang alam ng tao, 'yon lang din ba ang alam niya?*) So I thought, fine, do the interview. If you hire me, that's great. If not, that's okay!

Richard's experience showed that for many cruise workers, getting past initial job interviews meant having to circumvent stereotypes or biases about former migrants—particularly those who did more manual service labor. In this sense, cruise workers who occupied "front of house"[11] departments, such as hotel administration, entertainment, and dining, had a better chance of showcasing their ability to attend to customer needs for BPO companies. Meanwhile, those who worked in "back of house" roles in kitchens, laundries, or housekeeping departments were often cut from the list of potential applicants early in the job process. But this division did not map out as neatly in terms of interviewees' educational background.

Shayne, a waitress at a cruise ship café, had a bachelor's degree in tourism management but had worked in restaurants for her entire career. When the cruise industry shut down, she applied to a call center and went through multiple interviews with company representatives. To prove her skills at addressing customer needs, Shayne was also asked to perform a role-play with a "client," where she listened to a three-minute audio clip and then summarized in thirty seconds what was said. While initially questioned about her seafaring background, Shayne felt she was able to impress the company's recruiters by drawing comparisons to her cruise ship experience. "They asked me during the interview what I thought was my strongest quality. I said, as someone who works in the cruise industry, we know that we have to please the customer to stay in the business," she said. "I also know how to communicate. Of course, call centers are different—but I think we all know the basics of customer service."

To emphasize her service capabilities, Shayne was able to recall the many interactions she had had with foreign guests on her ship. These stories helped her draw parallels between call center work and cruise ship training, convincing company representatives of her potential skills. In contrast, her husband and fellow cruise worker, Alejandro, was rejected in his first interview. Like Shayne, Alejandro had completed four years of university education. He had majored in marine transportation but never had the chance to obtain his license. While his wife was assigned to the ship café, he entered the cruise industry as a room attendant for the housekeeping department. Alejandro shared that he actually interacted with guests often, responding to their many specific requests. However, he never spoke with them at length.

Shayne also had another advantage. Even as we spoke online, I could hear that she had adopted in her accent elements of American pronunciation and intonation, which I presume she picked up from the cruise travelers she met over the years. As Jeffrey Sallaz (2019) observed in his ethnography of call centers, accent is often a major criterion in hiring decisions, particularly for accounts that require voice calls. According to him, 90% of applicants to Philippine call centers failed to get past the interview process simply because they were "fluent yet too accented" (Sallaz 2019: 24).

True enough, many of the cruise workers I interviewed complained that they were often rejected from call center jobs because of the way they spoke English. This was the case for Clariza, another cruise ship waitress, who was unemployed for most of 2020. She gave up on applying to call centers after going through one unsuccessful interview:

> These call centers only take in people who really are super fluent in English. When you do an interview with them, your pronunciation needs to really be good, word for word, letter by letter. They want you to be polished. Like I might pronounce something as "lab-ly," for them it should be luh-vlee [as in the word "lovely"]. I can't pass those types of standards. I went for one interview and I'm never doing it again. I'll just get rejected.

While Clariza attributed her failure to not being "super fluent" in English, I actually found that she could understand and speak the language quite well. As we talked about her cruise work experiences, she would often code-switch between Tagalog and English, recounting conversations with foreign coworkers and supervisors. I felt that Clariza was rejected not so much for lack of English skills as for her inability to use the language in a manner deemed most appropriate to a mostly American clientele.[12]

Seeking call center jobs was an arduous process for many of my interviewees. If "recognition" means being seen as having some value or worth in the eyes of others (Bourdieu 1990), cruise workers felt often misrecognized by fellow Filipinos within the Philippines' BPO industry.[13] English fluency and accent did not always correlate with people's education and previous work experience, leading to rejections that my interviewees perceived as unfair. For example, in Clariza's case, her credentials were quite similar to Shayne's. Clariza had graduated with a university degree in business administration and had spent a longer period working in hotels and cruise ships than Shayne had. However, she could not secure a call center job because she was unable to produce the right accent for call center work. Such experiences were demoralizing, to say the least. "I'll probably start selling fish in the market since I can't even get into a call center," Clariza said half-jokingly. But her tone quickly became serious as she wondered about ever finding a job.

Glaiza, the former massage therapist at her ship's spa, was surprised to learn that fellow returnees could not get good jobs because of their English capabilities. Glaiza had never gone to university, but her accent was "neutral" enough to qualify her for a probationary contract at a call center near her home. She had applied along with coworkers who never made it to the final interview. "Well, maybe that's the problem, right?" she mused. "Employers in the Philippines are too perfectionist. In the ship, English is just a language. Here, we treat English like it is a sign of how smart you are."[14]

While Glaiza referred to English fluency as a symbol of "intelligence," cruise workers' stories also revealed a tendency for call center employers to conflate applicants' accent and fluency with other interpersonal capacities, such as selling company products or handling customer complaints. Even if cruise workers attempted to showcase their experience in international service, any shortcomings in terms of English delivery became a demerit in their performance.

In the end, cruise workers who took pride in their former jobs bemoaned the tendency of Philippine call centers to dismiss their potential as future employees. Nilo, a former cruise photographer, spoke at length about how working on a cruise ship had helped him build stronger social skills. Initially shy and reserved, Nilo had learned how to approach guests, promote the ship's travel photo packages, and cajole them into smiling and posing for the camera. Understandably, he was shocked when a local call center rejected him for his "lack of communication skills." He complained:

> I wanted to tell the interviewer, "I talk to different nationalities on the ship and they can understand how I speak!" . . . I've spent so many years onboard and now this Filipino senior manager is saying I'm incompetent and not ready to speak to other people? I don't know what kind of standard they have. I felt degraded. Really? Communication skills?

Nilo's experience was a prime example of how cruise workers struggled to find a place for their skills within their country's pandemic-stricken economy. Despite state efforts to encourage BPO work as an alternative career for former migrants, company representatives treated many cruise workers as low-skilled laborers, unfit for call center work.

This is not to say that BPO was the only industry that cruise workers could enter. Interviewees who could not access call centers went on to seek other online jobs, such as entering data, delivering food, or tutoring students in China and Korea. However, call center jobs still offered higher salaries and relatively stable benefits, such as health insurance. BPO also remained the best option for those who needed to start recouping their losses during the pandemic. As a result, those who tried and failed to obtain such jobs were left feeling disheartened, unable to find recognition for capabilities they had spent years honing onboard their ships.

Meaning in Service

Even among my interviewees who gained access to the Philippines' BPO industry, there remained a strong aspiration to return to their ships. While they felt lucky to be earning a regular salary in the midst of a pandemic, these former migrants saw little meaning in the work of call centers. Larry, formerly the head bartender of his ship's busiest bar, obtained a call center position that provided many benefits. The company paid him a decent wage and allowed him to conduct all his work from home. After nine years in the cruise line industry, he was grateful for the chance to be closer to his wife and children. Yet Larry admitted that if given a choice, he would prefer to be behind the bar, mixing drinks. Manning a bar was both mentally and physically demanding, as bartenders were expected to memorize dozens of cocktail recipes, stand for an entire shift, and keep an inventory of alcohol on stock. Still, he felt a stronger sense of purpose in ensuring that guests had a good time. As a call center agent, he was discouraged by the constant barrage of customer complaints and requests—many of which he was unable to truly address:

> To be honest, I don't find [call center work] interesting. Ninety percent of the calls that I receive are complaints. It gives you stress! Every time you take a call, they will shout at you, insult you, call you names. Then the only thing you can do is say sorry, even if you did not do anything. Right now, I feel like I've just become numb inside (*parang naging pusong bato*). Just deal with it. That's all you can do.

In many ways, Larry felt that being a call center agent was far from the special line of service he used to perform on the cruise ship. Even though he was assigned the exceptionally difficult task of receiving customer complaints, he argued that other call center tasks, such as sales or tech support, were simply boring. Another call center agent, Shayne, did not see her work as a form of service at all. When she was working in her ship's café, her supervisors had prioritized building relationships with customers and anticipating their needs. At the call center, managers were only interested in efficiency and reaching company goals. She explained:

> You need to hit a target number of calls per shift. So in one call, you can't go on talking to them for half an hour. For basic troubleshooting and payment, you need to get that done in three to five minutes. The longest you can take is probably ten minutes. When I was on the cruise, I could build relationships with customers. It takes time to build rapport. But at the call center, they want you to build rapport and settle everything in the shortest time!

While the Philippine government had promoted call centers as a natural place for former migrants, cruise workers argued that these jobs were a poor match for their talents and skills. Shayne complained that she often got told off for taking too long with her calls or failing to keep pace with the rest of her team. While the job paid relatively well, call center work seemed sadly impersonal and insincere. During our second interview in

2021, Shayne confided that she had followed up with her recruiter on possible positions on the cruise ship. When I asked why, she replied, "I miss my kind of work (*Nakakamiss ang trabaho sa linya ko talaga*)."

In highlighting my interviewees' unhappiness within local call centers, I do not mean to argue that money was not an important factor in their lives. After months of no income, they were happy to have local jobs that helped provide for their families. However, stories of workers like Larry and Shayne illustrate how years of working onboard ships had enriched a sense of pride and meaning in their work. As Rachel Sherman (2007) argues, some service workers derive dignity and pleasure from their work even if they are subject to the whims and demands of their much wealthier customers. Part of this comes from being granted some autonomy over how to perform their work, despite the subservient nature of their jobs. Similarly, my interviewees mentioned how much they missed the freedom to be creative and find ways to enhance their guests' experience onboard. Comparatively, call center work in the Philippines felt controlling and demeaning at the same time.

Cruise workers' misgivings about their local jobs underline how Philippine state officials had failed to properly understand how these former migrants perceived their skills as service professionals. In an effort to frame these workers' immobility in a positive light, Philippine state officials depicted service skills as capacities that could easily be abandoned or transferred to more relevant jobs in the domestic economy. What the government did not see was how cruise workers derived fulfillment from putting their service skills to use. As Hagan and her colleagues (2015) argue, return migrants are most successful when they are able to find work that utilizes the tacit knowledge and skills they have gained from their experiences abroad. For Filipino cruise workers, such occupations were found not at home, but onboard the ships they left behind.

Seeking Recognition Onboard

Toward the end of 2021, I found that cruise workers' views of their immobility had shifted once again. There was no doubt that the pandemic had made cruise work less lucrative and more dangerous than before. Still, the prospect of remaining in the Philippines had suddenly become an extended time of struggling to remain afloat. In failing to gain recognition for their skills, cruise workers could not imagine a future of permanent resettlement. Instead, staying in the Philippines was simply a period of being stuck at home, unable to move forward with their lives.

In many ways, government officials, in their efforts to construct former migrants' immobility, misunderstood a fundamental aspect of cruise workers' experiences. While state officials only saw them as unemployed migrants in need of reskilling, cruise workers themselves were frustrated with a domestic labor market that devalued their skills. Social scientists have long argued for the need to define "skill" beyond formal credentials, as the jobs we deem "unskilled" actually require the development of unique capacities through practice (Attewell 1990; Iskander 2021; Waldinger and Lichter 2003). Such was the case for the cruise workers I interviewed, regardless of their position onboard.

For my interviewees, cruise work required mastering particular skills to complete their daily tasks. A significant number of the cruise workers I spoke with had invested in learning such skills in university, where export-oriented educators promised to prepare them for a global hospitality industry. Clariza, who struggled to find call center work, grumbled that few people are aware of how difficult it is to become a waitress in a cruise ship's dining room. "We are expected to provide five-star service and so you need to keep to that standard. We go through lots of interviews. You need to know the different types of cuisine, wine, things like that," she explained. "And aside from food and beverage training, you also have safety training! You need to know what to do in case of an emergency." Failure would mean being asked to leave the ship.

Apart from the task of ensuring high standards in their work, cruise workers also took pride in their contributions to guest experiences onboard. In many of our conversations, interviewees shared how cruise travelers often celebrated special occasions on the ship, from birthdays to anniversaries and reunions. Cruise workers believed that they played an important role in making these moments happen, and "good" service often translated to generous tips at the end of every trip.

Cruise work also provided the possibility of moving up in the ship's hierarchy, without the usual barriers one would find at home. In Larry's case, the ship's free training program allowed him to move from folding towels by the pool to heading his own bar. There was an assurance that he would not be limited to only one type of work forever. Unlike the BPO industry, cruise ships had no explicit preference for the American-oriented English that made call center work seem so exclusive. While all cruise staff had to pass a language proficiency test to qualify for work onboard, the vast majority of workers onboard ships actually considered English a second language.

Larry's experience shows how cruise companies placed more emphasis on whether a person's skills fit the ship's needs, rather than on their academic background or credentials. This focus on performance determined promotions as well. Irrespective of position, cruise workers could engage in "cross-training" and move to higher status departments within the ship. Larry noted that many of his fellow bartenders had moved from more labor-intensive departments like sanitation and utilities. Basically, cruise workers willing to put in the effort were allowed to move into new positions regardless of educational attainment. For many of my interviewees, such pathways for social mobility were rare in the Philippines' service industry.

Even though cruise workers like Larry had benefited from the cruise ship's promotion structure, there were still inequalities in the ship hierarchy. Higher education remained a requirement for managerial positions, or for those who wanted to become higher rank officers. Cruise workers also noted that while employees from Asia filled the majority of low-rank positions in the most labor-intensive departments, those from Europe and North America were more likely to occupy office jobs that provided more interactions with guests.[15] Meanwhile, others complained about gender bias and co-ethnic favoritism, especially in kitchens, where there were fewer positions for head cooks and chefs.

However, cruise workers maintained that such problems existed in hotels and restaurants in the Philippines as well. They also believed that within the cruise ship, any effort poured into improving their skills would be better recognized with either a promotion or higher tips. In contrast, it was more difficult to derive satisfaction from service work in the Philippines, given that such work was often so poorly paid. As discussed earlier, remaining in the country meant having to tolerate the low value ascribed to one's skill.

Getting Back Onboard

Sometime in mid-2020, I chanced upon a newspaper article reporting the arrival of a flight bearing the remains of forty-nine Filipino migrant workers at Manila's international airport. These workers had died from the

COVID-19 virus while they were working abroad, and Philippine ambassadors had spent months finding ways to have their bodies returned home. Department of Labor secretary Silvestre Bello III made a statement to the media in attendance. "It's very painful to welcome dead heroes who served their families and country well," he said somberly. "I salute these fallen migrant workers. Fallen because like soldiers, they don't choose where to be taken. All they choose is to protect the future of their loved ones and their homeland" (*PNA* 2020b).

When I recounted this statement to Nilo, the former cruise photographer, he wondered if he would have been better off returning to the Philippines dead, instead of alive and unemployed. Unlike those who had perished overseas, former cruise workers like him were hardly treated as "heroes." "If you think about it, we're more like those soldiers who went off to war, got wounded, then were sent home," Nilo scoffed. "You served the nation, but now, you're no use to anyone because you lost your leg and can't even walk."

Nilo's statement reflects cruise workers' sentiment toward Philippine employers' inability to recognize their service skills and the state's emphasis on getting them to seek new capacities instead. For many, it seemed ironic that the skills they had accumulated through postsecondary training and hours of work experience were suddenly dispensable, despite generating millions of dollars in monetary remittances. Even worse, such skills had also become liabilities in a pandemic economy that shut down the hospitality and restaurant industry.

In the previous chapter, I described how the Philippine government tried to promote a narrative that portrayed cruise workers' return as a chance to start anew—a goal best achieved by reskilling for entrepreneurship. As state officials faced pressures to provide alternatives to self-employment, they also framed migrants' immobility as an opportunity to learn new skills or pivot to new industries. In contrast, this chapter illustrates how the devaluing of cruise workers' skill made it difficult for them to reintegrate into the Philippines' local economy. As such, they pushed their own narrative of immobility—one where staying home meant an endless cycle of debt and precarious work.

Such problems of misrecognition are not new. Numerous studies have shown how employers, state leaders, and even workers themselves can fail to see the unique capacities needed in performing jobs that may otherwise be seen as "low skilled" (Iskander 2021; Sherman 2007). In the service industry, a sector where immigrants are highly represented, this misrecognition is often worse. However, this chapter has shown how the low value accorded to returnees' skills can also shape how they interpret their own immobility. Unlike their nurse counterparts, cruise workers found that employers in their own country had little use for their capabilities as service professionals. State narratives celebrating the pandemic as a chance to start anew fell flat as cruise workers struggled to find gainful and fulfilling careers at home. Remaining in the country felt like treading water amid a constant wave of uncertainty, despite massive government support in funding migrants' reintegration. For the cruise workers I interviewed, the only way of moving forward was to get back onboard their ships. Eventually, this was a narrative that the state had no choice but to act on as well.

Conclusion

In March 2022, the Philippine government allowed all schools, work-places, and local businesses to open at full capacity, ending one of the world's longest lockdowns due to the COVID-19 pandemic (Associated Press 2022).[1] Six months later, the newly elected president, Ferdinand "Bongbong" Marcos Jr., dropped all restrictions at the country's border, easing the process of traveling in and out of the country (Gregorio 2022). By the time I flew to Manila in 2023, the World Health Organization had declared that COVID-19 was no longer an "international health concern," and I breezed through Philippine immigration without even a tempera-ture check (WHO 2023). It was my maternal grandmother's ninetieth birthday, and my parents had organized a party at a new Chinese restau-rant downtown. In attendance were four of her five children (two of whom had traveled from the United States), their partners, most of her sixteen grandchildren,[2] and dozens of other relatives and friends. Joining a large social gathering without the fear of contracting a deadly virus felt, for the lack of a better term, liberating. It was, in my father's words, "back to normal."

Still, it would be an understatement just to say that the COVID-19 pandemic had changed many aspects of our lives. For migration scholars, pandemic restrictions and border closures were a reminder of what we had taken for granted in our own research. From a concept that used to receive little attention within the field, immobility had become a popular topic in the "post-pandemic" era, spurring a proliferation of research on those who do not move. Scholars explored how immobility affects transnational connections, as migrant families navigate the challenges of maintaining lives across borders (Skovgaard-Smith 2021; Hoang and Zhang 2023). Meanwhile, others focused on how different groups of migrants—from contractual workers to international students—experience institutional controls over their movement (Deshingkar 2022; Liu and Peng 2023). Some had even gone on to proclaim an "immobility turn" in migration studies—a bold prediction of a drastic change in the field as a whole (Cairns and Clemente 2023).

Stuck at Home is a story of immobility set in the context of the COVID-19 pandemic. However, this book diverges from other studies in that it does not examine immobility as mainly an outcome of structural barriers or an aspect of migrants' individual experiences. Neither do I consider immobility a phenomenon that only became more salient with the coronavirus. Rather, this book argues that immobility has always been integral to the way states govern people's international movements. In the Philippine case, the consequences of remaining in place have long defined the state's emigration policies. Beyond merely exporting Filipino labor, administration officials must also attend to the interests of constituents who remained in the country. In this book, I show how doing so entails sometimes preventing people from moving or helping them stay in place. While COVID-19 created unprecedented disruptions in people's migration trajectories, it also magnified state practices that have long been in existence—policies that slowed people's progress toward emigration and programs that attempted to ensure successful return.

This book is an in-depth study of how immobility is a key part of how migrant-sending states govern emigration. Specifically, I argue that migration governance is not only about regulating people's cross-border movements but also about managing the meaning and implications of remaining in place. This process involves controlling the narrative as to why some are unable to leave the country and why others must be prevented from doing so at all. As a sociologist, I examined these stories in the "contexts of their telling" (Polleta et al. 2011: 110), tracing how state agencies and aspiring migrants negotiated the construction of a story that gave meaning to the latter's immobility. I studied the narratives that emerged around two groups of workers: nurses prevented from emigrating by the state's retention policies and former cruise workers unable to leave after COVID-19 shut down the global travel industry. I discussed how both administration officials and immobile workers tried to develop narratives that would gain support from other state representatives while also eliciting sympathy and commiseration from the Filipino public.

To date, migration scholars have paid scant attention to the role of nonmigrants in emigration governance. While local constituents are seen as influential stakeholders in the outcomes of *im*migration policy, they are largely invisible in discussions of how states regulate the *out*migration of their own citizens. *Stuck at Home* reveals the high stakes involved in telling the "right" story of immobility—one that provides a compelling rationale for how things ought to be. The sudden return of unemployed cruise workers could be framed as either an opportunity for permanent resettlement or a social problem that state agencies are ill equipped to handle. Meanwhile, banning the deployment of migrant nurses could be seen as an infringement on people's freedom to leave the country or as proof of how the state prioritizes its citizens' health and well-being. In the preceding chapters, I showed how the immobility narrative that prevailed eventually determined how Filipinos, in general, viewed their government's competence—a matter that became much more salient in the context of a global crisis.[3] These dominant narratives also affected how immobile workers were treated by others in their communities and how their government responded to their needs.

Coming to an End

How did the different stories of immobility featured in this book eventually play out? As international borders began to reopen in the pandemic's second year, I found that the outcomes were mixed for both aspiring Filipino migrants and the Philippine state.

While outgoing nurses and their political allies successfully pressured administration officials to loosen the conditions of the deployment ban, they failed to achieve their main goal: the free departure of all Filipino health care workers bound for jobs abroad. Even as the last COVID-19 regulations were removed in 2023, the Philippine state continued to enforce a limit of deploying only 7,500 nurses per year.[4] This number is far below the 22,133 nurses deployed in 2019.[5] It seemed that Philippine government officials had constructed a truly powerful story of health care workers' immobility—so much so that they later struggled to relax their own regulations over nurses' international movements.[6]

The salience of the state's narrative on nurses' immobility became especially apparent when government officials replaced the deployment ban with a cap on the number of nurses allowed to leave for overseas work. Commentators in the media were quick to note that the policy exempted nurses bound for countries that had existing bilateral labor agreements with the state.[7] Filipinos on social media raised concerns that destinations such as Germany and Kuwait were free to recruit as many nurses as they needed, given that local hospitals were still suffering from severe staff shortages. In an ironic plot twist, Bernard Olalia, the state official who had overseen the deployment ban in 2020, found himself having to defend nurses' outmigration. In one televised interview, the beleaguered administrator faced pointed questions about the state's capacity to manage the loss of health care workers. "How does the Philippine government stand to benefit if we allow certain governments to receive more health care workers from here?" asked one news anchor. "This is exactly the reason why we imposed the deployment ban," Olalia replied, clearly exasperated. "But considering the plight of nurses, they have been unemployed for some time, and they are ready to work abroad."

Even President Marcos Jr., son of the former president who established the Philippines' labor export policies, remained committed to keeping Filipino nurses "at home." In a meeting with American business executives, President Marcos Jr. was careful to emphasize the country's health needs despite heightened demand for Filipino nurses abroad. "Unfortunately, in terms of health care workers, we have become victims of our own success . . . Every leader I meet says, 'Can we have more Filipino med techs, doctors, and nurses?'" he lamented. "[But] we're having a shortage here . . . So we are trying to find schemes so as to alleviate that problem" (Lee-Brago and Romero 2023).[8] In many ways, the ominous image of understaffed hospitals and helpless patients continued to elicit public support for state limits on nurses' international migration. As such, Philippine officials maintained the narrative of their immobility as an emergency measure that needed to go on.

It did not help that nurses themselves were split into two groups. As discussed in chapter 3, some nurses refused the state's call to service, while others willingly entered local hospitals to gain the clinical experience needed for overseas work. The latter group became the state's symbol of national heroism, and those who pushed for outmigration were portrayed as selfish and unpatriotic.

Most of the nurses who entered the Philippines' pandemic hospitals (twenty-four out of twenty-seven) were still working in COVID-19 wards when my research team reached out for a follow-up interview at the end of 2020. At this time, the first wave of coronavirus infections had declined, and a mutated version of the virus was yet to emerge. Jenine, the derma nurse who gave up her job in Saudi Arabia, was grateful for the brief respite. However, the slowing down of COVID-19 infections had led to some uncertainty in the terms of her employment. As part of the country's urgent hiring scheme, Jenine's salary had been funded by the DOH. Then, as COVID-19 cases decreased, Jenine was told that the state's emergency funds had been depleted, and her salary would be coming from the public hospital where she worked, instead. "I'm just not sure what to expect," she sighed. "Are they going to remove our hazard pay and other benefits because the funds won't be coming from the DOH anymore? We're just worried that we'll lose out on some things when the hospital takes over." Jenine's anxiety reflected a broader concern that as the threat of the virus began to wane, the state would renege on its promise to care for health care workers. Perhaps for this reason, advocacy groups that first opposed the deployment ban eventually dropped their campaign for nurses' freedom to leave the country. By the time I began writing this book in 2022, these groups had shifted toward advocating for higher wages in local hospitals and ensuring the distribution of COVID-19 benefits (de Villa 2023; Tan 2023).

Among interviewees who refused to work in Philippine hospitals, only six out of twenty-eight were still in the country at the end of the pandemic's first year (see table 3.1). John Paul and Elmer, founders of the PrisoNurses, were able to fulfill their dreams of emigrating to the United Kingdom. Sadly, leaving the country was a bitter experience, as many Filipinos continued to berate those who left for abandoning the nation. The last time we spoke, I could tell that both nurses were eager to begin the next phase of their professional lives. John Paul and I exchanged a few messages on Facebook, where he updated me on his successful departure. However, he declined a follow-up interview; there was little time between shifts at his hospital. Elmer agreed to a short conversation. He was forced to retake his IELTS exam after his first certificate expired, but he managed to leave as soon as President Duterte announced that nurses with existing work contracts were exempted from the deployment ban. "I still get tagged as selfish because we chose not to serve the nation . . . but I'm not affected anymore. I'm now here in the UK. I am starting my new life here," he said. "There are still nurses who send me messages on Twitter, Facebook, asking for updates and what they can do next. Not everyone's problems are over." Elmer tries to provide moral support to a few dozen of their members who were still stuck in the Philippines. However, he had no interest in engaging any further with his government. "I don't know about you, Yasmin," he said. "I'm done with the Philippines."

While the state was successful in pushing an effective narrative of retention for outgoing nurses, it fell short in spinning a story of reintegration for former cruise workers. Philippine government officials tried to frame the pandemic as a time to "start anew," when cruise workers could work toward building alternative livelihoods at home. State agencies poured millions of pesos into promoting entrepreneurship and training programs among returnees. However, only a few of the cruise workers I interviewed took advantage of these supposed opportunities. Cruise workers valued the skills they had honed onboard their ships. As such, government efforts to reskill them for other jobs felt misplaced and insulting. Throughout the two years that my interviewees were stuck at home, they continuously sought aid from their local government representatives. However, they rejected any attempts to train for available "pandemic" jobs or start their own small businesses.

Eventually, the Philippine state was unable to maintain the story it was trying to tell, as doubtful politicians and migrants themselves poked holes in the image of the successful return. By the end of 2020, administration officials seemed to give up on pushing for reintegration and instead moved toward assuring the public that the cruise industry would eventually resume once again.

When I followed up with interviewees toward the end of 2021, all but four of the cruise workers we interviewed had either set sail or were preparing to leave soon. Unlike the case of the nurses, cruise workers' departures were celebrated by the government and the local media. Still, life did not simply go back to normal, despite the resumption of cruise travel. Manuel, the cruise worker who worked his way up from the galley to his ship's main restaurant, had already set sail when I reached out via Facebook. However, the cruise line decided to restructure restaurant positions to make up for financial losses. Suddenly, his position as wine steward no longer existed, and he was demoted to being a "runner" instead—literally running to ferry dishes from the kitchen to the dining room. Customer tips had also shrunk onboard his ship, given the limited number of guests that cruise lines were allowed to accept. It seemed that returning to cruise work had not solved his problems at home.

While the pandemic had revealed the vulnerable position of migrants working in the cruise industry, government officials continued to amplify cruise companies' recruitment efforts. Press releases from the state reported new openings for hospitality workers, with Carnival Corporation, for example, committed to recruiting at least 40,000 seafarers from the Philippines. Jaime J. Bautista, secretary of the Department of Transportation, heralded the possible deployment of more cruise workers as an opportunity for the nation. "I think there are other shipping companies that would want to have more Filipino seafarers," he declared triumphantly (Tabile 2023). A few media reports would mention reintegration programs for former migrants. However, it seemed that, in general, the state was ready to move back toward its usual practice of deploying cruise workers abroad.

Why were the outcomes of nurses' and cruise workers' immobilities so different? Any public narrative requires a subject that drives the plot forward, justifying the story to a broader audience (Somers 1997: 85). In the stories featured in this book, the notion of skill was the pivot point that determined how workers' immobilities were defined. For nurses, Philippine government officials framed health care workers' skills as a resource that was too essential to let go. This narrative rationalized the need to contain such capabilities within the country, conveniently ignoring how the state had actively exported nurses' labor before the pandemic. In contrast, the service skills of cruise workers, already devalued within the Philippines, had become even more dispensable in the context of the pandemic. Cruise workers wanted proper recognition of and compensation for the capabilities they had honed and developed onboard their ships. However, even Filipino employers were skeptical of whether cruise workers would permanently settle down in the Philippines. As a result, any narrative on their successful reintegration failed to gain ground.[9]

Despite their divergent outcomes, it was also striking how both nurses and cruise workers regarded their own skills in similar ways. For the Filipino workers in this book, coming to terms with one's immobility meant having to accept an abrupt shift in the reasons for one's education and training. Before the pandemic, learning nursing and service skills was a means toward becoming a global professional, able to market one's capacities to employers overseas. But in the context of the pandemic, societal perceptions of skills determined the broader narrative of who needed to remain in the country and who would be better off leaving. These struggles are invisible in a scholarship of migration governance centered only on questions of international mobility.

Moving On?

Among my interviewees, there were those whose stories failed to fit the new public narratives that emerged as nurse retention became more salient and discussions of cruise workers' reintegration receded from headline news.

Larry, the former bartender, was one of the very few cruise workers who chose not to return to his ship. He had been offered an opportunity to set sail in September 2021, but he decided to remain at home with his wife and two children. "When my company emailed me—you know, I was honored. There are thousands of Filipino cruise workers who are unemployed, and they chose me to go back," he recalled. "But then, when I went to sleep next to my wife that night, I realized that working on the ship would require me to spend another ten months lying in bed alone. That was my turning point."

Coincidentally, Larry was celebrating his thirty-third birthday at the time of our last interview. As he recounted his decision to remain at home, his wife was writing a list of groceries they needed to purchase for a big family dinner at his mother's home—something Larry had been unable to enjoy for the entire nine years he had spent working for the cruise line. "I couldn't even do video calls for my family to greet me happy birthday because of the time difference! The pandemic actually gave me two birthdays with my wife, family, and kids." Taking all these factors into account, he decided it was time to give up his career at sea.

In many ways, Larry had accomplished what the Philippine state had wanted all former migrants to do: find a place for themselves within the country's domestic labor market. Unlike many of his former colleagues, Larry was able to successfully establish a new career, working from home as a call center agent. But, as government officials pivoted back to deploying cruise workers, his purported achievement was unlikely to generate any public praise or celebration. Even Larry himself did not see his new career as a success. "I know it's cheesy, but I feel like I went through heartbreak, and I just need to move on," he shared. "Cruise work was my life for ten years. When I think about it, I feel emotional. It is the reason I was able to build the dreams I have right now."

The Philippines' restaurant industry seemed to have little regard for the skills Larry had gained working in the cruise industry. Having graduated with only a two-year associate's degree, Larry would need to invest in obtaining a bachelor's degree in order to qualify as head bartender for Manila's five-star hotels. The lack of recognition for returning migrants' skills has long frustrated reintegration efforts in the Philippines. Yet such challenges were now low on the Philippine state's priority list. In a "postpandemic" economy, officials were largely concerned about helping cruise workers return to their ships.

Rachel, the aspiring migrant nurse, was also heartbroken, but for completely different reasons. When I called her for a follow-up interview, I assumed that she had already left the country. As noted in the early chapters of this book, constant pressure from nursing groups had pushed state officials to loosen the initial conditions of the ban on nurses' overseas deployment. Rachel had been in the final stage of her departure for Ireland when we first spoke in June 2020. I was shocked when she told me that she had failed to leave, and the Irish nursing home had rescinded her job offer.

While Rachel was eventually exempted from the Philippines' deployment ban in August 2020, the recruitment agency processing her papers went out of business, further delaying her departure for Ireland. Unwilling to wait any longer, her supposed employer withdrew its offer and canceled her contract. Making things worse, the rest of Rachel's documents for overseas work expired one by one—from her English proficiency certificate to her letter of support from the Irish Nursing and Midwifery Board. She would need to apply for these papers once again before she could begin looking for a new employer. From being at the cusp of departure, Rachel's trajectory toward emigration went back to zero in the span of a few months.

Advocacy groups like the PrisoNurses had warned of the serious financial losses that nurses would suffer if they were prevented from leaving the country. Yet, as state adjustments to the ban allowed more health care workers to emigrate, stories like Rachel's failed to generate much concern or attention. Instead, both government agencies and nursing groups focused on the plight of nurses like Jenine, who continued to work in Philippine hospitals. Little was said about outgoing nurse migrants who remained stuck at home.

After her migration plans fell through, Rachel went through a deep depression. She disconnected from social media and all the PrisoNurses chat groups because she couldn't bear to see others share "happy pictures" in their destination countries. However, she assured me that she was ready to move on with her life. Her plan was to work as a call center agent for Shearwater Health, a company that specializes in providing services for American hospitals. A friend told Rachel that the company preferred Filipino nurses and would be willing to sponsor employees who wanted to take the US nursing board examinations. "I'm not saying I'll migrate to the US. I'm just thinking that if ever I decide to try for overseas work again, at least I have a possible ticket to the US," she explained. "My friend said the company will give me free review classes for six months and an allowance."

While the state's deployment ban had effectively disrupted Rachel's plans of working abroad, it failed to channel her toward the local hospitals that needed her labor. "The only reason I worked in the hospital is because I needed the experience to work abroad," she said, her voice rising in frustration. "Yes, it's a service to the people, but I can't feed my family by just serving others." The call center job still paid a salary higher than what local hospitals offered. And for Rachel, her clinical career in the Philippines had ended with her migration dreams to Ireland. "Hopefully, Ma'am Yasmin, if ever we speak again, I'll have a happier story to share with you," she said quietly.

The Dance of Migration Governance

In my introduction, I argued that the Philippines serves as an important case of how emigration governance goes beyond labor export. Migration scholars have mostly categorized the Philippine government as a neoliberal state driven mainly toward profiting off its citizens' labor. In contrast, this book shows how reaping the benefits of remittances is only one part of governing emigration. Beyond facilitating workers' departures, state institutions must also adhere to the needs and demands of local constituents. The sending state does not answer only to migrants and overseas employers. Rather, its legitimacy relies on a population of nonmigrants, most of whom are less concerned about maximizing remittances. When viewed through this lens, it is easy to see how negotiations over the meaning of immobility occur in many other sending and receiving nations across the world. Within Asia alone, countries such as Indonesia and India have seen contested discussions over state efforts to control people's international movements, either to leverage their interests to other nations or to pacify local constituents. The Philippines, as the "model" for migration management, serves as an important case of how state agencies and aspiring migrants engage in this negotiation and develop public narratives to support their own interests.

Ricardo Casco, the former bureaucrat who spent his career at the POEA, had described the state's role as a "dance" between global and local demands. In many ways, *Stuck at Home* reveals an essential part of this dance: managing the globally oriented workers when they should not or could not leave the country.

In 2023, I decided to pay Mr. Casco a visit, around the same time I returned to Manila for my grandmother's birthday. He had given a few public talks since the virtual conference he had hosted in 2021, the year we first met. Since then, he had mostly lived a retiree's life, tending to his garden and enjoying time with friends. As is typical of Filipino-style networking, I had added him to my Facebook list of "friends," but we never saw each other in person. In the discussions we had—both during the conference and through online messages—it was clear that we disagreed on the government's approach to retaining health care workers. He felt that the state had the mandate to prevent nurses from leaving when it was in the public's interest to do so. The COVID-19 pandemic was an unprecedented crisis, and the Philippines was not the only nation to restrict the movement of its health care professionals. The deployment ban was a necessary part of the dance that his former agency had long performed. While difficult for me to accept at first, these conversations eventually served as the foundation for this book. I wanted to personally thank Mr. Casco for his help. But there was also another reason why I wanted to meet with him.

Sometime before my trip to Manila, I learned that Mr. Casco had caught the first strain of COVID-19 in 2020, well before any vaccines were developed. His health deteriorated so rapidly that he was immediately sent to the intensive care unit and placed on oxygen support. His wife and daughter, both based in the United States, were unable to be with him due to border closures during the pandemic's first year. "It was like torture for them," he recalled.

Looking back, I wondered how Mr. Casco had felt about my arguments for nurses' departure. After all, the presence of competent nursing staff had saved his life, and perhaps those of many other Filipinos who suffered through the pandemic. While I still opposed the deployment ban, I wondered if perhaps the reason I could easily argue for nurses' emigration was because I didn't have a loved one whose life relied on their care. Questions about who gets to leave can be complicated by other national issues far beyond labor export. Perhaps these complications have been harder for scholars to see, mainly because studies of the emigration state are often conducted by those who don't live within its borders.

Mr. Casco didn't seem to take our disagreement personally. Over plates of tomato pasta and sliced fruit, he shared stories of establishing well-intentioned programs that inadvertently made life difficult for workers, as well as strong policies that made things better despite their lack of popularity. He, too, was critical of the poor work conditions for health care workers and the sudden implementation of a ban that upended the plans of those who had invested so much time, effort, and money in meeting requirements for departure. He told me how, while he was confined in the COVID-19 ward, a medical technologist who had come to draw his blood collapsed in front of him. His hospital room was already uncomfortably hot—COVID-19 was airborne, so all air conditioners were turned off in favor of keeping windows open to ensure that the wards were well ventilated—and Mr. Casco could tell that health care workers were also skipping meals and water breaks to conserve their PPE. "I didn't have a call button, so I couldn't even ask for help," he said. "I felt like crying, not for myself, but for what health care workers have to go through."

Still, Mr. Casco could see why the state was determined to retain its nurses. "In governing migration, you can't expect to make everyone happy," he said thoughtfully. "There are the migrants and there are the different stakeholders. It's really a balance."

True enough, the Philippine government has more to balance in the years beyond COVID-19. Although pandemic restrictions no longer exist, scholars argue that they will have created lasting changes in how countries govern international migration, perhaps at a scale comparable to the changes after the terrorist attacks of September 11, 2001, in the United States (Newland 2020). More migrants are also likely to experience more prolonged and sudden immobility, as global disruptions occur more frequently in the future. Amid all of this, state agencies and aspiring migrants must negotiate changes in the country's emigration policies, co-creating narratives of who gets to move and what should be done for those who stay in place.

Where will all this lead? A few months before I visited Mr. Casco, President Marcos Jr. decided the best way to deal with the country's nursing shortage would be to produce even more nursing skills. Realizing that it would be impossible to simply retain nurses within the country, the president ordered the Commission on Higher Education to ramp up the training of nursing graduates (Galvez 2023). Private universities responded in the same way they had in the early 2000s: by greatly expanding their nursing programs. Alongside this expansion, administration officials promised that they would offer government scholarships to keep nursing graduates tied to Philippine hospitals for a period of time. Still, beyond this new rhetoric of retention, it seemed that the country was on track toward making the same mistakes that had led to the glut in nurses only a decade before.

While Philippine health and labor officials broadcasted the campaign for keeping nurses at home, the Department of Tourism seemed to be priming the government to send even more of the country's service workers abroad. Newly appointed tourism secretary Christina Frasco announced her department's goal to establish the Philippines as the "cruising hub of Asia." Implicit in this plan was also the aggressive promotion of Filipinos as the ideal service workers. In a grand show of support, tourism officials held a welcome event for the *Silver Spirit*, a large luxury cruise line vessel that was at that moment docked in Manila's South Harbor. "One hundred eighty-one of the over 400 crew in this cruise ship are Filipinos, signaling the Filipino Brand of Service Excellence," Frasco declared proudly, as waitstaff distributed tropical drinks to alighting passengers. Switching to Tagalog, the secretary directed her statements to Filipinos in the audience. "I am thankful for these types of opportunities because it gives our overseas workers the chance to regain what the pandemic took away from them." This was the tourism official's only acknowledgment of the industry's vulnerability to future disruption—albeit one that offered no alternative for its service workers.

Perhaps, in performing the dance of migration governance, the sad truth is that states can end up circling back to where all their problems began: setting up the possibility of committing the very same missteps that disrupt people's lives. Researchers have long critiqued the inability of sending states to protect the interests of citizens who live and work overseas. In contrast, this book shows how emigration governance should also be about addressing the needs of immobile workers or those who remain in place. Just as others have called for more protections for immigrants abroad, this book seeks better ways of approaching the concerns of aspiring migrant workers who have yet to leave.

As one of the world's most organized systems of migration management, the Philippines has often been viewed by policymakers as a possible blueprint for other source countries to emulate in the future. But, as the cases of nurses and cruise workers show, negotiating the right narrative to define migrants' immobility has come with a cost. Amid the delicate balance of maximizing global opportunity while appealing to local constituents, individual migrants take on the labor of readjusting their plans for departure and coping with the repercussions of disruptions like the pandemic. In the end, this book shows that, within the process of how states choose to manage immobility, workers like Rachel and Larry bear the consequences of what it means to be stuck at home.

Appendix
(Field)Work from Home: Methodology

Stuck at Home is a story of how Filipino workers negotiated the meaning of their immobility with the labor-exporting state. However, I do not offer ethnographic accounts of their daily lives or an analysis defined by the experience of being "there." In conducting this study, I was unable to observe regular service on a cruise ship or witness the operations of a COVID-19 ward. Instead, I was in my faculty apartment in Singapore, speaking to nurses and cruise workers through Facebook Messenger and Skype. Rather than an immersive experience in the "field," I scheduled interviews in between grading student work, parenting my two children, and recording lectures for my undergraduate classes. As such, this book is very much a product of my own immobility as well as that of my interlocutors.

This project began in April 2020, amid a nationwide lockdown that shuttered my university as well as the elementary school that my children attended. Like many other parents, I found myself having to manage my job while helping my son and daughter navigate their online lessons. A year before the pandemic, my son was diagnosed with autism, and he needed to attend speech and communication therapy. With the lockdown, my husband Marvin and I took on the role of therapists at home as well. Whenever I had a scheduled interview, I would lock myself in our bedroom while Marvin tried to distract our children with other activities. Still, there were always small fights to mediate, snack requests, and just a general curiosity as to where I was hiding. Listening to my interview recordings, I can still hear their voices in the background. "Who are you talking to, *Nanay*?"

The divided attention I brought to this project made me extremely insecure about writing this book. Monographs based on qualitative research often draw from years of careful study, where scholars dedicate a significant period of their careers to investigating their research questions. I came to realize that, in many ways, the uneven pace of my project reflected the pandemic experience as a whole: frenetic, unpredictable, and difficult to plan. And perhaps the outcome of this project also provides one view of how qualitative researchers have been forced to cope with COVID-19: "hacking" our way through new challenges and restrictions, while making sense of people's experiences and doing justice to their stories.

My previous research had heavily relied on in-depth interviews; this project was the first where none of these conversations happened in person. For the entire duration of this study, Singapore's borders were strictly regulated. I remember hearing of international students who traveled to their home countries during the summer break, only to spend the next six months trying to get state approval to return. Even if I pushed through with fieldwork in the Philippines, it was also unlikely that I would be able to meet my research participants in person. Extended pandemic restrictions kept people isolated in their homes, and the disastrous effects of different COVID-19 variants had traumatized many Filipinos. Personal gatherings that used to come so naturally had become events that needed to be carefully planned and considered. I remember that when I first returned to my home city of Metro Manila in July 2022, my paternal grandmother requested that I refrain from visiting her and that we speak on the phone instead. While both of us were fully vaccinated, she was still worried about milder versions of the virus that continued to spread like the common cold. I would only see her in person a year later, when the WHO declared the end of the global pandemic.

This experience was a sobering reminder of how much the world had changed since 2020. I still find myself wondering how qualitative researchers will need to navigate new norms in relating with research participants, given that COVID-19 may not be the last health crisis the world will go through in the coming years.

The stories in this book are drawn mainly from online and phone interviews with fifty-five nurses and forty-five cruise workers in the Philippines (see table A.1). With a research team based in Manila and Singa-

TABLE A. 1. **Profile of Research Participants**

	Nurses	Cruise Workers
Gender		
Male	16	25
Female	39	20
Average age (years)	30	33
Educational attainment		
High school only	—	9
Associate's degree/diploma	—	5
Tech-voc certificate	—	1
Bachelor's degree	53	28
Master's degree	2	2

pore, I conducted a total of 208 interviews from April 2020 to December 2021. The first round of interviews took place at the onset of pandemic restrictions in the Philippines (between April and June 2020). We later invited our participants to a follow-up conversation six to eight months after their first interview. By this time, we found that a significant number of our nurse interviewees had been able to leave the country. Philippine government officials had eased the conditions of the deployment ban, and foreign employers were quick to facilitate the departure of nurses with existing job contracts overseas. In contrast, only one of the cruise workers we interviewed had returned to her ship. Leisure travel had yet to resume, and COVID-19 continued to upend attempts to restart cruise operations in large markets such as the United States and Europe. Given this situation, my research team and I decided to conduct a second round of follow-up interviews with cruise workers. This last set of interviews was held from October to December 2021. During this period, more than half of the cruise workers we interviewed were able to return to their ships. However, as I note in the chapters of this book, cruise work had also become considerably riskier and much less lucrative than it was before the pandemic.

Interviews for this project took place through a wide range of platforms. We disseminated our call for interviewees through personal networks, both offline and online. A few interviewees reached out to me through email after seeing my contact information in "e-posters" that we advertised through social media. However, we connected with most of our respondents through Facebook. In a country where internet access and mobile data are often unreliable, Facebook's free access for mobile phone users made it the best way to reach potential interviewees. We initially offered to hold interviews via Zoom or Skype, online platforms that allowed for video calls. Unfortunately, these conversations were often patchy due to the varying levels of internet speed in the Philippines. Many of our interviewees (cruise workers in particular) were not familiar with these tools and found them tedious and intimidating. Thus, most of our interviews were conducted through Messenger, an instant messaging application connected to Facebook. I only used Skype to call interviewees' phones because the platform's rates were cheaper than using my office landline in Singapore. While Messenger allowed for video, most respondents kept their cameras off. For many, only their profile photos allowed me to get a sense of what they looked like.

To examine the Philippine state's efforts in constructing the meaning of workers' immobility, we relied on a document analysis of newspaper reports, government press releases, and public statements from January 2020 to June 2022. For all the limitations the pandemic brought to our interviews, safety protocols made state discussions much easier to access. Work-from-home mandates prompted the Philippine Congress to move all meetings online. These meetings were either streamed live on Facebook or uploaded on YouTube, a video-sharing platform. Stranded nurses who organized "virtual meetings" with state officials made several of these recordings available on the internet as well. I was able to attend one meeting with the POEA because a nurse interviewee sent me the passcode for the online "meeting room." I would not have gained access to these gatherings if they were held in person. To supplement this public discourse, I decided to interview five current and former state officials. These interviews took place in 2023, well after the discovery of vaccines and the end of most pandemic restrictions. Ironically, these interviews also happened online, as my interviewees saw this as the most convenient way to speak!

By the end of the pandemic's first year, our project began to draw the attention of other migration scholars, many of whom had also been isolated in their homes due to government directives to stem the spread of the virus. Much of this attention centered on our lack of face-to-face interaction with our research participants. Given that few researchers were able to conduct fieldwork in 2020, I encountered many questions as to how my team conducted qualitative work given the many constraints over people's mobility.

On the one hand, I found that many were quick to praise our project as an example of "new" and "creative" ways of conducting research in a post-pandemic world. My team and I received several invitations to share our methodological "innovations" in various academic workshops, often organized under the theme of "digital tools and technology." Given that we had conducted most of our interviews through online platforms, others seemed eager to celebrate our project as a novel approach to doing qualitative research. However, I attended these events with a sense of trepidation. While conducting research in the middle of a global pandemic was truly a new experience, I was unsure as to whether the methods we used in implementing the project were actually as unique as others seemed to think.

On the other hand, I often felt pressured to explain how our team overcame the supposed limitations of digital media in conducting qualitative interviews. While the pandemic had pushed most scholars to adopt some technology in their research, the use of online platforms and digital media continued to be seen as a "less ideal" means of conducting in-depth interviews. Such critique came with the assumption that in-person research was still the gold standard for qualitative methods. While I did believe in the value of meeting my research participants in "real life," I began to wonder about the deficits we associate with online platforms and whether such critique was truly warranted in all interview situations.

My reflections on methodology arise from these divergent reactions to my project. Much like my early insecurity with this unexpected book project, I have come to see my methods as one example of how qualitative scholars can do research in a world that seems to be changing much more quickly. While imperfect, I also hope that this book's methodology will prompt migration scholars to consider how traditional methods used to signal quality and rigor are also built on privileges that many of us have taken for granted.

Old Tools for a "New" Situation

As this project came to a close in 2021, social science journals began to feature an increasing number of articles on how the COVID-19 pandemic had redefined what it means to conduct qualitative research. Researchers highlighted the benefits that "digital enhancements" can bring to the traditional interview—from chat boxes to automatic transcription and recording. Meanwhile, others discussed the ethical complexity of using "virtual" methods to examine people's everyday lives (Bandini, Rollison, and Etchegaray 2023; Keen, Lomeli-Rodriguez, and Joffe 2022; Tungohan and Catungal 2022). These studies acknowledged that the use of face-to-face online media was not necessarily new in itself. Even before the pandemic, researchers had investigated the use of programs like Skype in conducting qualitative interviews (Deakin and Wakefield 2014; Iacono, Symonds, and Brown 2016). However, scholars insisted that the pandemic had pushed such methods into the mainstream, forcing researchers to reflect on the impact of having interviews mediated with synchronous video.

I read these articles with much excitement, eager to find examples of studies that I could align with our project. But in the end, the only conclusion I came to was that my qualitative interviews were not innovative at all. Rather than charting new methodological pathways through synchronous video conversations, I realized that my team was merely conducting an online version of the classic phone interview. As noted earlier, poor internet access in the Philippines prevented many of my interviewees from using the cameras on their phones. Our conversations were much like the audio-only interviews that were already commonly used in a wide range of social science research (Irvine, Drew, and Sainsbury 2013; Trier-Bieniek 2012).

My team and I experienced many of the documented disadvantages of conducting audio-only interviews. There was the absence of bodily cues, our complete reliance on verbal prompts and affirmations to build rapport, and the awkwardness of intermittent silence. Still, this method also came with clear benefits, such as the ability to reach participants from a wider geographic area. While members of our team had done previous research on Filipino migrants, we were often limited to the region of Metro Manila, where our own families were based. I was ashamed to admit that many of our interviewees were in provincial towns and cities that I had yet to visit in person—even if these places were found within my own country. Their stories were vital in understanding how internal borders and state policy shape the meaning of immobility. I quickly realized that being "stuck at home" can be complicated when you live outside the capital city.

More important, these audio-only interviews became the perfect tool to deal with the unprecedented limits that the pandemic had created. For example, phone interviews allowed us to reach Filipino nurses who were working in COVID-19 hospitals at the height of the pandemic's first wave.

During this time, nurses either rented accommodations near the hospital or lived in temporary housing facilities built by government agencies. Most of our interviewees had mobile data, but they were hesitant to use their limited internet capacity to talk to researchers like me. Incoming calls are free for Philippine mobile subscribers, so I used my research funds to pay for my team members' mobile phone credits. However, "unlimited minutes" were only allowed if both callers were subscribed to the same telecommunications company. If a team member in Manila was to call a nurse who used a mobile plan from a different company, he or she would end up being charged by the minute. As such, I realized it was sometimes cheaper for me to use Skype to make long-distance calls to the Philippines.

Even then, my team's use of these "high-tech" tools seemed almost crude in many ways. Luis Macabasag, one of my team members based in Manila, took charge of recruiting nurses serving in local hospitals by sending them an SMS text (short messaging service). If they agreed to participate, he would note their preferred dates in a Google document that we shared online, and we would meet on Facebook Messenger to discuss how to divide the interviews. If I was the one assigned to a particular interviewee, Luis took charge of texting our interviewee to expect my call. We found that nurses avoided answering their phones if they saw a call from an unknown number. This convoluted procedure turned out to be the only way that we could talk to nurses as they went through their experiences in the COVID-19 wards. Although quite "old" in many ways, these tools proved to be the most effective means of coping with the new challenges of the pandemic.

Building Rapport through Online Interviews

In contrast to those researchers who celebrated online interviews as innovative and path-breaking, many more regarded these conversations as lacking in quality. Much of this skepticism seemed to be rooted in the belief that virtual or phone interviews impacted researchers' abilities to establish rapport with their interviewees (see Deakin and Wakefield 2013). As noted by Weller (2017: 614), qualitative researchers must create rapport with their interlocutors in order to establish trust. Failure to do so can impact "data quality" in terms of what participants may choose to disclose and share about their lives.

It would be dishonest to say that my research team did not face challenges with technology. Choppy internet connection sometimes stalled conversations, making it difficult to hear our interviewees. Even when the reception was clear, I sometimes struggled to express my commiseration when interviewees shared difficult experiences. I remember talking to one nurse, Ilyn, who began to cry as she relayed a story of a man who became infected with COVID-19 while receiving dialysis treatment at the hospital where she worked. While nurses tried their best to isolate infected patients from those who just needed regular hospital care, overwork and exhaustion made mistakes unavoidable. Ilyn believed that someone had used a blood pressure machine meant for COVID-19 patients on the man, inadvertently infecting him with the virus.

If I had been speaking to Ilyn in person, staying silent would have been enough for me to show that I was listening and that I empathized with her story. Yet, listening to her cry over the phone, my silence only seemed unresponsive and cold. Wanting to provide some comfort, I recall saying, "I'm so sorry this happened to you" again and again, in different ways. In the end, Ilyn had to reassure me that she was fine. "I know you're trying to make the interview light, but I just feel sad because this only happened yesterday," she said. This conversation was one of many instances when it pained me to not to be talking to my participants in person.

For cruise workers, audio-only interviews often amplified my limited knowledge of cruise travel. Since I had never gone on a cruise, I found it hard to imagine the contradictory spaces where they worked. Some parts of the ship sounded so huge; it was difficult to comprehend the scale of regular cruise operations. As one cruise waiter patiently explained, a regular ship's dining hall can serve up to a thousand guests in one seating. The kitchens took up an entire floor, and transporting dishes from one end to another meant walking almost a third of a mile each way. In contrast, the spaces crew members could inhabit on the ship seemed uncomfortably small. There was no hanging out on the deck or passing through guest areas. Crew cabins had no windows and felt even smaller when staff were forced to isolate in these rooms for weeks. Thankfully, the cruise workers we spoke to were patient enough to help us visualize their work environments and how these changed as they embarked on their long repatriation journeys home. Throughout these conversations, I tried to convey our determination to listen and to understand their stories, even if we were so far away from each other.

Despite these limitations, I do not think the audio-only interviews deterred me from building rapport with our research participants. I later found that other researchers felt the same way about online interview platforms as well (see Jenner and Myers 2019). Technically, good rapport is about establishing a sense of trust, and both the nurses and cruise workers we interviewed were open in sharing their experiences with our team. Whether their stories were of deferred departures or unhappy returns, interviewees seemed to take comfort in processing their struggles with a sympathetic listener, even if they knew that we could do little to help them. One stranded nurse admitted that he was happy to have someone else to talk to, given that his family was beginning to get tired of hearing about his anxieties. "I think everyone is just sick of me ranting," he laughed. "But if I don't talk about this, I feel like I'll go crazy." Our decision to conduct follow-up interviews was also an important part of rapport-building. Several of our interviewees admitted that they were happy to find that we stayed true to our promise to follow up with them after six months.

Within migration studies, many scholars develop deep bonds with their interlocutors, as the initial rapport established during the project grows into close and enduring friendships (Boccagni 2011; Francisco-Menchavez 2018). Academics have come to see these types of relationships as proof of the richness and validity of one's interview data. It is perhaps no surprise that people were often curious as to how "close" I had become to my interviewees. Whenever I shared the findings of this book in public seminars and workshops, members of the audience would always ask about how I dealt with "friend requests" from interviewees I recruited through Facebook. Adding someone as a "Facebook friend" meant giving them access to your personal profile, photos, and social media posts. Underlying this question was the assumption that the rapport built during the interview process would prompt my participants to want to be my "friends."

As such, fellow scholars were often surprised to hear that among the hundred workers who took part in our project, only three individuals (two nurses and one cruise worker) sent me "friend" requests on Facebook. To me, it was clear that while our interviewees trusted us enough to take part in our study, they had no desire to develop a relationship with the research team. They had no intention of becoming my friends. Nor did I see this as necessary in proving the authenticity of the stories they shared with us.

I believe that the distance between the research team and our interviewees was an advantage in terms of putting people at ease. Research participants can feel "pressures in presence," especially if they are less familiar with the research process (Weller 2017: 619). Audio-only interviews can mitigate many of the anxieties people have about taking part in a research interview. In our project, the nurses and cruise workers I spoke with seemed to take comfort in knowing that we were unlikely to see each other again after the research project was over. It seemed that, while developing close relationships does encourage more disclosure, ample distance can also make it easier for interviewees to speak about sensitive topics. A fellow sociologist, Aliya Rao, had argued that experiences of unemployment can be a source of embarrassment that people may find difficult to talk about, especially with close friends and family. In this sense, interviewees may feel more inclined to share certain experiences when talking to a researcher who is otherwise disconnected from the rest of their lives.

Such was the case with Philip, a bar waiter who was still unemployed in the Philippines when I called for our last interview toward the end of 2021. Philip's recruitment agency had called on him to complete his paperwork for immediate redeployment in August 2021. However, the cruise line wanted him to redo his medical exam, and this required getting vaccinated for hepatitis A. At that time, Philip had just received his second dose of the Pfizer vaccine for COVID-19, and he was told to wait at least two weeks before getting any other vaccine. Desperate to start working, Philip altered the dates in his vaccination history to ensure that the agency's clinic would allow him to receive a vaccine shot for hepatitis A.

Given the legal ramifications of tampering with one's vaccine record and the huge risk to his health, I was shocked that Philip had disclosed this story to me. Yet, over the phone, Philip said that he actually felt relieved to tell someone about what he had done. He was so ashamed for taking such a risk that he told no one about his secret—not even his wife, who was working as a nurse in Abu Dhabi. "I just shut my eyes and prayed that nothing would happen to me," he said, his voice filled with regret. "My wife would be so angry if she found out. She knows the risks. I mean, after all, she's a nurse." What made this secret even more painful was that Philip never made it to the ship. His contract was canceled after another wave of COVID-19 infections forced the cruise line to halt new voyages for several months.

Philip's story shows how the distance created by the audio-only interview can create the space that some interviewees need in making sense of experiences that they could not discuss with others within their families and communities. In Philip's case, he was assured that I did not know anyone in his life and there was little chance of me divulging his secrets to anyone in his personal network. Our interview provided him a chance to finally express his guilt and worries without having to be concerned as to how it might change the way others might view him. I like to think that this is something our project provided to those who took part in our study.

———————

While COVID-19 remained present throughout the entire project, I did manage to see a few of my research participants in person. In November 2020, I met with Dyan, Joshua, and Jonathan, three Filipino nurses who were bound for Singapore when the pandemic shut national borders and the Philippines' deployment ban went into effect. When we first spoke, they were stranded at home, praying that they would be allowed to finally leave the country. In fact, Joshua was my very first interviewee. He was also the one who messaged me on Facebook, letting me know that after three months of waiting, two weeks of quarantine, and a tumultuous journey through Manila, they had finally arrived in Singapore. I invited them to lunch at a local cafe, and we spent two hours chatting about their lives and their first impressions of their host country. The Filipina waitress who attended to our table served us a free honey cake with "Welcome to Singapore!" written in chocolate sauce script. This reunion felt both special and surreal at the same time.

Seven months later, I also had the opportunity to meet Phoebe, the only cruise worker who was able to return to her ship in early 2021. By some coincidence, Phoebe's company was offering a "cruise to nowhere" for Singapore residents, where passengers were invited to enjoy a four-day trip around the island with no port stops in between. With my collaborator Karen Liao, I decided to go on the cruise and meet with Phoebe onboard. We were so excited to see her that we assembled a "care package" as a gift. Unfortunately, we failed to properly coordinate what to buy. I wanted to give Phoebe something soothing and decided on lavender-scented hand cream from the mall next to my office. In contrast, Karen wanted a gift that would help Phoebe manage her homesickness. She purchased two bottles of *tuyo*, fish marinated in olive oil, from a Filipino grocery store on Orchard Road. We laughed over our gift's lack of sensory cohesion and how it seemed to reflect our own awkwardness. Fortunately, Phoebe was as gracious in person as she was in our Facebook interviews. Crew members were not allowed to sit with guests, so we stood by the ship's railing, looking out over the ocean. Phoebe was understandably exhausted, having just concluded a ten-hour shift, but she stayed with us for twenty minutes, telling us about how work had changed onboard. She said that if COVID-19 restrictions weren't so strict, she would have liked to give us a personal tour of the ship.

Looking back, I wondered if these meetings made a difference in terms of building rapport with these four interviewees. While these encounters were meaningful—and quite poignant in many ways—they did not make these interviewees stand apart from the other nurses and cruise workers whom we never met in person. I remember that after meeting Dyan, Joshua, and Jonathan for lunch, I asked if we could schedule a separate time to talk for a follow-up interview. They readily agreed, but requested that we have our conversation over Messenger once again. Their shifts at the hospital were so hectic, it was difficult to find time to meet in person, even if we were all in Singapore. In Phoebe's case, we contacted her for a follow-up interview a month after we met onboard. While she initially agreed, she did not respond to Karen's calls on the day of the interview. When our subsequent messages were left unanswered, we assumed that the stress of cruise life had taken over and we respected her decision to bow out of the project.

Perhaps these encounters signal how interviews mediated through online platforms need not be labeled as poor alternatives to in-person meetings. While such tools had become essential during the pandemic, their utility goes beyond times of crisis. The stories in this book show how the distance created by audio-only interviews can create spaces that provide less pressure and more accommodations for interviewees who do not have the luxury of time to meet. In terms of research methods, perhaps what our project reveals is how using such tools does not necessarily put good rapport out of reach.

Old Networks and "New" Immobilities

Eventually, I realized that *Stuck at Home* was not an account of methodological innovation or a cautionary tale regarding the problems of digital platforms. Rather, I have come to see this book as a story of how academics also came to terms with their own international immobility.

While underwhelming to some, I believe that the main factor that made this project possible was simply the presence of established social ties with fellow researchers in the Philippines. Access to research funds and digital tools allowed me to conduct interviews with our research participants despite pandemic restrictions. However, such resources would be of little use without Filipino collaborators who were also deeply embedded in the communities we hoped to reach.

When travel restrictions were first announced in the early months of 2020, I remember hearing how other scholars in Singapore were scrambling to find "local partners" in their overseas research sites. Unable to visit these countries themselves, it seemed that they were suddenly forced to find researchers located within the places they studied. In witnessing this rush to find local collaborators, I wondered if the pandemic had unintentionally revealed the tendency for social science research to rely heavily on scholars' international mobility. After all, a large proportion of research grants is often allotted to help researchers move from their universities to research sites elsewhere. Implied in this practice is the assumption that such travel is an essential means of studying social phenomena. I am not disputing the fact that researchers gain important insight by immersing themselves in their research sites. However, I do wonder if there is an inherent weakness in valorizing the image of the solo researcher, exploring new places overseas. Scholars have already raised concerns regarding the academic privileges that stem from powerful passports and visa-free mobility (Albayrak-Aydemir 2020; Courtois and Sautier 2022). Researchers have also questioned why we sometimes downplay the role of others in making fieldwork possible, whether friends within local communities or our own family members (de Silva and Gandhi 2019). This is not to say that collaborating with local scholars is completely absent in studies of migration. Still, I found quite telling how, in the pandemic's first year, the prevailing concern among other scholars around me was mainly their inability to travel overseas.

As I noted earlier, *Stuck at Home* was an unexpected project born out of pandemic disruptions. However, it was also the outcome of a joint effort with fellow Filipino researchers who had their own stake in documenting the stories of immobile workers in the Philippines.

Michael Joseph Diño was my first collaborator. When I met Michael in 2010, he was a clinical instructor at a large private university that offered degrees in both nursing and hospitality management. In 2020, Michael was supposed to begin his PhD program at the School of Nursing at Johns

Hopkins University. The closure of national borders and the Philippine government's health worker deployment ban left him stranded at home. I had messaged Michael, hoping that he could help me disseminate an early call for nurse interviewees. Having had his own departure deferred, Michael asked if he could join me in the project as well. For someone whose own future seemed so unstable during that period, Michael was the most determined to persevere with the project. We recruited our first batch of interviewees through his networks. When he finally left for the United States after a yearlong delay, he continued to amplify our results and push the project forward. Michael was undoubtedly the most resilient member of the team.

While Michael's networks helped us gain access to nurses who were in the final stages of leaving the country, our interviews with those serving in COVID-19 hospitals were largely due to the efforts of Luis Macabasag. Before the pandemic, Luis and I were already working on a separate project, tracing Filipino nurses' movements from large urban centers to rural health units within provincial towns and villages. A registered nurse himself, Luis had also pursued the profession as a stepping stone to emigration. He only gave up on this dream after overseas opportunities dried up in the 2010s. Finding his passion in research, he collaborated with me as a "side job" while working full time as a research assistant for a large public university. I reached out to Luis in the first weeks of the project, hoping that he could help me interview nurses affected by the deployment ban. Shortly after, the Duterte administration declared that the university hospital where he worked would become one of four COVID-19 treatment centers in Manila.

The hospital quickly received a deluge of patients, and as the first batch of health workers fell sick, administrators called on all employees with nursing degrees to serve as support staff in the wards. Luis assured me that this posting was temporary and that he would not be asked to interact with infected patients. Terrified for his safety, I told him to quit his job and stay at home instead. At that time, Filipino doctors were still struggling to find ways to treat the virus, and several health workers had already died from infection. However, Luis was determined to serve alongside his colleagues. His access to the COVID-19 wards inspired us to interview nurses who responded to the government's call to service. Such perspectives were vital in gaining a clearer understanding of how stranded nurses viewed their immobility. He remains the bravest member of our research team.

While the project began as a study focused on immobile nurses, news of extensive unemployment overseas made it difficult to ignore the experiences of Filipino workers forced to return home. To investigate this question, I turned to Karen Liao, an old friend who was writing her doctoral dissertation on how the Philippines repatriated distressed migrant workers. Karen was the only member of the team who was based in Singapore. She served as my coinvestigator when we applied for external funding to sustain the project. When one of my colleagues heard about our partnership, he questioned why I chose to collaborate with a graduate student. I explained that the reason I wanted to work with Karen was not because of her rank, but because of her expertise. To date, she is the only researcher who has extensively examined how Philippine state institutions and external agencies facilitate return in times of crisis.

Whenever I felt overwhelmed by the frustrations and loss in our interviewees' stories, Karen provided an important source of support and perspective. Her own work on repatriation had focused on migrants who had gone through abuse, armed conflict, and forced evacuation. It was Karen who advised me to empathize with our research participants but avoid crying during the interview. She also invited me to take long walks and indulge in baked treats—important reminders to care for our own mental health in the process of doing difficult research.

Toward the end of the project, Karen herself went through her own return journey home. After a year of writing her dissertation from a rented room in Singapore, she decided to return to Manila to be with her parents. In many ways, Karen experienced the same uncertainty that our cruise workers felt in returning to a nation still in the throes of an ongoing pandemic. I consider her the strongest member of the team.

As COVID-19 continued to stall research plans and immobilize researchers, migration scholars have faced the possibility of moving toward building more place-based collaborations. Ruminations on "post-pandemic" research have also called for more transdisciplinary approaches, emphasizing the need to coproduce knowledge with people within the communities that we study (Bandini, Rollison, and Etchegaray 2023; Marzi 2021). Of course, none of these arguments is necessarily new. Feminist scholars have long promoted the power of working with partners on the ground (see Dill and Zambrana 2009). In many ways, I wonder if the COVID-19 pandemic simply serves as a more urgent call to build such relationships.

Given that the research team was vital in completing the project, it was hard for me to imagine writing this book on my own. However, my collaborators helped me realize that our research study had many other stories that needed to be told. Michael wanted to write about the pandemic's impact on nurses' professional identities. Luis hoped to theorize the bodily experience of caring for patients while wearing layers of PPE. Meanwhile, Karen had her own analysis of the state's repatriation efforts during the pandemic. This project would not have been possible without my three collaborators, but they also made clear that the story of immobility within migration governance was my responsibility to tell. This book represents their contributions to this project as well as my attempt to do justice to their efforts.

Notes

Acknowledgments

1. This research was assisted by the Social Science Research Council's Rapid-Response Grants on Covid-19 and the Social Sciences, with funds provided by the SSRC, the Henry Luce Foundation, the William and Flora Hewlett Foundation, the Wenner-Gren Foundation, and the MacArthur Foundation.

Introduction

1. POEA was subsumed under the Department of Migrant Workers (DMW) in 2022.

2. The Philippine government repatriated 327,511 OFWs, with land-based workers making up 71% or 231,537 and the remaining 29% or 95,974 being sea-based workers from more than 150 cruise ships, oil tankers, and other bulk vessels (DFA 2020).

3. In December 2020, the Kuwaiti government sentenced Villavende's employer to death for her murder. Philippine state officials welcomed such news as evidence of the administration's effective response to the tragic incident (Santiago 2020).

4. The Philippines' relationship with Kuwait is particularly conflict-ridden and likely deserves a book of its own. Two years after I concluded my research for this book, another domestic worker was killed, this time by her Kuwaiti employer's seventeen-year-old son. While the newly formed Department of Migrant Workers (DMW) chose not to impose another deployment ban, other state officials called for pulling out all Filipino workers from Kuwait (Velasco 2023).

5. In line with this work, geographer Alan Gamlen (2008) suggests the emergence of an "emigration state" that grants membership rights to migrant citizens abroad and incorporates them into national projects. However, these studies have tended to look

outward, focusing only on what occurs after emigration (Lee 2017). Diaspora policies are also limited in that they mostly involve migrants who had permanently settled in their destination countries. Missing in these studies are stories of how sending states also manage the movements of temporary migrants who move back to their origin countries after completing work contracts abroad (Weinar 2017).

6. Karen Liao (2020) provides an important overview of how Philippine state agencies have organized repatriation efforts for overseas Filipinos caught in armed conflict or natural disasters. There have also been many instances when Philippine government officials chose to pause the deployment of workers to particular countries in order to negotiate for higher wages or better protections for Filipino migrants (Ruhs 2013).

7. Migration studies have shown how irregular migrants and refugees can become "stuck" between their planned destinations and their countries of origin. Stock's (2019) ethnography on African immigrants in Morocco provides a rich account of this period of extreme precarity and vulnerability.

8. Geographer Tim Cresswell (2010: 26) uses the concept of "friction" to refer to the structures, tools, and technologies that either slow people's mobility or stop them from moving altogether. Friction can be an "aid to power" when governments deliberately make it difficult for some groups to move while allowing the unimpeded mobility of others (Cresswell 2014: 111).

9. Julie Chu's (2010) ethnography on frustrated Chinese emigrants provides a compelling example of this phenomenon. Although her subjects were unable to leave their hometowns in Fuzhou, they continued to go about their lives in anticipation of an imagined future in the United States.

10. Currently, a growing literature on the experience of "waiting" has highlighted the parts of people's migration trajectories that involve keeping still because cross-border mobility requires would-be migrants to devote more time toward navigating the bureaucratic requirements of sending and receiving states (Bissell 2007; Conlon 2011; Janeja and Bandak 2018).

11. In her book on emigration policies in Morocco and Mexico, Iskander (2011) found that many of the "model" policies for migrant-sending states emerged from engagements between government agencies and overseas citizens. Few of these interactions were intentionally planned, often leading to unexpected outcomes for the state. In contrast, Filipino state officials have held consultations with individual migrants, even if these workers were not organized under a particular advocacy group (Rother 2022).

12. Emigration served as an important safety valve for the Marcos regime as well, providing an attractive solution to simmering discontent among members of the Filipino public (Acacio 2008).

13. For example, former president Corazon Aquino did little to dismantle Marcos's emigration policies after the fall of the latter's regime in 1986. Instead, her administration celebrated overseas Filipino workers as the country's new national heroes, given their contributions to the nation's economy (Encinas-Franco 2013). Meanwhile, former president Gloria Macapagal-Arroyo's administration intensified efforts to export skilled professionals in the 2000s, riding the wave of popular discourse about the knowledge-based economy (Ortiga 2018a).

14. The Philippine government ratified this law in response to the controversial execution of Flor Contemplacion, a domestic worker in Singapore. Singaporean courts declared Contemplacion guilty of killing another Filipino domestic worker and the latter's ward, sentencing her to the death penalty. Filipinos in the Philippines protested the conviction, but failed to overturn the decision.

Chapter 1

1. I document the association between overseas labor demands and Philippine higher education in my first book, *Emigration, Employability, and Higher Education in the Philippines* (Ortiga 2018a).

2. Migration scholars have long critiqued how the Philippine government has commodified the labor of Filipino women, marketing a racialized brand of "tender loving care" as a unique quality of Filipino culture (Guevarra 2010; Rodriguez and Schwenken 2013).

3. President Gloria Macapagal-Arroyo succeeded former president Joseph Estrada in 2001. The latter was ousted from the presidency due to charges of plunder and corruption.

4. Among private colleges and universities, only 339 institutions are sectarian. The rest are operated by either family-owned businesses or for-profit companies (CHED 2020).

5. Nursing schools were not the only private institutions that began to gain notoriety in the 2000s. The European Maritime Safety Agency had also raised concerns over the inferior quality of the country's maritime programs. These institutions also accepted large numbers of students but were found to suffer from "extremely low graduation rates, no shipboard training, inadequate equipment, and inexperienced instructors" (Siytangco 2017). Poor standards were such a concern that the European Union threatened to put the Philippines on a blacklist, thereby preventing Filipino seafarers from working in European fleets. These threats continued until the 2020s. Several administrations have since called for the reform of maritime education, but often with little success (Galam 2022).

6. Student fees for public colleges and universities are highly subsidized by state funds, making admissions extremely competitive. Students have to either be residents of a particular province or show proof of academic excellence. Faculty leaders in public institutions also have more power to push back on matters such as admissions and enrollment. In the University of the Philippines' College of Nursing, professors fought to maintain an enrollment of fewer than 150 students, despite pressure from administrators to increase the number of enrollees. One professor I spoke with argued that expanding the student body would only compromise the quality of classroom teaching (Ortiga 2018a).

7. The first nursing schools were established by the American colonial government in the early 1900s (Choy 2003: 31). Nurses are also well organized in mobilizing for their interests. To date, there are at least three nongovernment organizations that represent the profession's interest, namely, the Philippine Nursing Association, Filipino Nurses United, and Ang NARS. Despite this, nurses remain poorly paid and overworked within the public health care system. Much of this has to do with the devaluing of care work and the assumption that Filipino nurses will eventually leave for jobs overseas (Ortiga 2018a; 2018b).

8. Nursing is known as one of the most rigorous majors in Philippine higher edu-

cation. In addition to an already packed curriculum, students must go through at least twenty-four hours of hospital duty per week (Ortiga and Rivero 2019). I have also previously written about how the pressure to be more "globally relevant" has led to an increasing number of electives for nursing students (Ortiga 2014). For this reason, nursing programs also have some of the highest tuition fees in local universities.

9. In the past, there have been similar peaks and dips in the demand for migrant nurses abroad. However, the decline in opportunities in the mid-2000s was the first to occur at a time when Philippine nursing schools had produced so many nursing graduates.

10. Nurses who worked at private hospitals in Manila shared that they earned wages as low as PHP 10,000 a month (USD 200). This amount could go even lower in smaller hospitals outside big cities. The national minimum wage at that time was at least PHP 12,000 a month.

11. I elaborate on nurses' struggles with unemployment in chapter 3. I have also discussed the experiences of unemployed nursing graduates in my previous work (see Ortiga 2018b; Ortiga and Macabasag 2020; 2021).

12. Statistics provided by CHED.

13. Hospitality workers have a wide range of incomes. Based on my interviews, professionals working in marketing, guest relations, or sales can earn an average monthly salary of up to PHP 30,000 (USD 540). Entry-level waitstaff and kitchen staff would only earn a minimum wage of PHP 15,000 (USD 270). As noted in the chapter, service workers accept the low basic salary in anticipation of receiving a higher amount from customer gratuities and tips.

14. Filipino migrants are also highly represented in the seafaring industry. Roderick Galam (2018; 2019) has studied workers onboard international cargo ships.

15. There is extensive literature on how the exodus of health care workers affects countries such as Uganda, Kenya, and Nigeria (see Yeates and Pillinger 2019).

Chapter 2

1. The actual number of nurses impacted by the ban has varied, and government officials never released official statistics. A petition from stranded nurses had close to 1,000 signatures, while the advocacy group Filipino Nurses United counted roughly 600 nurses whose departures were deferred. However, these numbers may only include nurses who already had work visas and had finalized their travel plans. Constraints on nurse deployment also affected many more aspiring migrants who were in the process of applying for jobs overseas.

2. Rhacel Parreñas (2021b) had criticized the tendency to depict migration management as merely the disciplining of people into compliant and productive workers. She describes this approach as advancing a Marxist analysis of the state as exploiting labor to maximize the surplus gained from workers. She highlights how other forms of governance achieve goals beyond economic remittances.

3. The Migrant Workers and Overseas Filipinos Act of 1995 actually allows the Philippine government to "terminate or impose a ban on the deployment of migrant workers" on the condition that it serves national interests to do so (Romero 2020). The coun-

try's Bureau of Immigration is also notorious for its "offloading" practices—a colloquial term for preventing Filipinos from leaving the country if they were suspected victims of human trafficking. Hwang (2017: 132) defines the act of offloading as preventing "suspected victims of human trafficking, illegal recruitment, and undocumented workers from leaving the country."

4. At this time, the Philippines had bilateral agreements with Japan, Canada, Germany, and the United Kingdom.

5. In my first book, I argued that Philippine colleges and universities had sought to offer a variety of postsecondary degrees associated with overseas opportunities—from marine transportation to caregiving and hospitality management (Ortiga 2018a). However, nursing degrees were especially popular due to the demand in desirable destinations such as the United States and the United Kingdom. In 2006, the number of nursing schools in the country had expanded to 470 from only 40 schools in the 1980s (Masselink and Lee 2010). I also discuss these trends in chapter 1.

6. Exequiel Cabanda (2017b) provides an in-depth analysis of the development of the Philippine Nursing Act of 2002.

7. Eventually, the Philippine Nursing Act of 2002 did mandate a salary increase for entry-level nurses in government hospitals to receive a monthly salary of PHP 30,531 (approximately USD 560). However, this provision was challenged multiple times in both the country's courts and the Philippine Congress. In 2019, nursing groups scored a victory by having the Philippine Supreme Court uphold the salary increase as mandated by the law (Pulta 2019). However, ensuring that hospitals are implementing this mandate properly has become another problem—one that has become more difficult due to the pandemic (Cabico 2022). It is also important to note that the Philippine Nursing Act of 2002 does not include nurses working in private hospitals.

8. In an informal survey conducted in 2006, a significant number of nurses expressed an intention to stay in the Philippines if their salaries were raised to a minimum of PHP 30,000 a month. At this time, people were skeptical that such a change would happen. As one journalist wrote, "Easier said than done. At current rates, even nursing directors don't earn close to that amount" (Cueto 2006).

9. I discuss the factors behind this decline in the introduction to this book. I also document how nurses had grappled with this decline in my previous publications (Ortiga 2018b; Ortiga and Macabasag 2021).

10. Most Filipino nursing graduates aspire to work in tertiary hospitals after obtaining their license, mainly because they see these jobs as the types of work they had trained for as nursing students. However, clinical experience is also important for aspiring nurse migrants. Most destination countries, such as the United States, require at least two years of work experience in a tertiary hospital (see Ortiga and Macabasag 2021). I discuss this in more detail in chapter 4.

11. In 2012, the exchange rate was USD 1 = PHP 44.

12. I describe the state's attempt to channel nurses to other industries as a strategy of pushing them "sideways" toward alternative careers. Given that nursing graduates had invested so much time and money in their professional training, aspiring migrants could

not be pushed "downward" to low-wage jobs, such as caregiving or domestic work. Encouraging them to pursue other health-related careers within the Philippines served as the state's bid to appease unemployed nursing graduates and make use of their labor (Ortiga 2021).

13. There is a burgeoning scholarship on how the Philippines had marketed a specific brand of care that is both racialized and gendered (see Parreñas 2015; Guevarra 2010).

14. In a strange parallel to the case of stranded nurses, the outmigration of pilots and mechanics also prompted a local congressman, Roseller Barinaga, to call on administration officials to protect the domestic aviation industry. Congressman Barinaga claimed that the exodus of these workers would have "serious national security implications and economic repercussions as they affect air transportation, tourism, commerce, construction, and chains of economic linkages in the country" (*Manila Standard* 2006).

15. It is interesting to note that this logic of "dwindling supply" was also apparent in the discourse surrounding essential commodities, such as masks and medicines. In March 2020, former US president Donald Trump called on companies such as 3M to stop exporting their N95 masks overseas and divert production for American needs (Swanson, Kanno-Youngs, and Haberman 2020). The parallels in how Filipino officials talked about nurses show that they continued to regard nurses mainly as commodities, albeit ones that now needed to be redirected to local hospitals.

16. Since 2006, the POEA had issued similar directives targeted at assembly technicians and computer machinists (POEA 2012; 2013). Workers listed as having such skills were required to provide Filipino employers with at least six months' notice before leaving their companies for overseas work. Outgoing workers had to provide a certificate proving this before leaving the country. However, none of these previous efforts to stem the migration of mission-critical skills involved an outright ban on their deployment.

17. This quotation is from a recorded excerpt of a Zoom meeting between nurses and DOLE officials. A portion of this recording is featured in the documentary "Nurses Wanted: Philippines," https://www.youtube.com/watch?v=3F1qTKPeft4.

18. This quotation was taken from a personal communication with Mr. Ricardo Casco.

19. There were many missteps before administration officials were able to develop an urgent hiring scheme that could attract health workers to COVID-19 treatment centers. Initially, the DOH actually sought to augment hospital manpower by calling for volunteers ("health care heroes"). This move was immediately met with anger and disbelief. Social media users flooded the department's Facebook page with accusations that the Philippine government was exploiting health workers, with nurses being the most vocal in their displeasure. In response, the DOH offered to pay health workers an allowance of PHP 500 per day (USD 10), along with free food and accommodation for one month (Magsambol 2020). Still, advocacy groups protested that the allowance was below the Philippine daily minimum wage. As one health activist drily noted, "Altruism has no price. But if you put a tag on it, make sure it is not insulting" (Sabillo 2020). The DOH then quickly retracted the policy and was forced to request emergency funds to hire nurses at higher salaries. This series of events reveals how the pandemic itself did not really shift how the state viewed the value of nurses. It was public pressure from individ-

ual citizens, nursing groups, and allied politicians that led to the state's sudden change of heart.

20. Up until 2019, Filipino nurses in the Philippines earned between PHP 8,000 and PHP 13,500 per month (USD 158 to USD 267), making them the lowest paid in Southeast Asia (Jazul 2020). In contrast, those who entered the state's urgent hiring scheme would receive PHP 33,000 (USD 650) every month.

21. It is interesting to note that the image of "the migrant" has long been used to rationalize policies that call either for better treatment or for more stringent policing of people moving across borders (Allen et al. 2018; Brigden and Mainwaring 2016). However, existing studies have been concentrated on the experiences of migrant-receiving countries, where state officials are mainly concerned with restricting entry into their territories. In the Philippine case, government officials had the opposite problem: they needed to justify keeping their own citizens in the country after previously encouraging them to work overseas. In this sense, legitimizing the deployment ban meant creating a convincing image of the aspiring migrant whose immobility would be seen as essential and reasonable.

22. Before the pandemic, OECs were only issued to outgoing nurses a week before their departure.

23. A recording of this webinar can be found on YouTube: https://www.youtube.com/watch?v=lrFUj-D8pWY.

Chapter 3

1. Chapter 2 in this book provides an extensive background and analysis of the Philippines' ban on the deployment of health workers.

2. Recent work on people's aspirations to stay have sought to move beyond the rational calculation of monetary costs and benefits. Specifically, scholars have highlighted motivations such as the need to care for family, the desire to contribute to one's community, and the comfort of being in a familiar place. Chand Somaiah and her colleagues (2020) have advocated for using these alternative lenses in assessing would-be migrants' views of their own immobility.

3. My previous research has been largely focused on documenting the struggles of nurses who were unable to leave after the downturn of overseas opportunities in the mid-2000s (see Ortiga 2018b; 2020; Ortiga and Macabasag 2021).

4. Chapter 2 provides an in-depth discussion of how the popularity of nursing as a step toward overseas jobs eventually led to an oversupply of nursing graduates that hospital administrators were quick to exploit.

5. Out of the fifty-five nurses we interviewed, fifty-two were actively working toward leaving the Philippines. However, we acknowledge that there are also those who did decide to remain in place. In previous work, I have discussed how perspectives of time can lead some nurses to forgo their original migration aspirations. For these nurses, migration itself comes to be seen as only a short-term benefit, given that most migrant contracts only last for a few years (see Ortiga and Macabasag 2020). Still, Megha Amrith (2021) would argue that the decision to stay is not set in stone, either. Nurses can restart their migration

plans when life plans change and opportunities for overseas jobs become more available.

6. It was interesting to note that nurses who worried about expiring skill were bound for a wide range of destination countries. Nurses bound for the United Kingdom were the obvious majority. However, I also interviewed nurses who were headed to Kuwait, New Zealand, Qatar, Singapore, and the United States. In many ways, these nurses' concerns about certificates and tests reveal how the profession is highly controlled and how nurses who wish to emigrate must provide proof of their competency and abilities.

Chapter 4

1. By the time all *Diamond Princess* passengers and crew had disembarked from the ship, health officials recorded 712 infections and 8 deaths (Sim 2020b; Westbrook 2020).

2. Before news of the *Diamond Princess* reached the Philippines, the country's foreign affairs agency had already sent teams to repatriate Filipino workers who were stranded in cities in China. Karen Liao (2020) provides a detailed outline of these efforts during the first few months of 2020.

3. In early February, Genting Cruise Lines' *World Dream* ship had to disembark all 3,600 passengers in Hong Kong after three passengers who had sailed on a previous voyage were later found to have contracted the virus (BBC 2020). Unfortunately, fears of further infection affected other ships as well. As stories of the *Diamond Princess* circulated in the news, port officials began to prevent all cruise ships from docking on their shores. One ship, Holland America's MS *Westerdam*, skipped port calls in Hong Kong, Japan, and Guam despite having no known cases of the virus and no passengers in quarantine (Witsil 2020).

4. Soon after the US Centers for Disease Control and Prevention (CDC) declared its "no sail" order, the Cruise Lines International Association (CLIA) announced that it would be "voluntarily and temporarily suspending cruise ship operations from the US" (CLIA 2020).

5. Secretary Locsin's bold pledge to care for all overseas Filipinos reflects a common discourse among modern migrant-sending states. Recognizing the benefits brought by both monetary and social remittances, more nations have claimed responsibility over citizens working abroad, despite these migrants' absence at home (Fitzgerald 2012; Ho 2011).

6. It is important to note that India, another large migrant-sending nation, also allocated millions of dollars to migrant reintegration programs. However, state initiatives were criticized for poor implementation and not enough support given to international migrants (compared with internal migrants) (Khan and Arrokiaraj 2022).

7. OWWA was later attached to the Department of Migrant Workers (DMW), a new department established by the Duterte administration. Former OWWA administrator Hans Cacdac became the new DMW secretary in 2024.

8. International policymakers have long praised the Philippines as a model for how migrant-sending nations must not only deploy workers but also ensure their successful return (Liao 2020). However, evidence of successful reintegration remains quite limited despite the presence of several government agencies, such as the OWWA.

9. One benefit of the pandemic's restrictions on large gatherings was that all meetings

at the Philippine Congress were recorded and uploaded on YouTube. This is the link to the webinar I cite: https://www.youtube.com/watch?v=SEt1uIZrxrs.

10. I cite newspaper accounts of this meeting, but I also took notes after watching the entire hearing myself. The recording is available online: https://www.youtube.com/watch?v=uAI6kHjxgVI.

11. Cacdac had spoken about these two strategies before (Aquino 2020c; Torregoza 2020b). These were the same two approaches that defined his agency's approach to all Filipino migrants who returned to the country. For the first half of 2020, OWWA initiatives focused mainly on disbursing cash for emergency needs. Filipino workers who lost their jobs overseas were eligible for immediate aid, the most popular being a one-time payment of PHP 10,000 to tide them over the crisis (Damicog 2020; *Manila Bulletin* 2020).

12. The International Organization for Migration (IOM) deemed the 10.3% unemployment rate one of the worst in recent years. In comparison, the joblessness rate was only 5.1% in 2019.

13. Small-business grants were disbursed by a wide range of Philippine government agencies. The OWWA was the best known among migrant workers. However, other agencies, such as the Department of Trade and Industry, also offered larger grants for migrant associations and their families.

14. This survey was conducted by the National Reintegration Center for OFWs, a unit under DOLE. According to the same survey, the top businesses for former migrants are sari-sari stores (neighborhood sundry stores), *bigasan* (rice depots), water-refilling stations, eateries or *carinderias*, meat processing, and farming and livestock raising (https://www.rappler.com/brandrap/announcements/coca-cola-philippines-ofw-rise-program/).

15. The recording of this Senate hearing is available online: https://www.youtube.com/watch?v=SEt1uIZrxrs.

16. In the pandemic's first year, Filipinos entering the country from abroad were required to isolate themselves in a local hotel in order to stem the spread of the coronavirus. Given the large number of returnees, quarantine periods often dragged on for weeks, worsening the incidence of anxiety and depression.

17. The recording of the interview is available online: https://www.youtube.com/watch?v=qLIzRVJHFe8.

18. Milk tea is a specialty drink made from milk, tea, and sweet toppings such as tapioca, aloe vera, and pudding. It is especially popular in Asia and has become a booming business in the Philippines.

19. Lazada and Shopee are popular online shopping platforms in Asia.

20. The video is available online: https://www.youtube.com/watch?v=89vdGUGvvCg.

21. BPO companies offer a wide range of services, from data entry to medical transcription. However, the highest paid accounts were often those that involved voice calls. These call centers had proliferated in the Philippines beginning in the early 2000s and remain one of the largest contributors to the national economy. According to Sallaz (2019: 20), call center revenues had surpassed migrant remittances as "the largest source of foreign exchange flowing into the country."

22. There is considerable variety in what call center agencies require of their appli-

cants. However, a relevant college major was definitely not a barrier to entry. In the mid-2000s, call centers were one of the largest employers of unemployed nursing graduates who were unable to work in local hospitals. Jan Padios (2018) discusses this contradiction in her book.

23. At first, companies insisted that call center agents return to the office as "essential workers." Some of my interviewees were told that management did not trust employees (especially newly hired ones) to be able to work from home. Given that many of my interviewees lived far from the business districts where these companies were located, they did not bother trying to apply for these jobs. However, as the pandemic became more serious, call center companies eventually allowed workers to work from home.

24. While I cite newspaper reports on this particular webinar, I supplement these accounts with notes from watching the actual event. Organizers uploaded the webinar for public viewing at https://www.youtube.com/watch?v=JT30qLls4FI.

Chapter 5

1. Scholars such as Kuschminder (2017) argue that successful reintegration also entails having migrants' cultural and social identities accepted in the country of origin. The assumption is that migrants change as they spend longer periods away from home and may feel out of place when they return to their communities (see also Fitzgerald 2009). Yet, as I argue in this chapter, cultural differences were not a big barrier to cruise workers' reintegration. Few of the cruise workers I interviewed saw themselves as working on the ship forever. Their frequent visits home also kept them well connected to their families and communities in the Philippines.

2. The POEA differentiated "sea-based" jobs on ocean vessels and cruise ships from other "land-based" work found within a specific country's territory. Most land-based jobs in domestic work, retail, or factory work require at least a two-year contract. These workers are usually only able to return home for vacation after they complete their contracts.

3. The Maritime Labour Convention states that all employment contracts for seafarers must not exceed twelve months (ILO 2006). Several of our older interviewees recalled serving ten-month contracts in the 1990s. However, in recent years, cruise companies have shortened crew employment contracts to four to eight months.

4. Cruise workers shared that they prioritized spending time with family and friends during their time at home. Several also used the time between contracts to earn extra money by taking on side jobs. Before the pandemic, there were plenty of part-time positions available in local hotels and restaurants. While few of these jobs paid well, there were always opportunities for people looking for work.

5. Severe acute respiratory syndrome (SARS) became a serious outbreak between 2003 and 2004. Meanwhile, H1N1 or swine flu was also raised as a possible problem in 2009. As my interviewees note, none of these previous diseases had come close to shutting down the global cruise industry.

6. Some of the cruise workers I interviewed mentioned receiving aid from their cruise companies immediately after they were repatriated home. The amount varied between

USD 100 and USD 200. Not all companies offered such aid to their employees.

7. Chapter 4 provides a more detailed discussion of what BPO companies are and what services they provide in the Philippines (see also Fabros 2016; Padios 2018; Sallaz 2019).

8. Out of the forty-five cruise workers, twenty-nine respondents had university degrees, six had two-year associate degrees, and nine were high school graduates. Only one respondent had a master's degree.

9. However, as Jan Padios (2018) noted, the industry's location in urban centers and its use of technology often relied on an image of "higher order, white-collar labor" that requires more mental acumen than other forms of service work. It was this "professional" image that made cruise workers feel inadequate and excluded.

10. Pierre Bourdieu (1990) defines "cultural capital" as the knowledge, behaviors, language, and ways of viewing the world that dominant groups in society regard as desirable and of value. As I discuss in this chapter, many of the ideal attributes of "successful" call center agents are actually largely associated with the Philippines' middle-class culture.

11. The term "front of house" is used to refer to service workers who have frequent interactions with guests within a restaurant or hotel. These positions usually involve waitstaff and front office staff. Meanwhile, "back of house" positions encompass jobs where there are minimal interactions with customers. Common examples include housekeepers, cleaning staff, and technical staff.

12. Jan Padios (2018) argues that the emphasis on mimicking anglophone accents is part of a desire for what she calls Filipino/American relatability or a performance of having familiarity and affinity with Americans and America. She argues that this relatability allows Philippine call centers to reinforce their status in the market and drive the growth of the industry. In Clariza's case, I noticed that she had a strong Filipino accent (saying "jab" instead of "job"). However, I thought that she could understand and speak the language easily.

13. Pierre Bourdieu (1990) used the concept of "misrecognition" to describe how society accords more value and importance to the knowledge, lifestyles, and behaviors of dominant classes. I use this concept in discussing the BPO industry's preferences for Filipino middle-class culture and the use of "English skills" to weed out applicants unable to embody this "professional" status. However, as Padios (2018) argues, the image of the ideal call center agent is also intertwined with the country's postcolonial history and current ties with the United States.

14. It is interesting to note that cruise line staff actually need to pass an English proficiency exam to qualify for work onboard ship. All my interviewees had passed the exam and did not consider it a particularly arduous requirement. In some sense, English-language capacities took on a different meaning within call center agencies. One assistant cook, Rogelio, recalled scoring an 89 out of 100 in his proficiency exam. Despite this, he was not confident enough to apply for call center jobs. While he can understand the language, he has trouble keeping conversations going. "It takes too long for me to think of what to say (*Kasi kailangan ko pa mag-isip*)."

15. There are important studies on racism and discrimination onboard ships (Chin 2008; Terry 2011). A number of my interviewees mentioned unpleasant interactions with

guests. However, the general sentiment was that cruise ships still offer better work conditions than remaining in the Philippines.

Conclusion

1. Critics have blamed the Philippines' long lockdowns on the inefficiency of the national government in procuring vaccines for Filipinos. Meanwhile, state agencies have mostly blamed Filipinos themselves for failing to follow protocols that called for "social distancing" and quarantine.

2. My grandmother has quite a transnational group of grandchildren as well, scattered across the United States, Australia, and the United Arab Emirates. In true Filipino fashion, everyone unable to attend sent in birthday messages, and my brother compiled them in a tribute video that we showed after dinner.

3. The work of Sarah Wolff and her coauthors also discusses how states have sought to frame people's immobility during crises like the pandemic. However, they situate their work mainly in the context of Schengen countries (Wolff, Servent, and Piquet 2020).

4. This number does not include nurses deployed through government-to-government agreements like Germany's Triple Win or the Japan-Philippines Economic Partnership Agreement.

5. This data is provided by the POEA (now renamed the Department of Migrant Workers). This number does not include nurses who were "rehired" or who had renewed their contracts with employers based overseas.

6. Officials from the Philippine Department of Health (DOH) continued to reinforce this narrative as well. In June 2022, DOH representatives called for stricter measures to stem the outmigration of nurses from the country. Undersecretary Maria Rosario Vergeire argued, "We are urging the government to act on this since it should be a whole-of-government approach. The so-called brain drain in the country needs to be addressed by the government, because we need our health care workers to stay here in the country to help our health care system" (Pinlac 2022).

7. Even before the pandemic, the Philippine state had worked to establish bilateral ties with major receiving nations, such as Kuwait, Canada, and Japan. Exequiel Cabanda (2020) provides a thorough analysis of the work behind such agreements.

8. Despite President Marcos Jr.'s assurances, nursing groups continued to complain about the slow disbursement of COVID-19 benefits, such as hazard pay (Manahan 2023).

9. Within migration studies, ideas of "skill" have long been a central part of the broader narratives that revolve around emigration. In these stories, skill is what drives people's ability to move, as well as their treatment within destination countries (Iskander 2021; Liu-Farrer, Yeoh, and Baas 2020). In the Philippine case, skills were the resources that educators and labor officials needed to produce, enhance, and promote to a global market for migrant workers (Guevarra 2010; Ortiga 2018a; Rodriguez 2010; Tyner 2004).

References

Aben, Elie. 2020. "Philippines Imposes Total Ban on Sending Workers to Kuwait." Arab News, January 16. Retrieved on July 7, 2023, from https://www.arabnews.com/node/1614086/world.

Acacio, Kristel Ann S. 2008. "Managing Labor Migration: Philippine State Policy and International Migration Flows, 1969–2000." *Asia and Pacific Migration Journal* 17(2): 103–132.

Acacio, Kristel Ann S. 2011. "Getting Nurses Here: Migration Industry and the Business of Connecting Philippine-Educated Nurses with United States Employers." PhD diss., University of California, Berkeley.

Aguilar, Filomeno V. 2009. *Maalwang Buhay: Family, Overseas Migration, and Cultures of Relatedness in Barangay Paraiso.* Philippines: Ateneo de Manila University Press.

Albayrak-Aydemir, Nihan. 2020. "The Hidden Costs of Being a Scholar from the Global South." *LSE Higher Education Blog*, February 20. Retrieved from: https://blogs.lse.ac.uk/highereducation/2020/02/20/the-hidden-costs-of-being-a-scholar-from-the-global-south.

Ali, Syed. 2007. "'Go West Young Man': The Culture of Migration among Muslims in Hyderabad, India." *Journal of Ethnic and Migration Studies* 33(1): 37–58.

Allen, William, Bridget Anderson, Nicholas Van Hear, Madeleine Sumption, Franck Düvell, Jennifer Hough, Lena Rose, Rachel Humphris, and Sarah Walker. 2018. "Who Counts in Crises? The New Geopolitics of International Migration and Refugee Governance." *Geopolitics* 23(1): 217–243.

Altbach, Philip G. 1989. "Twisted Roots: The Western Impact on Asian Higher Education." *Higher Education* 18(1): 9–29.

Amrith, Megha. 2017. *Caring for Strangers: Filipino Medical Workers in Asia*. Copenhagen: NIAS Press.

Amrith, Megha. 2021. "The Linear Imagination, Stalled: Changing Temporal Horizons in Migrant Journeys." *Global Networks* 21(1): 127–45.

Aning, Jerome. 2006a. "Palace Asks Hospitals to Consider '06 Nurses." *Philippine Daily Inquirer*, August 30.

Aning, Jerome. 2006b. "POEA Restricts Deployment of Pilots Overseas." *Philippine Daily Inquirer*, April 19.

Aquino, Leslie Ann. 2020a. "136,000 OFWs Transported to Home Provinces." *Manila Bulletin*, August 13.

Aquino, Leslie Ann. 2020b. "Bello Turns Down Lifting of Health Workers' Deployment Ban." *Manila Bulletin*, September 17.

Aquino, Leslie, Hannah Torregoza, and Genalyn Kabiling. 2020. "POEA Recommends Deployment of Healthcare Workers with Completed Contracts." *Manila Bulletin*, September 11.

Arowolo, Oladele O. 2000. "Return Migration and the Problem of Reintegration." *International Migration* 38(5): 59–82.

Associated Press. 2022. "Traffic Jams Back in Philippine Capital As Officials Ease Pandemic Restrictions." *NBC News*, March 1. Retrieved from https://www.nbcnews.com/news/world/philippines-lifts-pandemic-restrictions-rcna18073.

Attewell, Paul. 1990. "What Is Skill?" *Work and Occupations* 17(4): 422–488.

Avendano, Christine O. 2017. "Duterte Bares Creation of OFW Department." *Inquirer.net*, April 16.

Bagaoisan, Andrew Jonathan, and Mark Angelo Ching. 2009. "Defying CHED Rules, Substandard Nursing Schools Churn Out Graduates." *GMA News*, July 16.

Bakewell, Oliver. 2008. "'Keeping Them in Their Place': The Ambivalent Relationship between Development and Migration in Africa." *Third World Quarterly* 29(7): 1341–1358.

Bandini, Julia I., Julia Rollison, and Jason Etchegaray. 2023. "Journaling among Home Care Workers during the COVID-19 Pandemic: A Promising Method for Qualitative Data Collection." *Qualitative Social Work* 22(2): 340–356.

Banta, Vanessa L. 2023. "Unsettling Migrant Reintegration: The Serial Risk-Taking of Returning Overseas Filipino Workers (OFWs) to Cordillera, Philippines." *Antipode* 55(1): 27–48.

Banta, Vanessa L., and Geraldine Pratt. 2021. "Surplused in Dubai: Filipino Professionals as Surplus Entrepreneurs." *Geoforum* 126: 471–82.

Batistella, Graziano, and Maruja B. Asis. 2013. *Country Migration Report: Philippines*. Makati City, Philippines: Scalibrini Migration Center and the International Organization for Migration.

Bélanger, Danièle, and Rachel Silvey. 2020. "An Im/Mobility Turn: Power Geometries of Care and Migration." *Journal of Ethnic and Migration Studies* 46(16): 3423–3440.

Bissell, David. 2007. "Animating Suspension: Waiting for Mobilities." *Mobilities* 2(2): 277–298.

Boccagni, Paolo. 2011. "From Rapport to Collaboration . . . and Beyond? Revisiting Field Relationships in an Ethnography of Ecuadorian Migrants." *Qualitative Research* 11(6): 736–754.

Bourdieu, Pierre, 1990. *The Logic of Practice*. Cambridge, UK: Polity Press.

Brigden, Noelle, and Ċetta Mainwaring. 2016. "Matryoshka Journeys: Im/mobility during Migration." *Geopolitics* 21(2): 407–434.

British Broadcasting Corporation [BBC]. 2020. "Coronavirus: Thousands on Cruise Ship Allowed to Disembark after Tests." February 2.

Brock, Gillian, and Michael Blake. 2015. *Debating Brain Drain: May Governments Restrict Emigration?* Oxford, UK: Oxford University Press.

Buchan, James, Fiona O'May, and Gilles Dussault. 2013. "Nursing Workforce Policy and the Economic Crisis: A Global Overview: Nursing and the Economic Crisis." *Journal of Nursing Scholarship* 45(3): 298–307.

Business Mirror. 2020a. "IATF Backs Lifting of Deployment Ban on Health Staff with Contracts." April 14.

Business Mirror. 2020b. "Ople Center Warns of Rise in Trafficking as Pandemic Cuts Jobs." December 15.

Cabanda, Exequiel. 2017a. "Identifying the Role of the Sending State in the Emigration of Health Professionals: A Review of the Empirical Literature." *Migration and Development* 6(2): 215–231.

Cabanda, Exequiel. 2017b. "Higher Education, Migration and Policy Design of the Philippine Nursing Act of 2002." *Higher Education Policy* 30(4): 555–575.

Cabanda, Exequiel. 2020. "'We Want Your Nurses!' Negotiating Labor Agreements in Recruiting Filipino Nurses." *Asian Politics and Policy* 12(3): 404–431.

Cabico, Gaea Katreena. 2022. "Higher Pay, Regularization Needed to Address Exodus of Nurses." *Philippine Star*, June 21.

Cabreza, Vincent, and Leila Salaverria. 2007. "Nurses Retake Exams, Seek Leakage Closure." *Philippine Daily Inquirer*, June 11.

Cahiles-Magkilat, Bernie. 2020. "Coke PH Expands Balik Pinas Program for Repatriated OFWs." *Manila Bulletin*, October 26.

Cairns, David, and Mara Clemente. 2023. *The Immobility Turn: Mobility, Migration and the COVID-19 Pandemic*. Bristol, UK: Bristol University Press.

Canlas, Jomar. 2020. "Govt to Release P5B for OFW Repatriation." *Manila Times*, August 10.

Carling, Jørgen. 2002. "Migration in the Age of Involuntary Immobility: Theoretical Reflections and Cape Verdean Experiences." *Journal of Ethnic and Migration Studies* 28(1): 5–42.

Carling, Jørgen, and Kerilyn Schewel. 2018. "Revisiting Aspiration and Ability in International Migration." *Journal of Ethnic and Migration Studies* 44(6): 945–963.

Carr, Austin. 2020. "The Cruise Ship Suicides." *Bloomberg,* 30 December. https://www.bloomberg.com/features/2020-cruise-ship-suicides/.

Casey, Ruairi. 2020. "Cruise Industry in Choppy Seas As Coronavirus Fears Swell." *Al Jazeera*, March 13.

Cassarino, Jean-Pierre. 2004. "Theorising Return Migration: The Conceptual Approach to Return Migrants Revisited." *International Journal on Multicultural Studies* 6(2): 253–279.

Cassarino, Jean-Pierre. 2014. "A Case for Return Preparedness." In Graziano Battistella, ed., *Global and Asian Perspectives on International Migration*, 153–165. Cham, Switzerland: Springer.

Centers for Disease Control and Prevention [CDC]. 2020. *No Sail Order and Other Measures Related to Operations.* Washington, DC: US Department of Health and Human Services.

Cerojano, Teresa. 2006. "17 Charged in Philippine Nursing Exam Cheating Scandal." *Associated Press*, October 12.

Chan, Carol. 2017. "In Between Leaving and Being Left Behind: Mediating the Mobilities and Immobilities of Indonesian Non-Migrants." *Global Networks* 17(4): 554–573.

Channel News Asia [CNA]. 2012. "More Filipinos Taking Up Hotel and Restaurant Management Courses." November 30.

Chin, Christine B. N. 2008. "Labor Flexibilization at Sea." *International Feminist Journal of Politics* 10(1): 1–18.

Choy, Catherine Ceniza. 2003. *Empire of Care: Nursing and Migration in Filipino American History.* Durham, NC: Duke University Press.

Chu, Julie Y. 2010. *Cosmologies of Credit: Transnational Mobility and the Politics of Destination in China.* Durham, NC: Duke University Press.

CNN Philippines. 2020a. "Philippines OKs Total Deployment Ban of Workers to Kuwait." January 15.

CNN Philippines. 2020b. "Hospitals Close Doors to COVID-19 Patients after Reaching Capacity." March 24.

CNN Philippines. 2020c. "Restaurants Look for Different Business Model As Country Shifts To 'New Normal.'" May 12.

CNN Philippines. 2020d. "Locsin Pushes IATF to Lift Deployment Ban on Nurses or 'Pay Big Money.'" August 28.

Cohen, Jeffrey H. 2004. *The Culture of Migration in Southern Mexico.* Austin: University of Texas Press.

Colcol, Erwin. 2020. "DOLE Urged to Stop Sending Nurses Abroad amid Effort vs COVID-19." *GMA News Online*, March 30.

Collins, Francis L. 2021. "'Give Me My Pathway!' Multinational Migration, Transnational Skills Regimes and Migrant Subjectification." *Global Networks* 21(1): 18–39.

Commission on Higher Education [CHED]. 2020. Higher Education and Data Indicators. Manila, Philippines. https://ched.gov.ph/wp-content/uploads/Higher-Education-Data-and-Indicators-AY-2009-10-to-AY-2019-20.pdf.

Conlon, Deirdre. 2011. "Waiting: Feminist Perspectives on the Spacings/Timings of Migrant (Im)mobility." *Gender, Place & Culture* 18(3): 353–360.

Cook-Martin, David. 2013. *The Scramble for Citizens: Dual Nationality and State Competition for Immigrants.* Stanford: Stanford University Press.

Corrales, Nestor. 2017. "Working Abroad Will Soon Just Be an Option, Duterte Tells OFWs." *Philippine Daily Inquirer*, March 23.

Cortes, Patricia, and Jessica Pan. 2015. "The Relative Quality of Foreign Nurses in the United States." *Journal of Human Resources* 50(4): 1009–1050.

Courtois, Aline, and Marie Sautier. 2022. "Academic Brexodus? Brexit and the Dynamics of Mobility and Immobility among the Precarious Research Workforce." *British Journal of Sociology of Education* 43(4): 639–657.

Cox, Caitriona L. "'Healthcare Heroes': Problems with Media Focus on Heroism from Healthcare Workers during the COVID-19 Pandemic." *Journal of Medical Ethics* 46(8): 510–513.

Cresswell, Tim. 2010. "Towards a Politics of Mobility." *Environment and Planning D: Society and Space* 28(1): 17–31.

Cresswell, Tim. 2012. "Mobilities II: Still." *Progress in Human Geography* 36(2): 645–653.

Cresswell, Tim. 2014. "Friction." In Peter Adey, David Bissell, Kevin Hannam, Peter Merriman, and Mimi Sheller, eds., *Routledge Handbook of Mobilities*, 107–115. London: Routledge.

Crismundo, Kris M. 2014. "Tourism Industry Pays Highest Entry Level Salary." *Philippines News Agency*, April 7.

Crisostomo, Sheila. 2012. "Aspiring Nurses Urged to Explore Other Fields." *Philippine Star*, March 4.

Crisostomo, Sheila. 2020. "Only 25 Nurses Applied for DOH Emergency Hiring Program." *Philippine Star*, August 22.

Cruise Lines International Association [CLIA]. 2020. "Cruise Lines International Association (CLIA) Announces Voluntary Suspension in U.S. Cruise Operations." https://www.prnewswire.com/news-releases/cruise-lines-international-association-clia-announces-voluntary-suspension-in-us-cruise-operations-301023348.html.

Cueto, Francis. 2006. "Exodus of Nurses Still Triggers Touchy Debate." *Manila Times*, August 7.

Cuttitta, Paolo. 2018. "Repoliticization through Search and Rescue? Humanitarian NGOs and Migration Management in the Central Mediterranean." *Geopolitics* 23(3): 632–660.

Damicog, Jeffrey. 2020. "Nurses Appeal Lifting of Deployment Ban." *Manila Bulletin*, August 21.

D'Appollonia, Ariane Chebel. 2012. *Frontiers of Fear: Immigration and Insecurity in the United States and Europe*. Ithaca, NY: Cornell University Press.

Deakin, Hannah, and Kelly Wakefield. 2014. "Skype Interviewing: Reflections of Two PhD Researchers." *Qualitative Research* 14(5): 603–616.

de Haas, Hein. 2005. "International Migration, Remittances and Development: Myths and Facts." *Third World Quarterly* 26(8): 1269–1284.

Depasupil, William. 2020. "500K Medical Workers Jobless." *Manila Times*, August 30.

Department of Foreign Affairs, Philippines [DFA]. 2020. "DFA Repatriates 327,511 Overseas Filipinos in 2020." https://dfa.gov.ph/dfa-news/dfa-releasesupdate/28480-dfa-repatriates-%20327-511-overseas-!lipinos-in-2020.

Department of Labor and Employment, Philippines [DOLE]. 1995. *Annual Report*. Manila, Philippines.

Department of Labor and Employment, Philippines [DOLE]. 2003. *Annual Report.* Manila, Philippines.

Depasupil, William, and Darwin Pesco. 2020. "Displaced OFWs Assured of Govt Aid." *Manila Times*, October 3.

Deshingkar, Priya. 2022. "Navigating Hyper-Precarity: Im(mobilities) during the COVID Pandemic in India." *Social Change* 52(2): 175–186.

de Silva, Menusha, and Kanchan Gandhi. 2019. "'Daughter' As a Positionality and the Gendered Politics of Taking Parents into the Field." *Area* 51(4): 662–669.

de Villa, Kathleen. 2023. "Gov't Still Owes 20,000 Healthcare Workers P1.94 billion in Backpay." *Philippine Daily Inquirer,* April 23.

Dill, Bonnie T., and Ruth E. Zambrana, eds. 2009. *Emerging Intersections: Race, Class, and Gender in Theory, Policy, and Practice.* Piscataway, NJ: Rutgers University Press.

Dulay, Dean, Janica Magat, and Mateo V. Chaparro. 2021. "Precarity and Preferences for Redistribution in Weak States: Evidence from the Philippines." Unpublished paper.

Eckstein, Susan, and Giovanni Peri. 2018. "Immigrant Niches and Immigrant Networks in the U.S. Labor Market." *RSF: The Russell Sage Foundation Journal of the Social Sciences* 4(1): 1.

Elemia, Camille. 2020. "Germany to Fly in Filipino Nurses to Care for Their Coronavirus Patients—Report." *Rappler*, March 21. https://amp.rappler.com/nation/255388 -germany-hesse-filipino-nurses-coronavirus-patients-covid-19.

Encinas-Franco, Jean. 2013. "The Language of Labor Export in Political Discourse: 'Modern-day Heroism' and the Constructions of Overseas Filipino Workers." *Philippine Political Science Journal* 34(1): 97–112.

Encinas-Franco, Jean. 2016. "Filipino Women Migrant Workers and Overseas Employment Policy: An Analysis from Women's Rights Perspective: Praxis: A Review of Policy Practice." *Asian Politics & Policy* 8(3): 494–501.

Encinas-Franco, Jean. 2023. "Dreams Interrupted: Migrant Filipino Nurses, Gendered Nationalism and Ontological (In)Security during the COVID-19 Pandemic" In Radha Adhikari and Evgeniya Plotnikova, eds., *Nurse Migration in Asia: Emerging Patterns and Policy Responses*, 115–134. London: Routledge.

Estuye, Josine. 2013. "Clinical Experience in PH Could Open Doors." *Philippine News Agency,* August 30.

Fabros, Alinaya. 2016. *Outsourceable Selves: An Ethnography of Call Center Work in a Global Economy of Signs and Selves.* Manila: Ateneo de Manila University Press.

Fitzgerald, David. 2009. *A Nation of Emigrants: How Mexico Manages Its Migration.* Berkeley: University of California Press.

Fitzgerald, David. 2012. "Citizenship à la Carte: Emigration and the Strengthening of the Sovereign State." In Peter Mandaville and Terrence Lyons, eds., *Politics from Afar: Transnational Diasporas and Networks.* New York: Columbia University Press.

Francisco-Menchavez, Valerie. 2018. *The Labor of Care: Filipina Migrants and Transnational Families in the Digital Age.* Urbana: University of Illinois Press.

Galam, Roderick. 2018. "An Exercise in Futurity: Servitude As Pathway to Young Filipino Men's Education-to-Work Transition." *Journal of Youth Studies* 21(8): 1045–1060.

Galam, Roderick. 2019. "Utility Manning: Young Filipino Men, Servitude and the Moral

Economy of Becoming a Seafarer and Attaining Adulthood." *Work, Employment, and Society* 33(4): 580–595.

Galam, Roderick. 2022. "The Philippines and Seafaring Labour Export: State, Non-State and International Actors in the Assembly and Employability of Filipino Seafarers." *International Migration.* https://doi.org/10.1111/imig.13092.

Galvez, Daphne. 2023. "Marcos Orders CHED to Address Shortage of Nurses Due to Migration." *Philippine Daily Inquirer,* 29 March.

Gamlen, Alan. 2008. "The Emigration State and the Modern Geopolitical Imagination." *Political Geography* 27: 840–856.

Gamolo, Nora. 2008. "RP Nurses Seen As Prime Export Commodity." *Manila Times,* March 10.

Geddes, Andrew. 2021. *Governing Migration beyond the State: Europe, North America, South America, and Southeast Asia in a Global Context.* Oxford, UK: Oxford University Press.

Geducos, Argyll Cyrus. 2020a. "Higher Salary for Public Hospital Nurses Eyed." *Manila Bulletin,* September 4.

Geducos, Argyll Cyrus. 2020b. "Duterte Tells Filipino Health Workers: Please Stay for a While." *Manila Bulletin,* September 22.

Gillin, Nicola, and David Smith. 2020. "Overseas Recruitment Activities of NHS Trusts 2015–2018: Findings from FOI Requests to 19 Acute NHS Trusts in England. *Nursing Inquiry* 27(1): e12320.

Gita-Carlos, Ruth A. 2020. "Duterte OKs Total OFW Deployment Ban to Kuwait." *Philippine News Agency,* January 17.

Glick Schiller, Nina, and Noel B. Salazar. 2013. "Regimes of Mobility across the Globe." *Journal of Ethnic and Migration Studies* 39(2): 183–200.

Goh, Charmian, Kellynn Wee, and Brenda S. A. Yeoh. 2017. "Migration Governance and the Migration Industry in Asia: Moving Domestic Workers from Indonesia to Singapore." *International Relations of the Asia-Pacific* 17(3): 401–433.

Graviano, Nicola, Andrea Götzelmann, Nazanine Nozarian, and Anita Jawadurovna Wadud. 2017. *Towards an Integrated Approach to Reintegration in the Context of Return.* Geneva: International Organization for Migration.

Green, Nancy L., and François Weil. 2007. *Citizenship and Those Who Leave: The Politics of Emigration and Expatriation.* Urbana: University of Illinois Press.

Gregorio, Xave. 2022. "Philippines Set to Loosen Travel Restrictions to Boost Tourism." *Philippine Star,* October 25.

Guevarra, Anna Romina. 2010. *Marketing Dreams, Manufacturing Heroes: The Transnational Labor Brokering of Filipino Workers.* New Brunswick, NJ: Rutgers University Press.

Guevarra, Anna Romina. 2014. "Supermaids: The Racial Branding of Global Filipino Care Labour." In B. Anderson and I. Shutes, eds., *Migration and Care Labour.* London: Palgrave Macmillan.

Hagan, Jacqueline M., Rubén Hernández-León, and Jean-Luc Demonsant. 2015. *Skills of the "Unskilled": Work and Mobility among Mexican Migrants.* Berkeley: University of California Press.

Hagan, Jacqueline M., and Joshua T. Wassink. 2020. "Return Migration around the World: An Integrated Agenda for Future Research." *Annual Review of Sociology* 46: 533–552.

Hage, Ghassan. 2009. *Waiting*. Melbourne, Australia: Melbourne University Press.

Hannam, Kevin, Mimi Sheller, and John Urry. 2006. "Editorial: Mobilities, Immobilities and Moorings." *Mobilities* 1(1): 1–22.

Harkison, Tracy, Jill Poulston, and Jung-Hee Ginny Kim. 2011. "Hospitality Graduates and Managers: The Big Divide." *International Journal of Contemporary Hospitality Management* 23(3): 377–392.

Harris, Sophia. 2020. "'This Has Been a Nightmare': Canadian Passengers on Virus-stricken Cruise Finally Headed for Home." *CBC News*, April 2.

Harvey, William S. 2008. "Brain Circulation?" *Asian Population Studies* 4(3): 293–309.

Hiemstra, Nancy. 2012. "Geopolitical Reverberations of US Migrant Detention and Deportation: The View from Ecuador." *Geopolitics* 17(2): 293–311.

Hines, Morgan. 2020. "No Cruising in US Waters until 2021 As Industry Voluntarily Extends Suspension." *USA Today*, November 3.

Ho, Elaine Lynn-Ee. 2011. "'Claiming' the Diaspora: Elite Mobility, Sending State Strategies and the Spatialities of Citizenship." *Progress in Human Geography* 35(6): 757–772.

Hoang, Lan Anh, and Juan Zhang. 2023. "Migrant Immobilities beyond the Pandemic: Changing Migration Patterns and Aspirations." *Asia and Pacific Migration Journal* 32(2).

Hollifield, James F. 2004. "The Emerging Migration State." *International Migration Review* 38(3): 885–912.

Hwang, Maria Cecilia. 2017. "Offloaded: Women's Sex Work Migration across the South China Sea and the Gendered Antitrafficking Emigration Policy of the Philippines." *WSQ: Women's Studies Quarterly* 45(1–2): 131–147.

Hyndman, Jennifer, and Wenona Giles. 2011. "Waiting for What? The Feminization of Asylum in Protracted Situations." *Gender, Place & Culture* 18(3): 361–379.

Iacono, Valeria, Paul Symonds, and David H. K. Brown. 2016. "Skype as a Tool for Qualitative Research Interviews." *Sociological Research Online* 21(2): 103–117.

International Labour Organization [ILO]. 2006. "Text and Preparatory Reports of the Maritime Labour Convention, 2006," https://www.ilo.org/global/standards/maritime-labour-convention/text/lang--en/index.htm.

International Organization for Migration [IOM]. 2021. *COVID-19 Impact Assessment on Returned Overseas Filipino Workers*.: Manila: IOM.

Irvine, Annie, Paul Drew, and Roy Sainsbury. 2013. "'Am I Not Answering Your Questions Properly?' Clarification, Adequacy and Responsiveness in Semi-Structured Telephone and Face-to-Face Interviews." *Qualitative Research* 13(1): 87–106.

Iskander, Natasha. 2011. *Creative State: Forty Years of Migration and Development Policy in Morocco and Mexico*. Ithaca, NY: Cornell University Press.

Iskander, Natasha. 2021. *Does Skill Make Us Human? Migrant Workers in 21st Century Qatar and Beyond*. Princeton: Princeton University Press.

Janeja, Manpreet, and Andreas Bandak, eds. 2018. *Ethnographies of Waiting: Doubt, Hope and Uncertainty*. London: Routledge.

Jaymalin, Mayen. 2009. "More Nurses, Teachers Will Go Abroad with Pay Hike Rejection—Recruiters." *Philippine Star*, May 25.

Jaymalin, Mayen. 2020a. "Philippines Stops Deployment Abroad of Health Workers." *Philippine Star*, April 7.

Jaymalin, Mayen. 2020b. "DOLE Rolls Out Employment Recovery Plan." *Philippine Star*, December 29.

Jazul, Noreen. 2020. "FNU Calls for Lifting of Deployment Ban of Nurses." *Manila Bulletin*, September 2.

Jenner, Brandy M., and Kit C. Myers. 2019. "Intimacy, Rapport, and Exceptional Disclosure: A Comparison of In-Person and Mediated Interview Contexts." *International Journal of Social Research Methodology* 22(2): 165–177.

Jimenez, Josephus. 2020. "Total Ban on Kuwait: Too Late, Too Little, Too Overacting?" *Philippine Star*, January 20.

Johnson, Mark, and Johan Lindquist. 2020. "Care and Control in Asian Migrations." *Ethnos* 85(2): 195–207.

Kandilige, Leander, and Geraldine Adiku. 2020. "The Quagmire of Return and Reintegration: Challenges to Multi-Stakeholder Co-ordination of Involuntary Returns." *International Migration* 58(4): 37–53.

Keen, Sam, Martha Lomeli-Rodriguez, and Helene Joffe. 2022. "From Challenge to Opportunity: Virtual Qualitative Research during COVID-19 and Beyond." *International Journal of Qualitative Methods*, https://doi.org/10.1177/16094069221105075.

Khan, Asma, and H. Arokkiaraj. 2021. "Challenges of Reverse Migration in India: A Comparative Study of Internal and International Migrant Workers in the Post-COVID Economy." *Comparative Migration Studies* 9(1): 49.

Kingma, Mireille. 2006. *Nurses on the Move: Migration and the Global Health Care Economy*. Ithaca, NY: Cornell University Press.

Kuschminder, Katie. 2017. *Reintegration Strategies: Conceptualizing How Return Migrants Reintegrate*. Cham, Switzerland: Palgrave Macmillan.

La Porta, Rafael, and Andrei Shleifer. 2014. "Informality and Development." *Journal of Economic Perspectives* 28(3): 109–126.

Lee, Suzy K. 2017. "The Three Worlds of Emigration Policy: Towards a Theory of Sending State Regimes." *Journal of Ethnic and Migration Studies* 43(9): 1453–1471.

Lee, Suzy K. 2021. "Migrating beyond Networks: The Mechanisms of Sending State Intervention." *Migration and Development* 10(3): 342–358.

Lee-Brago, Pia, and Alexis Romero. 2023. "Marcos on Nurse Exodus: We're Victims of Our Success." *Philippine Star*, July 11.

Liao, Karen Anne S. 2020. "Operation 'Bring Them Home': Learning from the Large-Scale Repatriation of Overseas Filipino Workers in Times of Crisis." *Asian Population Studies* 16(3): 310–330.

Liao, Karen Anne S. 2024. "The Grey Window of Temporary Reintegration: The Involuntary Return and Crisis-Induced Immobility of Filipino Migrant Workers." *International Migration Review*. https://doi.org/10.1177/01979183241255666.

Liao, Karen Anne, and Maruja Asis. 2020. "Back to the Philippines: Connecting Aspirations, Return and Social Remittances in International Student Migration." *Asia and Pacific Migration Journal* 29(3): 402–421.

Lim Uy, Sasha. 2020. "Through COVID-19, Top Philippine Restaurants Just Want to

Survive." *Rappler*, November 5. https://www.rappler.com/life-and-style/food-drinks/top-philippines-restaurants-just-want-survive.

Lin, Weiqiang, and Brenda S. A. Yeoh. 2021. "Pathological (Im)mobilities: Managing Risk in a Time of Pandemics." *Mobilities* 16(1): 96–112.

Lindstrom, David P., and Nathaniel Lauster. 2001. "Local Economic Opportunity and the Competing Risks of Internal and US Migration in Zacatecas Mexico." *International Migration Review* 35(4): 1232–1256.

Liu, Jiaqi, and Rui Jie Peng. 2023. "Mobility Repertoires: How Chinese Overseas Students Overcame Pandemic-Induced Immobility." *International Migration Review*. https://doi.org/10.1177/01979183231170.

Liu-Farrer, Gracia, Brenda S. Yeoh, and Michiel Baas. 2020. "Social Construction of Skill: An Analytical Approach toward the Question of Skill in Cross-Border Labour Mobilities." *Journal of Ethnic and Migration Studies* 47(10): 2237–2251.

Lorenzo, Fely Marilyn E., Jaime Galvez-Tan, Kriselle Icamina, and Lara Javier. 2007. "Nurse Migration from a Source Country Perspective: Philippine Country Case Study." *Health Services Research* 42(3p2): 1406–1418.

Loyola, James. 2017. "STI, Royal Caribbean Train Pinoys to Man Cruise Ships." *Manila Bulletin*, September 26.

Magsambol, Bonz. 2020. "DOH Asks for Volunteer Health Workers Vs Coronavirus, To Be Paid P500 a Day." *Rappler*, March 27. https://www.rappler.com/nation/volunteer-health-workers-philippines-compensation-fight-coronavirus.

Manahan, Job. 2023. "Marcos to Increase Deployment Cap of Nurses Abroad." *ABS-CBN News*, September 1.

Manila Bulletin. 2008a. "RP has 400,000 Surplus Nurses—PRC." September 1.

Manila Bulletin. 2008b. "Overseas Workers Urged to Seek Jobs in Healthcare, Education." December 22.

Manila Bulletin. 2013a. "Providing Students with the Best Career Opportunities." July 4.

Manila Bulletin. 2013b. "83 Nursing Schools Closed." March 23.

Manila Bulletin. 2014. "UAE Expo Creates Jobs for Filipinos." February 8.

Manila Bulletin. 2016. "Filipinos Make Cruising Experience a Lot Better." February 24.

Manila Bulletin. 2020. "More OFWs to Receive Cash Aid under DOLE Program for Displaced Migrant Workers." July 19.

Manila Standard. 2004. "Only a Law Can Stop Exodus of Doctors—CHED." September 22.

Manila Standard. 2006. "Pilots' Exodus Endangers Local Aviation Industry?" March 23.

Manila Times. 2004. "Malacañang Restrains CHED." November 18, A4.

Manila Times. 2007. "Nursing Schools Set to Explode with Record Enrollees—TUCP." June 13.

Manongdo, Jenny, David Cagahastian, Roy Mabasa, and Fred Roxas. 2006. "Nurses' Alliance Reiterates Stand on No Retake of Exam." *Manila Bulletin*, October 11.

Marcus, Kanchan, Gabriella Quimson, and Stephanie D. Short. 2014. "Source Country Perceptions, Experiences, and Recommendations regarding Health Workforce Migration: A Case Study from the Philippines." *Human Resources for Health* 12(1): 1–10.

Marzi, Sonja. 2021. "Participatory Video from a Distance: Co-Producing Knowledge during the COVID-19 Pandemic Using Smartphones." *Qualitative Research.* https://doi .org/10.1177/14687941211038171.

Masselink, Leah E., and Shoou-Yih Daniel Lee. 2010. "Nurses, Inc.: Expansion and Commercialization of Nursing Education in the Philippines." *Social Science & Medicine* 71(1):166–172.

Massey, Douglas, Jorge Durand, and Nolan J. Malone. 2002. *Beyond Smoke and Mirrors: Mexican Immigration in an Era of Economic Integration.* New York: Russell Sage Foundation.

Massey, Douglas, and Emilio Parrado. 1998. "International Migration and Business Formation in Mexico." *Social Science Quarterly* 79(1): 1–20.

Mata-Codesal, Diana. 2015. "Ways of Staying Put in Ecuador: Social and Embodied Experiences of Mobility–Immobility Interactions." *Journal of Ethnic and Migration Studies* 41(14): 2274–2290.

Mata-Codesal, Diana. 2017. "Gendered (Im)mobility: Rooted Women and Waiting Penelopes." *Crossings: Journal of Migration & Culture* 8(2): 151–162.

McCormick, Erin, and Patrick Greenfield. 2020. "Revealed: 100,000 Crew Never Made It Off Cruise Ships amid Coronavirus Crisis." *Guardian,* April 30.

Mercado, Neil Arwin. 2020. "DOH to Deploy 857 Healthcare Workers in Three Covid-19 Referral Hospitals." *Philippine Daily Inquirer,* April 12.

Milena, Belloni, and Georgia Cole. 2022. "The Right to Exit As National and Transnational Governance: The Case of Eritrea." *International Migration.* https://doi.org/10 .1111/imig.13078.

Ministry of Education [MEC]. 1984. *Annual Report.* Manila.

Mountz, Alison, and Nancy Hiemstra. 2014. "Chaos and Crisis: Dissecting the Spatiotemporal Logics of Contemporary Migrations and State Practices." *Annals of the Association of American Geographers* 104(2): 382–390.

Napallacan, Jhunnex, and Ritchie Umel. 2006. " 'Don't Let Them Take No. 9 Away from Me.' " *Philippine Daily Inquirer,* October 8.

Natter, Katharina. 2018. "Rethinking Immigration Policy Theory beyond 'Western Liberal Democracies.' " *Comparative Migration Studies* 6(1): 4.

Natter, Katharina, and Hélène Thiollet. 2022. "Theorising Migration Politics: Do Political Regimes Matter?" *Third World Quarterly* 43(7): 1515–1530.

Newland, Kathleen. 2020. "Will International Migration Governance Survive the COVID-19 Pandemic?" Migration Policy Institute, October.

Ortiga, Yasmin Y. 2014. "Professional Problems: The Burden of Producing the 'Global' Filipino Nurse." *Social Science & Medicine* 115 (August): 64–71.

Ortiga, Yasmin Y. 2017. "The Flexible University: Neoliberal Education and the Global Production of Migrant Labor." *British Journal of Sociology of Education* 38(4): 485–499.

Ortiga, Yasmin Y. 2018a. *Emigration, Employability and Higher Education in the Philippines.* London: Routledge.

Ortiga, Yasmin Y. 2018b. "Learning to Fill the Labor Niche: Filipino Nursing Graduates and the Risk of the Migration Trap." *RSF: The Russell Sage Foundation Journal of the Social Sciences* 4(1): 172.

Ortiga, Yasmin Y. 2018c. "Education as Early Stage Brokerage: Cooling Out Aspiring Migrants for the Global Hotel Industry." *Pacific Affairs* 91(4): 727–748.

Ortiga, Yasmin Y. 2021. "Shifting Employabilities: Skilling Migrants in the Nation of Emigration." *Journal of Ethnic and Migration Studies* 47(10): 2270–2287.

Ortiga, Yasmin Y., Meng-Hsuan Chou, Gunjan Sondhi, and Jue Wang. 2019. "Working within the Aspiring Centre: Professional Status and Mobilities among Migrant Faculty in Singapore." *Higher Education Policy* 32(2): 149–166.

Ortiga, Yasmin Y., and Romeo Luis A. Macabasag. 2020. "Temporality and Acquiescent Immobility among Aspiring Nurse Migrants in the Philippines." *Journal of Ethnic and Migration Studies* 47(9): 1976–1993.

Ortiga, Yasmin Y., and Romeo Luis A. Macabasag. 2021. "Understanding International Immobility through Internal Migration: 'Left Behind' Nurses in the Philippines." *International Migration Review* 55(2): 460–481.

Ortiga, Yasmin Y., and Jenica Ana Rivero. 2019. "Bodies of Work: Skilling at the Bottom of the Global Nursing Care Chain." *Globalizations* 16(7): 1184–1197.

Ostergaard-Nielsen, Eva. 2003. *International Migration and Sending Countries Perceptions, Policies and Transnational Relations.* London: Palgrave Macmillan.

Oyogoa, Francisca. 2016. "Cruise Ships: Continuity and Change in the World System." *Journal of World-Systems Research* 22(1): 31–37.

Ozkan, Umut Riza. 2018. "Foreign Qualification Recognition Regimes for Internationally Trained Professionals: The Case of Pharmacists." *Journal of International Migration and Integration* 19(2): 367–389.

Padios, Jan M. 2018. *A Nation on the Line: Call Centers As Postcolonial Predicaments in the Philippines.* Durham, NC: Duke University Press.

Parreñas, Rhacel S. 2021a. *Unfree: Migrant Domestic Work in Arab States.* Stanford: Stanford University Press.

Parreñas, Rhacel S. 2021b. "Discipline and Empower: The State Governance of Migrant Domestic Workers." *American Sociological Review* 86(6): 1043–1065.

Patterson, Shawn, Jr. 2021. "The Politics of Pandemics: The Effect of Stay-at-Home Orders on COVID-19 Mitigation." *State Politics and Policy Quarterly* 22(1): 1–23.

Pettit, Harry, and Wiebe Ruijtenberg. 2019. "Migration As Hope and Depression: Existential Im/mobilities in and beyond Egypt." *Mobilities* 14(5): 730–744.

Philippine Daily Inquirer [PDI]. 2020a. "Repatriation Biggest Ever in PH History." August 2.

Philippine Daily Inquirer [PDI]. 2020b. "600 to 900 Nurses with Complete Documents Allowed to Leave PH–DOLE." August 21.

Philippine Daily Inquirer [PDI]. 2020c. "Nurses Chafe at New DBM Classification, Deployment Ban." September 4.

Philippine News Agency [PNA]. 2012. "Genting Expands with $1.2B in PHL." October 11.

Philippine News Agency [PNA]. 2020a. "248 Seafarers Return from Miami amid Covid-19 Crisis." April 3.

Philippine News Agency [PNA]. 2020b. "Health Workers with Contracts as of March 8 Can Leave PH." April 14.

Philippine News Agency [PNA]. 2020c. "Welcome and Farewell: Final Respects for 'Fallen Heroes.'" July 29.

Philippine Overseas Employment Administration [POEA]. 2006. *Governing Board Resolution No. 01, Series of 2006*. Manila: Department of Labor and Employment.

Philippine Overseas Employment Administration [POEA]. 2012. *Memorandum Circular No. 03: Additional Mission Critical Skills (MCS) Category*. Manila: Department of Labor and Employment.

Philippine Overseas Employment Administration [POEA]. 2013. *Memorandum Circular No.01: Additional Mission Critical Skills (MCS)*. Manila: Department of Labor and Employment.

Philippine Overseas Employment Administration [POEA]. 2020. *Governing Board Resolution No. 09, Series of 2020*. Manila: Department of Labor and Employment.

Pinlac, Beatrice. 2022. "DOH Urges Gov't to Stop Exodus of PH Health Workers." *Philippine Daily Inquirer*, June 18.

Polleta, Francesca, Pang Ching Bobby Chen, Beth G. Gardner, and Alice Motes. 2011. "The Sociology of Storytelling." *Annual Review of Sociology* 37: 109–130.

Powell, Walter W., and Kaisa Snellman. 2004. "The Knowledge Economy." *Annual Review of Sociology* 30: 199–220.

Pulta, Benjamin. 2019. "SC Upholds SG 15 Minimum Pay for Gov't Nurses." *Philippine News Agency,* 9 October.

Punter, Dagmar E., Hasse van der Veen, Enrike van Wingerden, and Darshan Vigneswaran. 2019. "A 'Distributive Regime': Rethinking Global Migration Control." *Political Geography* 70 (April): 117–126.

Ragazzi, Francesco. 2014. "A Comparative Analysis of Diaspora Policies." *Political Geography* 41 (July): 74–89.

Raghuram, Parvati. 2021. "Interjecting the Geographies of Skills into International Skilled Migration Research: Political Economy and Ethics for a Renewed Research Agenda." *Population, Space and Place* 27(5).

Raghuram, Parvati, and Eleanore Kofman. 2004. "Out of Asia: Skilling, Re-skilling and Deskilling of Female Migrants." *Women's Studies International Forum* 27: 95–100.

Ramirez, Robertzon. 2020. "Deployment Ban on Health Workers to Be Reviewed." *Philippine Star*, April 12.

Ranada, Pia. 2020. "Cainta Nurse Gets P60 Daily Hazard Pay and Dies of COVID-19 before Receiving It." *Rappler*, August 13. https://www.rappler.com/newsbreak/in-depth/cainta-nurse-maria-theresa-cruz-dies-covid-19-before-getting-hazard-pay.

Riaño, Yvonne. 2022. "Migrant Entrepreneurs as Agents of Development? Geopolitical Context and Transmobility Strategies of Colombian Migrants Returning from Venezuela." *Journal of International Migration and Integration.* https://doi.org/10.1007/s12134-022-00959-w.

Rodriguez, Robyn. 2010. *Migrants for Export: How the Philippine State Brokers Labour to the World*. Minneapolis: University of Minnesota Press.

Rodriguez, Robyn M., and Helen Schwenken. 2013. "Becoming a Migrant at Home: Subjectivation Processes in Migrant-Sending Countries Prior to Departure." *Population, Space and Place* 19(4): 375–388.

Romero, Alexis. 2020. "Duterte Allows More Health Workers to Leave." *Philippine Star*, September 22.

Ronquillo, Charlene, Geertje Boschma, Sabrina T. Wong, and Linda Quiney. 2011. "Beyond Greener Pastures: Exploring Contexts Surrounding Filipino Nurse Migration in Canada through Oral History." *Nursing Inquiry* 18(3): 262–275.

Rother, Stefan. 2022. "The 'Gold Standard' for Labour Export? The Role of Civil Society in Shaping Multi-Level Philippine Migration Policies." *Third World Quarterly* 43(7): 1607–1626.

Ruhs, Martin. 2013. *The Price of Rights: Regulating International Labor Migration*. Princeton: Princeton University Press.

Ruiz, Neil. 2014. "Made for Export: Labor Migration, State Power, and Higher Education in a Developing Philippine Economy." PhD diss., Massachusetts Institute of Technology.

Sabillo, Kristine. 2020. "Doctors, Health Workers Outraged at DOH's P500 Daily Allowance for COVID-19 Hospital Volunteers." *ABS-CBN News*, March 27.

Saguin, Kidjie. 2020. "Returning Broke and Broken? Return Migration, Reintegration and Transnational Social Protection in the Philippines." *Migration and Development* 9(3): 352–368.

Salazar, Noel B. 2011. "The Power of Imagination in Transnational Mobilities." *Identities* 18(6): 576–598.

Salazar, Noel B. 2021. "Immobility: The Relational and Experiential Qualities of an Ambiguous Concept." *Transfers* 11(3): 3–21.

Salazar, Noel B., and Alan Smart. 2011. "Anthropological Takes on (Im)mobility." *Identities* 18(6): i–ix.

Sallaz, Jeffrey. 2019. *Lives on the Line: How the Philippines Became the World's Call Center Capital*. Oxford, UK: Oxford University Press.

San Juan, Epifanio. 2009. "Overseas Filipino Workers: The Making of an Asian-Pacific Diaspora." *Global South* 3:99–129.

Santiago, Maxxy. 2020. "Kuwaiti Woman Sentenced to Death for Torturing, Killing Pinay Maid." *ABS-CBN News*, December 30.

Santos, Rudy. 2020a. "IATF Wants Health Workers' Deployment Ban Lifted." *Philippine Star*, April 14.

Santos, Rudy. 2020b. "Recruiters Want Deployment Ban on Nurses Lifted." *Philippine Star*, August 24.

Saxenian, Ann. 2005. "From Brain Drain to Brain Circulation: Transnational Communities and Regional Upgrading in India and China." *Studies in Comparative International Development* 40(2): 35–61.

Schewel, Kerilyn. 2015. "Understanding the Aspiration to Stay: A Case Study of Young Adults in Senegal." International Migration Institute, University of Oxford.

Schewel, Kerilyn. 2020. "Understanding Immobility: Moving beyond the Mobility Bias in Migration Studies." *International Migration Review* 54(2): 328–355.

Schewel, Kerilyn, and Sonja Fransen. 2022. "Who Prefers to Stay? Voluntary Immobility among Youth in Ethiopia, India, and Vietnam," *Journal of Ethnic and Migration Studies*. DOI: 10.1080/1369183X.2022.2092085.

Setijadi, Charlotte. 2023. *Memories of Unbelonging: Ethnic Chinese Identity Politics in Post-Suharto Indonesia*. Honolulu: University of Hawai'i Press.

Sherman, Rachel. 2007. *Class Acts: Service and Inequality in Luxury Hotels*. Berkeley: University of California Press.

Shoichet, Catherine. 2020. "Covid-19 Is Taking a Devastating Toll on Filipino American Nurses." *CNN,* December 11.

Showers, Fumilayo. 2023. *Migrants Who Care: West Africans Working and Building Lives in US Health Care*. New Brunswick, NJ: Rutgers University Press.

Shrestha, Tina. 2018. "Aspirational Infrastructure: Everyday Brokerage and the Foreign-Employment Recruitment Agencies in Nepal." *Pacific Affairs* 91(4): 673–693.

Sim, Walter. 2020a. "Coronavirus: Cruise Ships Quarantined Off Japan and Hong Kong As Passengers Test Positive." *Straits Times,* February 5.

Sim, Walter. 2020b. "Cruise Ship Off Japan Carries Largest Cluster outside China." *Straits Times,* February 13.

Siytangco, Deedee. 2017. "Call for Raising Standards in Maritime Higher Education." *Manila Bulletin*, April 3.

Skovgaard-Smith, Irene. 2021. "Transnational Life and Cross-border Immobility in Pandemic Times." *Global Networks* 23(1): 59–74.

Smets, Kevin. 2019. "Media and Immobility: The Affective and Symbolic Immobility of Forced Migrants." *European Journal of Communication* 34(6): 650–660.

Smith, David M., and Nicola Gillin. 2021. "Filipino Nurse Migration to the UK: Understanding Migration Choices from an Ontological Security-Seeking Perspective." *Social Science & Medicine* 276: 113881.

Somaiah, Bittiandra Chand, Brenda S. A. Yeoh, and Silvia Mila Arlini. 2020. " 'Cukup for Me to Be Successful in This Country': 'Staying' among Left-behind Young Women in Indonesia's Migrant-sending Villages." *Global Networks* 20(2): 237–255.

Somers, Margaret. 1997. "Deconstructing and Reconstructing Class Formation Theory: Narrativity, Relational Analysis, and Social Theory." In John R. Hall, ed., *Reworking Class*, 73–106. Ithaca, NY: Cornell University Press.

Sprague-Silgado, Jeb. 2017. "The Caribbean Cruise Ship Business and the Emergence of a Transnational Capitalist Class." *Journal of World-Systems Research* 23(1): 93–125.

Stock, Inka. 2019. *Time, Migration and Forced Immobility*. Bristol, UK: Bristol University Press.

Stokes-DuPass, Nicole. 2015. *Integration and New Limits on Citizenship Rights: Denmark and Beyond*. New York: Palgrave Macmillan.

Swanson, Ana, Zolan Kanno-Youngs, and Maggie Haberman. 2020. "Trump Seeks to Block 3M Mask Exports and Grab Masks from Its Overseas Customers." *New York Times*, April 3.

Tabile, Justine D. 2023. "Seafarer Deployment to Reach Pre-pandemic Level by Yearend—DMW." *Business World Online*, June 27.

Tadalan, Charmaine. 2020. "Filipinos from Virus-hit Cruise Ship to Come Home." *Business World,* February 20.

Talani, Leila Simona. 2021. *The International Political Economy of Migration in the Globalization Era*. Cham, Switzerland: Springer.

Tan, Edita. 2011. "What's Wrong with Philippine Higher Education?" *Philippine Review of Economics* 48(1): 147–184.

Tan, Maria. 2023. "Nurses Push for 50K Living Wage." *ABS-CBN News*, April 12.

Terrazola, Vanne Elaine. 2020a. "Livelihood Program for Balikbayan OFWs Eyed by OWWA." *Manila Bulletin*, August 26.

Terrazola, Vanne Elaine. 2020b. "DOLE Recommends Lifting Deployment Ban for 600 Nurses." *Manila Bulletin*, August 26.

Terrazola, Vanne Elaine. 2020c. "OWWA Vows Strict Screening of Applicants for OFW Livelihood Assistance Program." *Manila Bulletin*, August 30.

Terrazola, Vanne Elaine. 2020d. "Villanueva Wants Clear Policy on Deployment Ban of Healthcare Workers." *Manila Bulletin*, September 9.

Terry, William. 2011. "Geographic Limits to Global Labor Market Flexibility: The Human Resources Paradox of the Cruise Industry." *Geoforum* 42(6): 660–670.

Terry, William. 2014. "The Perfect Worker: Discursive Makings of Filipinos in the Workplace Hierarchy of the Globalized Cruise Industry." *Social & Cultural Geography* 15(1): 73–93.

Teves, Oliver. 2006. "Test Cheating Scandal Clouds Future of Philippine Nurses." *Associated Press*, August 27.

Thalang, Chanintira na, and Chontida Auikool. 2018. "The Immobility Paradox in Thailand's Southern Border Provinces." *South East Asia Research* 26(4): 315–329.

Thompson, Maddy. 2019. "Everything Changes to Stay the Same: Persistent Global Health Inequalities amidst New Therapeutic Opportunities and Mobilities for Filipino Nurses." *Mobilities* 14(1): 38–53.

Thompson, Maddy, and Margaret Walton-Roberts. 2019. "International Nurse Migration from India and the Philippines: The Challenge of Meeting the Sustainable Development Goals in Training, Orderly Migration and Healthcare Worker Retention." *Journal of Ethnic and Migration Studies* 45(14): 2583–2599.

Timmons, Stephen, Catrin Evans, and Sreelekha Nair. 2016. "The Development of the Nursing Profession in a Globalised Context: A Qualitative Case Study in Kerala, India." *Social Science & Medicine* 166:41–48.

Torpey, John. 2007. "Leaving: A Comparative View." In Nancy Green and Francois Weil, eds., *Citizenship and Those Who Leave: The Politics of Emigration and Expatriation*. Urbana: University of Illinois Press.

Torregoza, Hannah. 2020. " 'Provide P10,000 Cash Grant, Other Aid to Repatriated OFWs'—Sen. Villanueva." *Manila Bulletin*, August 11.

Trier-Bieniek, Adrienne. 2012. "Framing the Telephone Interview As a Participant-Centred Tool for Qualitative Research: A Methodological Discussion." *Qualitative Research* 12(6): 630–644.

Tungohan, Ethel, and John Paul Catungal. 2022. "Virtual Qualitative Research Using Transnational Feminist Queer Methodology: The Challenges and Opportunities of Zoom-Based Research during Moments of Crisis." *International Journal of Qualitative Methods*. https://doi.org/10.1177/16094069221090062.

Tyner, James. 2004. *Made in the Philippines: Gendered Discourses and the Making of Migrants*. London: Routledge.

Vathi, Zana, Russell King, and Barak Kalir. 2022. "The Shifting Geopolitics of Return Migration and Reintegration." *Journal of International Migration and Integration.* https://doi.org/10.1007/s12134-022-00974-x.

Velasco, Raheema. 2023. "Tulfo Bats for Total Deployment Ban in Kuwait." *CNN Philippines,* January 29.

Villegas, Bernardo. 2017. "Restaurant Business As Sunrise Sector," *Manila Bulletin,* January 2.

Waldinger, Roger, and Michael Ira Lichter. 2003. *How the Other Half Works: Immigration and the Social Organization of Labor.* Berkeley: University of California Press.

Walton-Roberts, Margaret. 2021. "Bus Stops, Triple Wins, and Two Steps: Nurse Migration In and Out of Asia." *Global Networks* 21(1): 84–107.

Wassink, Joshua T., and Jacqueline M. Hagan. 2018. "A Dynamic Model of Self-Employment and Socioeconomic Mobility among Return Migrants: The Case of Urban Mexico." *Social Forces* 96(3): 1069–1096.

Weinar, Agnieszka. 2017. *Emigration and Diaspora Policies in the Age of Mobility.* Cham, Switzerland: Springer.

Weller, Susie. 2017. "Using Internet Video Calls in Qualitative (Longitudinal) Interviews: Some Implications for Rapport." *International Journal of Social Research Methodology* 20(6): 613–625.

Westbrook, Lauren. 2020. "Covid-19 Survivors: Hong Kong Passengers Relive Time Trapped on Diamond Princess Cruise—First Major Cluster outside China." September 12. https://www.scmp.com/news/hong-kong/health-environment/article/3101259/covid-19-survivors-hong-kong-passengers-relive.

Witsil, Frank. 2020. " 'We Are Floating around the Ocean': Cruise Ship with No Coronavirus Shut Out of Ports." *USA Today,* February 9.

Wolff, Sarah, Ariadna Ripoll Servent, and Agathe Piquet. 2020. "Framing Immobility: Shengen Governance in Times of Pandemics." *Journal of European Integration* 42(8): 1127–1144.

World Health Organization [WHO]. 2006. *The World Health Report 2006: Working Together for Health.* Geneva.

World Health Organization [WHO]. 2023. "Statement on the Fifteenth Meeting of the IHR (2005) Emergency Committee on the COVID-19 Pandemic." Geneva.

Wyngaarden, Sara, Sally Humphries, Kelly Skinner, Esmeralda Lobo Tosta, Veronica Zelaya Portillo, Paola Orellana, and Warren Dodd. 2022. " 'You Can Settle Here': Immobility Aspirations and Capabilities among Youth from Rural Honduras." *Journal of Ethnic and Migration Studies.* https://doi.org/10.1080/1369183X.2022.2031922.

Xiang, Biao. 2016. "Beyond Methodological Nationalism and Epistemological Behaviouralism: Drawing Illustrations from Migrations within and from China." *Population, Space and Place* 22(7): 669–680.

Xiang, Biao, William L. Allen, Shahram Khosravi, Hélène Neveu Kringelbach, Yasmin Y. Ortiga, Karen Anne S. Liao, Jorge E. Cuéllar, Lamea Momen, Priya Deshingkar, and Mukta Naik. 2022. "Shock Mobilities during Moments of Acute Uncertainty." *Geopolitics* (July): 1–26.

Xiang, Biao, Brenda S. A. Yeoh, and Mika Toyota. 2013. *Return: Nationalizing Transnational Mobility in Asia.* Durham, NC: Duke University Press.

Yang, Calvin, Osmond Chia, and Dominic Low. 2021. "Dream Cruises Ship Turns Back to Singapore after COVID-19 Case Found on Board." *Straits Times*, July 15.

Yap, DJ, and Tina G. Santos. 2020. "Health Workers with Jobs Abroad Allowed to Leave." *Philippine Daily Inquirer*, April 14.

Yeates, Nicola. 2012. "Global Care Chains: A State-of-the-Art Review and Future Directions in Care Transnationalization Research." *Global Networks* 12(2): 135–154.

Yeates, Nicola, and Jane Pillinger. 2019. *International Health Worker Migration and Recruitment: Global Governance, Politics, and Policy*. London: Routledge.

Yee, Jovic. 2020. "Only 25 Grabbed DOH Job Offer to Health Workers." *Philippine Daily Inquirer*, August 22.

Yee, Karol Mark R. 2024. "At All Costs: Educational Expansion and Persistent Inequality in the Philippines." *Higher Education* 87(6): 1809–1827.

Yuval-Davis, Nira, Georgie Wemyss, and Kathryn Cassidy. 2019. *Bordering*. Cambridge, UK: Polity Press.

Zolberg, Aristide. 2007. "The Exit Revolution." In Nancy Green and Francois Weil, eds., *Citizenship and Those Who Leave: The Politics of Emigration and Expatriation*. Urbana: University of Illinois Press.

Zurbano, Joel. 2020. "2k OFWs Brought Home, Total Repatriates Now 316k." *Manila Standard*, December 26.

Index

nurses (*cont.*)
  Philippine wages of, 42, 43, 158n10, 159n7, 161n20; requirements for aspiring migrant, 63, 159n10; rise and fall in demand for, 32, 33, 158n9; temporary employment for, 48, 52; work experience of, 63–65
nursing: board examination scandal, 28–29; filling skills gaps in, 66–71; growth in number of schools, 159n5; solution to shortage, 137

OFW. *See* overseas Filipino workers
Olalia, Bernard, 46, 47, 128
OEC. *See* Overseas Employment Certificate
Overseas Employment Certificate, 50
overseas Filipino workers: deployment during pandemic, 85; heroism of, 13, 156n13, 87
Overseas Workers Welfare Administration: monitoring aid recipients, 94, 162n8, 163n13; reintegration efforts, 84; support for migrant businesses, 85, 86 table 4.1, 88, 89, 92, 163n11
outmigration, 1, 15, 16, 17, 31, 46, 55, 127, 128, 129, 160n14, 166n6
OWWA. *See* Overseas Workers Welfare Administration

Padilla, R., 42
Padios, J., 165n9, 165nn12–13
Parreñas, R., 158n2
permanent resettlement, 18, 86, 90, 95, 97, 98, 102, 105, 109,
Philippine Nursing Act of 2002, 41, 159nn6–7
Philippine Overseas Employment Administration: ban on health care workers, 40, 44, 45, 46, 47, 48, 49, 51 (*see also* deployment ban); function of, 1; on the difference among Filipino migrant workers, 164n2; policies on other

professions, 160n16; role in export-oriented education, 26
POEA. *See* Philippine Overseas Employment Administration
Polleta, F., 14
post-pandemic: cruise workers, 131; limits for nurse deployment, 128; policies in the Philippines, 133; studies of, 126–127
PRC. *See* Professional Regulation Commission
preparedness to return, 106
PrisoNurses: formation of, 74; opposition to deployment ban, 60, 61, 73, 74, 80, 133; post-lockdown situation of members, 129–31, 134
private schools: course development, 26; problems with, 27; role in the Philippines, 25
Professional Regulation Commission, 28, 42

Ramos, Fidel, 16
reintegration: efforts, 84, 87, 94, 96, 103; funds for, 84, 86 table 4.1, 162n6 (*see also* cash aid); key to, 109, 112
remain in place, 3, 13, 14, 19, 61, 138, 161n5
repatriation, 6, 16, 83, 93, 98, 111, 146, 153, 154, 156n6
returning migrant workers: alternative careers for, 99–101; entrepreneurial skills training for, 88; financial assistance for, 85, 93; lack of support for, 83; repatriation programs for, 86 table 4.1; reskilling for, 98, 99, 100; self-employment programs for, 163n14; small-business grants for, 94, 163n13
Riaño, Y., 97
Rodriguez, R., 8
Rodriguez, Rufus, 39
Roque, Harry, 53, 56
Royal Caribbean Cruises Limited, 25, 36

The authorized representative in the EU for product safety and compliance is:
Mare Nostrum Group B.V.
Mauritskade 21D
1091 GC Amsterdam
The Netherlands
Email address: gpsr@mare-nostrum.co.uk

KVK chamber of commerce number: 96249943